Warcraft II™: Battle.net Edition
Prima's Official Strategy Guide

D1315116

Prima Games
A Division of Prima Communications, Inc.
3875 Atherton Road
Rocklin, CA 95765
(916) 632-4400
www.primagames.com

Project Editors: Patrick Cunningham, Brooke Raymond
Product Manager: Jon W. Goetzman

ISBN: 7615-1944-0
Library of Congress Catalog Card Number: 98-67932

Printed in the United States of America

01 02 BB 10 9 8 7 6

Chapter 7, continued

Chapter 8: The Alliance...of Dwarves, Elves, and Men 106

Chapter 9: The Orcish Hordes 130

Chapter 10: Cheat Codes 154

Chapter 11: Battle.net Maps (listed alphabetically) 155

Part 1: Tides of Darkness
Chapter 1
Warcraft II Armies

From lowly workers to elite spellcasters, the might of any army is judged by the quality, as well as the number, of its soldiers. This chapter describes all the talents and shortcomings of every combatant on both sides of the war.

Alliance Unit Statistics

Unit	Visual Range	Hit Points	Magic Points	Build Time	Gold	Lumber	Oil	Attack Range	Armor	Basic Damage	Piercing Damage	Effective Damage	Speed	Explosive Damage
Ballista	9	110	—	250	900	300	—	8	0	80	0	25–80	5	—
Battleship	8	150	—	140	1,000	500	1,000	6	15	130	0	50–130	6	—
Dwarven Demolition Squad	4	40	—	200	700	250	—	1	0	4	2	1–6	4	400
Elven Archer	5	40	—	70	500	50	—	4	0	3	6	3–9	10	—
Elven Destroyer	8	100	—	90	700	350	700	4	10	35	0	2–35	10	—
Elven Ranger	6	50	—	70	500	50	—	4	0	3	6	3–9	10	—
Footman	4	60	—	60	600	—	—	1	2	6	3	2–9	10	—
Gnomish Flying Machine	9	150	—	65	500	100	—	—	2	—	—	—	17	—
Gnomish Submarine	5	60	—	100	800	150	900	4	0	50	0	10–50	7	—
Gryphon Rider	6	100	—	250	2,500	—	—	4	5	0	16	8–16	14	—
Knight	4	90	—	90	800	100	—	1	4	8	4	2–12	13	—
Mage	9	60	255	120	1,200	—	—	2	0	0	9	5–9	8	—
Oil Tanker	4	90	—	50	400	200	—	—	10	—	—	—	10	—
Paladin	5	90	255	90	800	100	—	1	4	8	4	2–12	13	—
Peasant	4	30	—	45	400	—	—	1	—	3	2	1–5	10	—
Transport	4	150	—	70	600	200	500	1	0	—	—	—	10	—

ALLIANCE UNITS

Ballista

Ballistae launch steel-tipped bolts to impale all in their paths. Because an awesome amount of force must be exerted on their bowstrings, these machines of war are reinforced with lumber from the precious Ironwood trees. The Ballista, a product of Human design and Elven craftsmanship, is the most devastating weapon of the Alliance.

Battleship

The Alliance relies on its great Battleships to control the seas. These hulking behemoths possess armor and weaponry far greater than that of any other Alliance vessel. Their combination of devastating weaponry and substantial armor more than compensates for their somewhat sluggish speed in sea combat.

Dwarven Demolition Squad

From the subterranean halls of Khaz Modan, the Dwarven Demolition Squad comes to aid the Alliance. As masters of explosives, the Demolition Squad can demolish any obstacle—from a mighty wall to a bulwark of solid stone.

Elven Archer

Out of the forests of Quel'thalas come the Elven Archers to aid the Alliance. These agile woodsmen are unmatched in their use of the bow. Unencumbered by helmet or heavy armor, Archers are keen of eye and fleet of foot.

Elven Destroyer

Elven Destroyers are powerful warships from the fleets of Quel'thalas. Manned by highly skilled Elven seafarers, these swift vessels constitute a critical part of the Alliance naval defense force.

Elven Ranger

Rangers are a special group of Elven Archers who are intimately bound to the wildlands of Lordaeron. Their mastery in Longbow, Marksmanship, and Scouting makes them even deadlier than their brothers. Although their numbers are few, their presence can change the course of the war if they are deployed wisely.

Footman

Footmen are the initial line of defense against the Horde. Arrayed in hardened steel armor, they courageously wield broadsword and shield in hand-to-hand combat against their vile Orcish foes.

Gnomish Flying Machine

The Gnomes of Khaz Modan compensate for their lack of physical strength with ingenuity and daring. They are the inventors and pilots of the astounding Flying Machines. Although these awkward contraptions' armor and armament are too light for them to serve as weapons of mass destruction, Flying Machines can be used to survey vast areas of terrain, making them invaluable for discovering the movements of the Horde.

Gnomish Submarine

The resourceful Gnomish Inventors have designed an amazing craft known as the Submarine. This watertight vessel can submerge itself beneath the waves and surreptitiously keep watch on enemy forces above the surface. The use of cunning to carry out surprise attacks on more powerful enemies makes the Submarine an invaluable part of the Lordaeron armada.

Gryphon Rider

From the peaks of Northeron come the Dwarven Gryphon Riders. These Dwarves wield the mystic Stormhammers, forged deep within the secret chambers of their Aviaries. They have allied themselves only with the Elves of Quel'thalas, distrusting their Dwarven cousins and Humans alike. When the call to battle is sounded, however, they fight alongside any who oppose the Horde.

Knight

The Knights of Lordaeron are the fiercest fighting force of the Alliance. They are protected by suits of heavy armor and carry mighty warhammers. Astride great warhorses, these honorable warriors symbolize order to the people of Lordaeron in these dark times.

Mage

Once students of the Conjurers of Azeroth, the members of this new order of Mages have discovered untapped magical forces. The Conjurers who fell during the First War were unprepared. Determined to avoid a similar fate, the Mages have dedicated themselves to the command of more aggressive and destructive magicks. Whether in the Violet Citadel in Dalaran or on the battlefields of Lordaeron, the Mages are resolute in their efforts to defend the people.

Mage Spells

Image	Spell	Spell Point Cost	Effect
	Blizzard	25/area	Ice storm that affects a large area
	Fireball	100	Launches ball of flame into its target
	Flame Shield	80	Functions as a fiery barrier and weapon
	Invisibility	200	Makes caster and target invisible (any interaction other than movement terminates spell)

Mage Spells, continued

Image	Spell	Spell Point Cost	Effect
	Lightning	0	Bolts of energy that strike victim regardless of armor
	Polymorph	200	Turns victim into a harmless animal
	Slow	50	Temporarily slows target's movement and reflexes

Oil Tanker

Oil Tankers are the only ships that do not require oil for their construction. They are manned by mariners who search for the rich oil deposits that lie beneath the waves. The crew of every Tanker is skilled in building Oil Platforms and ferrying the oil back to a Shipyard or Oil Refinery where it may be processed and put to use.

Paladin

Paladins are a holy order of warriors. The Archbishop Alonsus Faol perceived that the pious Clerics of Northshire were ill prepared for the dangers of combat. Therefore, he sought only those of the greatest virtue among the knighthood of Lordaeron and tutored them in the ways of magic. These Paladins—christened the Knights of the Silver Hand—must now heal the wounds sustained in combat and restore faith in the promise of freedom from Orcish tyranny.

Paladin Spells

Image	Spell	Spell Point Cost	Effect
	Exorcism	4/HP	Causes injury to enemy undead (can be cast on a group or single target)
	Healing	6/HP	Heals wounded
	Holy Vision	70	Shows all terrain (& all inhabitants temporarily)

Peasant

Peasants are trained citizens of the kingdoms of Lordaeron. Because they mine gold and harvest lumber to meet the needs of the fighting force, they are the backbone of the Alliance. Trained in the construction and maintenance of buildings, both civilian and military, they take great pride in the service they provide. Peasants use both pick and axe for their own defense if threatened.

Transport

Transports are a vital part of the Alliance, for these sturdy vessels allow troops to traverse various waterways to engage in battle. Designed to carry and deliver several ground units directly onto the shore, Transports are slow and unarmed. Hence, they must rely on Destroyers and Battleships for protection.

Units of the Orcish Horde

Unit	Visual Range	Hit Points	Magic Points	Build Time	Gold	Lumber	Oil	Attack Range	Armor	Basic Damage	Piercing Damage	Effective Damage	Speed	Explosive Damage
Catapult	9	110	—	250	900	300	—	8	0	80	0	25–80	5	—
Death Knight	9	60	255	120	1,200	—	—	3	0	—	9	5–9	8	—
Dragon	6	100	—	250	2,500	—	—	4	5	0	16	8–16	14	—
Giant Turtle	5	60	—	100	800	150	900	4	0	50	0	10–50	7	—
Goblin Sapper	4	40	—	200	700	250	—	1	0	4	2	1–6	11	400
Grunt	4	60	—	60	600	—	—	1	2	6	3	2–9	10	—
Ogre	4	90	—	90	800	100	—	1	4	8	4	2–12	13	—
Ogre Juggernaught	8	150	—	140	1,000	500	1,000	6	15	130	0	50–130	6	—
Ogre-Mage	5	90	0	90	800	100	—	1	4	8	4	2–12	13	—
Oil Tanker	4	90	—	50	400	200	—	—	10	—	—	—	10	—
Peon	4	30	—	45	400	—	—	1	0	3	2	1–5	10	—
Transport	4	150	—	70	600	200	500	—	0	—	—	—	10	—
Troll Axethrower	5	40	—	70	500	50	—	4	0	3	6	3–9	10	—
Troll Berserker	6	50	—	70	500	50	—	4	0	3	6	3–9	10	—
Troll Destroyer	8	100	—	90	700	350	700	4	10	35	0	2–35	10	—
Zeppelin	9	150	—	65	500	100	—	—	2	—	—	—	17	—

UNITS OF THE ORCISH HORDE

Catapult

Sharpened horns, crimson with blood, mark the appearance of the Orcish Catapult. Its grim exterior is enough to make the weak Human troops flee in stark terror. This cumbersome, wheeled machine launches deadly incendiary shots that explode on impact. The Catapult is feared and respected throughout the land.

Death Knight

These soldiers of darkness were created by Gul'dan to replace the slaughtered Warlock clans. Assembled from the corpses of the Knights of Azeroth slain in the First War, these abominations were then animated with the ethereal essence of the Shadow Council. Further empowered with magical energies culled from the slain Necrolytes, the Death Knights wield a terrifying arsenal of spells.

Death Knight Spells

Image	Spell	Spell Point Cost	Effect
	Death and Decay	25	Dark clouds that affect a large area
	Death Coil	100	Drains targeted unit of its energy, which is given to the caster
	Haste	50	Temporarily speeds up target's movement and reflexes
	Raise Dead	50/skeleton	Brings fallen soldiers back to life
	Touch of Darkness	0	Energy that strikes victim regardless of armor
	Unholy Armor	100	Uses one half of target's life force to make him/her temporarily invulnerable
	Whirlwind	100	A damaging, chaotic wind

Dragon

Dragons are native to the untamed northlands of Azeroth. Rend and Maim, the Chieftains of the Black Tooth Grin clan, captured the Dragon Queen, Alexstrasza. With their Queen held captive, the Dragons have been forced into subservience by the Horde. Their tremendous destructive powers and keen intellects make them the single most powerful force within the Horde. Their powerful wings allow them to soar tirelessly through the skies, and the devastating flame that issues from the mouths of older serpents can level enemy troops.

Giant Turtle

Giant Turtles are native to the southern seas; they were captured by the Stormreaver clan. These lumbering monstrosities are fitted with watertight canopies on the backs of their shells and are used as submersible Orcish craft. By submerging themselves under the waves, the Giant Turtles can steal up on unsuspecting enemy craft and report their positions to the Horde fleet.

Goblin Sapper

The mischievous Goblin Sappers are known for their tremendous aptitude for destruction. These Goblins are armed with explosives that enable them to level enemy structures and weapon emplacements.

Grunt

Grunts epitomize the merciless spirit of the Horde. Equipped with mighty axes and battle-worn armor, they are prepared to fight to the death.

Ogre

The Ogres were brought through the Portal by the Warlock Gul'dan after the First War. The Ogres act as enforcers in an effort to quell needless infighting between the Orc clans. Owing to the constant bickering between their two heads, the Ogres exhibit less intelligence than even the lowly Peon. The Ogres' enormous strength and unnatural toughness, however, place them among the fiercest warriors in the Horde.

Ogre Juggernaught

These gargantuan ships of war are the main armament in the dark armada of the Horde. Heavily armed and armored, the Juggernaughts are veritable floating fortresses. Though not as swift as the Troll warships, these ruinous craft have quickly come to be feared across the seas of Azeroth for their unrelenting onslaughts against the Alliance.

Ogre-Mage

The Ogre-Magi were originally a small band of loyal Ogre enforcers, transformed by Gul'dan into sorcerers. By warping the Elf-magicks of the Runestone at Caer Darrow, Gul'dan was able to infuse the magical abilities of long-dead Warlocks into the bodies of these unsuspecting hosts. The Ogre-Magi can direct their death magicks as easily as their lesser cousins would deliver a crushing blow. The Ogre-Magi have also become extremely cunning and insidious, serving the Horde only as they see fit.

Ogre-Mage Spells

Image	Spell	Spell Point Cost	Effect
	Bloodlust	50	Causes target to inflict more damage to opponents
	Eye of Kilrogg	70	Conjures magical eye unit that acts like a Zeppelin—but is fast
	Runes	200	Exploding trap that cannot discern friend from foe; causes damage to adjacent areas

Oil Tanker

The Orcish Oil Tanker is crudely constructed because its purpose is to bear cargo rather than weapons or troops. The Tanker is crewed by a mob of Orcs scarcely more capable than the lowly Peons. Other than piloting the craft, the crew of the Tanker builds Oil Platforms and returns cargo to be processed and used as the overseer directs.

Peon

The label of Peon denotes the lowest station among those in the Orcish Horde. Deficient in all important skills, these inferior folk are assigned to menial tasks such as harvesting lumber and mining gold. Their labor is also required for the construction and maintenance of the buildings that support the vast undertakings of the Horde.

Transport

Transports are huge skeletal ships charged with ferrying Horde troops across large bodies of water. Being slow and bulky, Transports rely upon magical armor to repel enemy fire. Although the Horde usually defends its Transports with Destroyers and Juggernaughts, some reckless crews will sail straight into naval engagements to deliver their troops to land.

Troll Axethrower

The Trolls of Lordaeron have suffered ages of attrition at the hands of the Humans, Dwarves, and Elves. More agile than the brutish Orcs, Trolls employ throwing axes—along with a cunning attack-and-retreat strategy—to assail their foes. This combination of speed and range makes them a valuable addition to the Orcish Horde.

Troll Berserker

Berserkers are a bloodthirsty sect of Trolls dedicated to the total annihilation of their hated enemies, the Elves. Numerous experiments by the Goblin Alchemists have given the Berserkers many strange abilities that make them all but unstoppable in the heat of battle. A Berserker may also enter into a battle-rage, which transforms him into a veritable cyclone of death and destruction.

Troll Destroyer

The Troll Destroyers are swift, ill-formed longboats designed to cut through enemy armadas and deal damage to enemy vessels. The savage Troll crewmen are eager to enter into combat against Alliance ships of war and hungrily await any chance to stand mast-to-mast against the Elven Destroyers.

Zeppelin

Zeppelins are ingenious inventions that allow small teams of Goblins to soar above the countryside and spy on enemy positions. The Zeppelins are cumbersome and awkward and maintain no armament. Their airborne capabilities and their extensive line of sight, however, make them an integral part of the Horde's spy network.

Chapter 2
Warcraft II Structures

Medieval armies don't have the luxury of having everything shipped in for a battle. Artisans and workers must set up villages near the battle site to provide housing, food, and weapons in preparation for war. The sections that follow detail every structure and unit and what it takes to build and upgrade each, for both Alliance and Horde.

ALLIANCE STRUCTURES

Alliance Structures

Structure	Visual Range	Hit Points	Build Time	Gold Cost	Lumber Cost	Oil Cost	Armor	Production	Basic Damage	Piercing Damage	Effective Damage
Barracks	3	800	200	700	450	—	20	—	—	—	—
Blacksmith	3	775	200	800	450	100	20	—	—	—	—
Cannon Tower	9	160	190	1,000	300	—	20	—	50	0	10–50
Castle	9	1,600	200	2,500	1,200	500	20	Gold 100+20	—	—	—
Church	3	700	175	900	500	—	20	—	—	—	—
Elven Lumber Mill	3	600	150	600	450	—	20	Lumber 100+25	—	—	—
Farm	3	400	100	500	250	—	20	—	—	—	—
Foundry	3	750	175	700	400	400	20	—	—	—	—
Gnomish Inventor	3	500	150	1,000	400	—	20	—	—	—	—
Gryphon Aviary	3	500	150	1,000	400	—	20	—	—	—	—
Guard Tower	9	130	140	500	150	—	20	—	4	12	6–16
Keep	6	1,400	200	2,000	1,000	200	20	Gold 100+10	—	—	—
Mage Tower	3	500	125	1,000	200	—	20	—	—	—	—
Oil Platform	3	650	200	700	450	—	20	—	—	—	—
Oil Refinery	3	600	225	800	350	200	20	Oil 100+25	—	—	—
Scout Tower	9	100	60	550	200	—	20	—	—	—	—
Shipyard	3	1,100	200	800	450	—	20	—	—	—	—
Stables	3	500	150	1,000	300	—	20	—	—	—	—
Town Hall	4	1,200	255	1,200	800	—	20	—	—	—	—

Barracks

Barracks are large, fortified structures that offer training and housing to the many warriors of the Alliance. An integral part of any defended community, the Barracks foster unity and goodwill between the races. Human Footmen live alongside Elven Archers; all train together under one roof. The training of Ballista crews and the construction of these war machines also take place within the Barracks compound.

Options

Train Footman

Train Archer

Requires Lumber Mill.

Train Ranger

Requires Keep, Lumber Mill, Ranger upgrade. Replaces Archer.

Train Ballista

Requires Lumber Mill, Blacksmith.

Train Knight

Requires Stables.

Train Paladin

Requires Stables, Church, Paladin upgrade. Replaces Knight.

Blacksmith

Blacksmiths are important to many settlements that depend on military protection. Although the metals Blacksmiths forge are vital for constructing advanced buildings, Blacksmiths are renowned for their skillful weapon crafting and armoring. The smiths of Lordaeron, occasionally aided by Dwarven allies, produce some of the finest-quality weapons in the northlands. The Blacksmiths and Elves are rumored to be developing a machine that may alter the course of the war against the Horde.

Options

Upgrade Swords 1
Damage +2
Build Time: 200
Gold: 800

Upgrade Shields 1
Armor +2
Build Time: 200
Gold: 300
Lumber: 300

Upgrade Swords 2
Damage +2
Build Time: 250
Gold: 2,400

Upgrade Shields 2
Armor +2
Build Time: 250
Gold: 900
Lumber: 500

Upgrade Ballista 1
Damage +15
Build Time: 250
Gold: 1,500

Upgrade Ballista 2
Damage +15
Build Time: 250
Gold: 4,000

Cannon Tower

Although twice as expensive as Guard Towers, Cannon Towers provide a formidable stationary defense and a slightly longer firing range. A row of these along a shoreline can pelt enemy ships and sink them long before they pose any threat.

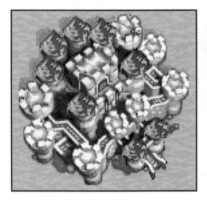

Castle

The mighty Castles of Lordaeron are the centers of large military cities. As in the lesser Keeps, Peasants may take gold and lumber there for distribution to sustain the war effort. Fortified battlements protect these bastions against invasion and render them virtually indestructible.

Options

 Train Peasant

Church

Churches are where the citizens of Lordaeron seek spiritual enlightenment. Once led by devout Clerics, Churches now depend on Paladins to minister to the masses in this time of war. In these places of healing and serenity, the holy warriors gather to deepen their faith. Through meditation, communion, and tithing at these sacred sites, Paladins discover new ways to channel their healing and spiritual powers.

Options

Upgrade Knights to Paladins
Build Time: 250
Gold: 1,000

Research Healing
Build Time: 200
Gold: 1,000

Research Exorcism
Build Time: 200
Gold: 2,000

Elven Lumber Mill

Seeking insight into the mysteries of the great Ironwood trees of Northeron, the Elves of Quel'thalas constructed Lumber Mills and became exceptional craftsmen. The Elves offered their superior skills to the Alliance, providing more efficient means for processing lumber and making it possible to produce ships and war machines.

Lumber Mills produce the perfectly crafted arrows that make the Elven Archers feared throughout the Horde. Given the necessary resources, Elven craftsmen can upgrade the quality of these arrows, increasing the damage they inflict. After training at the Barracks, Elven Rangers gather at the mills, honing their skills in the Longbow, Marksmanship, and Scouting.

Options

Upgrade Arrows 1
Damage +1
Build Time: 200
Gold: 300
Lumber: 300

Upgrade Arrows 2
Damage +1
Build Time: 250
Gold: 900
Lumber: 500

Elven Ranger Training
Requires Keep
Build Time: 250
Gold: 1,500

Scouting Research
Sight 9
Build Time: 250
Gold: 1,500

Longbow Research
Range +1
Build Time: 250
Gold: 2,000

Marksmanship Research
Damage +3
Build Time: 250
Gold: 2,500

Farm

Farms are a vital part of the many communities in Lordaeron. Producing various grains and foodstuffs, Farms generate sustenance for peasants, workers, and armies. The overall amount of food a town's Farms can produce is a major factor in determining how many new workers and soldiers a community can accommodate. You must monitor this production at all times to keep the population well-fed and the town running smoothly.

Foundry

Foundries make it possible to construct mighty Transports and Battleships. The skilled Foundry artisans need only sufficient resources to design better armor and weaponry for the fleet. Located on the coast to supplement the Alliance Shipyards, Foundries are an integral part of warship maintenance.

Options

Upgrade Ship Cannons 1
Damage +5
Build Time: 200
Gold: 700
Lumber: 100
Oil: 1,000

Upgrade Ship Armor 1
Armor +5
Build Time: 200
Gold: 500
Lumber: 500

Upgrade Ship Cannons 2
Damage +5
Build Time: 250
Gold: 2,000
Lumber: 250
Oil: 3,000

Upgrade Ship Armor 2
Armor +5
Build Time: 250
Gold: 1,500
Lumber: 900

Gnomish Inventor

Gnomish Inventors are adept at creating clever contraptions for the military. Among the many inventions created by the Gnomes are Flying Machines and Submarines. Gnomes have perfected techniques for extracting chemical compounds from oil to make gunpowder and explosives.

Options

Build Flying Machine

Train Dwarven Demolition Squad

Gryphon Aviary

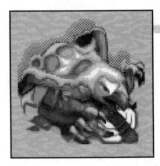

This colossal structure was hewn from solid rock by the Dwarves of Northeron. Their Aviary inspires dread in the foes of these Gryphon Riders. Deep inside this massive edifice are Gryphon aeries and Dwarven workshops, where saddles and harnesses are crafted.

Most sacred to the Dwarves is the enchanted forge that lies at the heart of each Aviary, where the magical Stormhammers are fashioned. A Stormhammer, when thrown, strikes with the fury of lightning and the force of thunder. This destructive weapon and the Gryphon Riders' indomitable spirit justifies their reputation as masters of the skies.

Options

Train Gryphon Rider

Guard Tower

Once upgraded, the Guard Tower houses a small Ballista for limited stationary defense. Such a structure cannot be upgraded again into a Cannon Tower.

Keep

In large, well-defended settlements, the Keep replaces the Town Hall as the center of commerce, where Peasants deliver shipments of gold and lumber for processing. The Keep is also a military structure protected by high granite walls that make it difficult to destroy. As control of a town becomes more critical, you may need to upgrade the Keep into a Castle.

Options

Train Peasant

Upgrade to Castle

Requires Stables, Blacksmith, Lumber Mill

Mage Tower

Serpentine spires of living rock form the Mage Towers' foundations. There, glowing spheres of mystic energy replenish and focus the awesome magicks wielded against the Orcish Horde. These Towers hold ominous secrets that none but the Mages of Lordaeron dare explore. As extensions of the Violet Citadel in Dalaran, these Towers allow the Mages to research arcane spells unhindered by the affairs of the temporal plane.

Options

 Train Mage

 Research Slow
Build Time: 100
Gold: 500

 Research Flame Shield
Build Time: 100
Gold: 1,000

 Research Invisibility
Build Time: 200
Gold: 2,500

 Research Polymorph
Build Time: 200
Gold: 2,000

 Research Blizzard
Build Time: 200
Gold: 2,000

Oil Platform

Harvesting the vast amounts of oil beneath the sea is critical to the construction of ships and war machines. Because the oceans are rich with this substance, Tankers must construct platforms where the oil is plentiful. Only then can the Tankers collect their dark cargo.

Oil Refinery

These large, steel-clad buildings are where raw oil is refined for use in constructing and maintaining the Alliance fleets, and for creating unconventional war machines. Like a Shipyard, a Refinery is built on the coast so Tankers can deliver their cargo directly. Oil can be processed in a Refinery far more efficiently than in a Shipyard alone.

Scout Tower

Scout Towers are tall, sturdy structures that guard the borders of many settlements. From these sites, the defenders of Lordaeron can spot enemy troops from high above, making it difficult for the Orcs to launch surprise attacks. The presence of these structures in the wildlands ensures the swift deployment of armies to meet any Orc incursion.

Options

Upgrade to Guard Tower
Requires Lumber Mill.

Upgrade to Cannon Tower
Requires Blacksmith.

Shipyard

The Shipyards' dedicated sailors and shipwrights strive tirelessly to keep the Alliance naval fleet running smoothly. Shipyards also are where Alliance warships are constructed. Elevated on strong pillars of Ironwood, these waterfront structures also receive and process the oil necessary to construct ships of war.

Options

 Build Oil Tanker

 Build Destroyer

 Build Battleship
Requires Foundry.

 Build Transport
Requires Foundry.

 Build Gnomish Submarine
Requires Gnomish Inventor.

Stables

Stables are maintained to breed and house Lordaeron's prized warhorses. These brave, loyal stallions carry Knights into battle (and contribute precious fertilizer to the bountiful farms about Lordaeron).

Town Hall

Town Halls serve as centers for the community and commerce of the various towns and military outposts in Lordaeron. As the chief economic centers in all settlements, these sites are equipped to process vital resources, such as lumber and gold. The steady stream of Peasants, who harvest and transport resources, creates constant activity near the Town Hall. The training Peasants need to assist in the growth of their community is provided here. In time, you may improve and upgrade the Town Hall into a Keep.

Options

Train Peasant

Upgrade to Keep
Requires Barracks.

HORDE STRUCTURES

Orcish Structures

Structure	Visual Range	Hit Points	Build Time	Gold Cost	Lumber Cost	Oil Cost	Armor	Production	Basic Damage	Piercing Damage	Effective Damage
Altar of Storms	3	700	175	900	500	—	20	—	—	—	—
Barracks	3	800	200	700	450	100	20	—	—	—	—
Blacksmith	3	775	200	800	450	—	20	—	—	—	—
Cannon Tower	9	160	190	1,000	300	—	20	—	50	0	10–50
Dragon Roost	3	500	150	1,000	400	—	20	—	—	—	—
Fortress	9	1,600	200	1,600	1,200	500	20	Gold 100+20	—	—	—
Foundry	3	750	175	700	400	400	20	—	—	—	—
Goblin Alchemist	3	500	150	1,000	400	—	20	—	—	—	—
Great Hall	4	1,200	255	1,200	800	—	20	—	—	—	—
Guard Tower	9	130	140	500	150	—	20	—	4	12	6–16
Ogre Mound	3	500	150	1,000	300	—	20	—	—	—	—
Oil Platform	3	650	200	700	450	—	20	—	—	—	—
Oil Refinery	3	600	225	800	350	200	20	Oil 100+25	—	—	—
Pig Farm	3	400	100	500	250	—	20	—	—	—	—
Scout Tower	9	100	60	550	200	—	20	—	—	—	—
Shipyard	3	1,100	200	800	450	—	20	—	—	—	—
Stronghold	6	1,400	200	1,000	1,000	200	20	Gold 100+10	—	—	—
Temple of the Damned	3	500	125	1,000	200	—	20	—	—	—	—
Troll Lumber Mill	3	600	150	600	450	—	20	Lumber 100+25	—	—	—

Altar of Storms

Carved from the Runestone at Caer Darrow, the Altar of Storms channels dark to pervert the Runestone's innate Elven magicks. These energies, lost after the Doomhammer destroyed the Orc Warlocks, are used now to create the powers of the Ogre-Magi. Here the Ogre-Magi receive new spells and skills to aid them in their fight against the Alliance.

Options

Ogres to Ogre-Magi
Build Time: 250
Gold: 1,000

Research Bloodlust
Build Time: 100
Gold: 1,000

Research Runes
Build Time: 150
Gold: 1,000

Barracks

Barracks maintain the facilities necessary for training Orc, Troll, and Ogre troops for battle. The clash of cold steel and the war cries of Troll Axethrowers can be heard from dawn to dusk, providing a constant reminder of the Horde's warring mentality.

Options

 Train Grunt

 Train Axethrower
Requires Lumber Mill.

 Build Catapult
Requires Blacksmith.

 Build Two-Headed Ogre
Requires Ogre Mound.

 Train Berserker
Requires Stronghold, Lumber Mill, Berserker upgrade.

 Train Ogre-Mage
Requires Ogre Mound, Altar of Storms, Ogre-Mage upgrade.

Blacksmith

The Orcs that live and work in the Blacksmith shops are veteran warriors themselves. They understand the value of strong steel, so they continually develop new techniques to improve their weapons and armor. The steel they forge is essential for manufacturing the devastating Catapult. Often their expertise is required in constructing advanced structures as well.

Options

Upgrade Weapons 1
Damage +2
Build Time: 200
Gold: 500
Lumber: 100

Upgrade Shields 1
Armor +2
Build Time: 200
Gold: 300
Lumber: 300

Upgrade Weapons 2
Damage +2
Build Time: 250
Gold: 1,500
Lumber: 300

Upgrade Shields 2
Armor +2
Build Time: 250
Gold: 900
Lumber: 500

Upgrade Catapults 1
Damage +15
Build Time: 250
Gold: 1,500

Upgrade Catapults 2
Damage +15
Build Time: 250
Gold: 4,000

Cannon Tower

Although twice as expensive as Guard Towers, Cannon Towers provide a formidable stationary defense and a slightly longer firing range. A row of these along a shoreline can pelt enemy ships and sink them long before they become a threat.

Dragon Roost

Mighty chains of adamantine steel bind the most powerful creature in all of Azeroth—Alexstrasza, the Dragon Queen. Captured and charmed by the Dragonmaw clan, Alexstrasza is kept in a constant state of weakness and pain. As the unwilling slave of the Horde, the Queen is closely watched as she lays her precious eggs. The Dragonmaw clan then raises her young to fight for the Horde, slaying them when they become too powerful to be controlled. Efforts are made constantly to break Alexstrasza's will so her captors can master control of the more mature Dragons.

Options

 Build Dragon

Fortress

As the military and economic center for the largest Orc cities, the Fortress can hold and process all the gold and lumber the Peons can harvest. Protected by obsidian spires, the Fortress is all but impervious to the attacks of the feeble Human forces.

Options

 Train Peon

29

Foundry

Known by the trio of towering smokestacks that surround it, the Foundry is instrumental in creating the massive armor plates and lethal cannons of the greatest Orc warship–the Juggernaught. Heat emanates from all openings as Foundry workers pour molten slag into casts for new cannons, and the pounding resounds for miles along the coasts as they shape ore into new armor.

Options

Upgrade Ship Cannons 1
Damage +5
Build Time: 200
Gold: 700
Lumber: 100
Oil: 1,000

Upgrade Ship Armor 1
Armor +5
Build Time: 200
Gold: 500
Lumber: 500

Upgrade Ship Cannons 2
Damage +5
Build Time: 250
Gold: 2,000
Lumber: 250
Oil: 3,000

Upgrade Ship Armor 2
Armor +5
Build Time: 250
Gold: 1,500
Lumber: 900

Goblin Alchemist

Goblin Alchemists are masters of volatile chemicals, explosives, and obscure mechanical devices. In constructing Zeppelins to soar above the battlefield and watertight pilot-shacks for use on the Giant Turtles, the Goblins defy the very laws of nature.

Options

 Build Goblin Zeppelin

 Train Goblin Sappers

Great Hall

This structure is the gathering place and command center for most Orcish settlements. The lowly Peons are trained here to perform the menial tasks of construction, repair, and harvesting. This is also where vital raw materials are gathered for processing and distribution. When a settlement achieves greater prosperity and requires stronger defenses, the Great Hall can be reinforced to make it a Stronghold.

Options

 Train Peon

 Upgrade to Stronghold
Requires Barracks

Guard Tower

Once upgraded, the Guard Tower houses a small Ballista for limited stationary defense. Such a structure can't be upgraded again into a Cannon Tower.

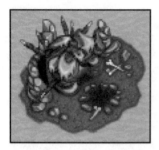

Ogre Mound

After training in the rudiments of combat at the Barracks, Ogres congregate in these crude stone huts to enhance their endurance, strength, and speed. These two-headed titans hurl and crush giant rocks to increase their already formidable strength and resilience; those who escape the pounding delivered by their brethren find themselves the quicker for it.

Oil Platform

The vast amounts of oil beneath the sea must be used in the construction of ships and various war machines. The oceans are rich with this substance, and so Tankers construct Oil Platforms where the oil is most plentiful. Only then can the Tankers collect their dark cargo.

Oil Refinery

The Oil Refinery uses the large, arching pipelines on either side of the main structure to pump oil from the Tankers into its processing holds. Built on the rim of the sea, Refineries are under constant threat from waterborne enemy vessels. Because a Refinery processes oil far more efficiently than a Shipyard alone, warships commonly are deployed to defend these structures.

Pig Farm

Farms provide the raw foodstuffs for sustaining both the slave labor force and the war parties in the field. Acquiring new units is impossible without a sufficient food supply. The basic diet of the Orcs—as well as their Troll and Ogre kin—is fresh meat. To satisfy this hunger for flesh, wild pigs are trapped and bred for food.

Scout Tower

Rising high above the timberline, Scout Towers resemble primitive huts bedecked with animal bones and giant tusks. These insubstantial (but useful) lookouts are ideal for spotting the Human forces from above, making Scout Towers a vital part of any Orcish settlement's defenses.

Shipyard

It may be a haphazard collection of stone, mortar, and cheap lumber, but the shabby Orc Shipyard is perhaps the most important structure in the Horde's war effort. As construction sites for Battleships, Transports, and Tankers, Shipyards provide vital links among the clans scattered across Lordaeron. These sites also have crude processing facilities, so Tankers can deliver shipments of oil there.

Options

 Build Oil Tanker

 Build Transport
Requires Foundry.

 Build Juggernaught
Requires Foundry.

 Build Destroyer

 Build Giant Turtle
Requires Goblin Alchemist.

Stronghold

The massive, jagged spires of the Orc Stronghold are a constant reminder of Orcish power and dominance. As the center of a large Orcish settlement, the Stronghold can process gold and lumber in the same fashion as a Great Hall. These intimidating steel and stone structures are built to serve as strong barriers, greatly reducing the damage attacking forces inflict. Convinced of their superiority as warriors, Ogres and Troll Berserkers act only under the direction of an overseer who has proved himself capable of establishing a Stronghold. As needs and resources dictate, a Stronghold can be reinforced and refitted as a Fortress.

Options

 Train Peon

 Upgrade to Fortress
Requires Ogre Mound,
Blacksmith, Lumber Mill.

Temple of the Damned

Temples of the Damned—called *Grombolar* ("bowels of the giant") in the Orcish tongue—are the dwellings of the dead. Created by Gul'dan to house his blasphemous Death Knights, the Temples were formed from the petrified carcasses of the race of giants that inhabited the Orcish homeworld. The Temple's subterranean labyrinth contains the fetid halls where the Death Knights dwell. There, the Death Knights practice their depraved necromancy on fallen warriors harvested from the battlefields above.

Options

 Train Death Knight

 Research Haste
Build Time: 100
Gold: 500

 Research Raise Dead
Build Time: 100
Gold: 1,500

 Research Whirlwind
Build Time: 150
Gold: 1,500

 Research Unholy Armor
Build Time: 200
Gold: 2,500

 Research Death and Decay
Build Time: 200
Gold: 2,000

Troll Lumber Mill

Carved from the trunk of an ancient Ironwood tree, the Troll Lumber Mill is a vital part of the Horde's lumber-processing operation. Having lived in the forests of the far north for centuries, the Trolls have devised a unique method of harvesting. By treating a group of trees with a volatile alchemical solvent, the Trolls can deaden and weaken large sections of wood.

Trolls are adept at fashioning a special sort of throwing axe. The manufacture and use of this weapon are always being perfected. Troll Berserkers frequent the Ironwood trees to digest potions they get from the Goblin Alchemists in their environs. These potions sharpen the Berserkers' sight or give them the ability to throw their axes farther. It is said that ingesting the correct potion can increase the speed at which healing occurs. This process of regeneration, or "fast healing," is one of the most unusual and awesome powers of the Troll Berserkers.

Options

Upgrade Throwing Axes 1
Damage +1
Build Time: 200
Gold: 300
Lumber: 300

Upgrade Throwing Axes 2
Damage +1
Build Time: 250
Gold: 900
Lumber: 500

Berserker Upgrade
Requires Stronghold
Build Time: 250
Gold: 1,500

Berserker Scouting
Sight: 9
Build Time: 250
Gold: 1,500

Research Lighter Axes
Range +1
Build Time: 250
Gold: 2,000

Berserker Regeneration
Build Time: 250
Gold: 3,000

Chapter 3
The Annals of the Great Alliance

I am Milan of the Elven House of Scribes. I have been given the honor of inscribing these Annals in preparation for the impending invasion by the Orcish Horde. For the first time in history, the Great Alliance of Lordaeron has brought together Humans, Elves, Dwarves, and Gnomes under the same banner to destroy our common enemy. I know not whether these Annals will describe our victory or our miserable defeat, but it is my hope that our ancestors will read and learn from these pages, whatever the outcome.

Therefore, I am concentrating on the military aspects of our endeavors—so that future leaders may study them in the event of our demise. The preservation of knowledge is paramount, for the Horde comes to destroy all we have learned and all we love about these lands. I have sworn a great oath to the Alliance to protect these words with my life and to pass this knowledge on. Tomorrow, I travel to Hillsbrad to record the maps, orders, and tactics of our most promising Human commander. May the Gods favor us.

ACT I: THE SHORES OF LORDAERON
Mission One: Hillsbrad

Orders: Because of your position as regional commander of the southern defense forces, Lord Terenas orders you to raise an outpost in the Hillsbrad foothills. It is rumored that Orcish marauders have been raiding coastal towns in the area, but whether these attacks are part of a greater Horde offensive is, as yet, unknown.

Your outpost is to provide food and information for Alliance troops and, therefore, should consist of at least four Farms. You must also construct a Barracks in order to safeguard the Hillsbrad operation. Your base will give advanced warning of Orcish troop movements in the area; it is an essential part of securing Alliance operations.

Objective: Build four Farms and a Barracks.

Opening Maneuvers: We have converted a large stone mansion into a Town Hall; the owner has graciously provided his servants and his Farm to assist us as well. Our first task was to plow more farmland for the arrival of more troops while training more servants for construction and mining. An old mine, nearby to the north, was reopened after the second Farm was completed, and all available workers helped gather the necessary materials for building. The forest was strangely quiet today. Our units of Footmen stayed close to the Hall.

Even Peasants can gang up and kill an enemy.

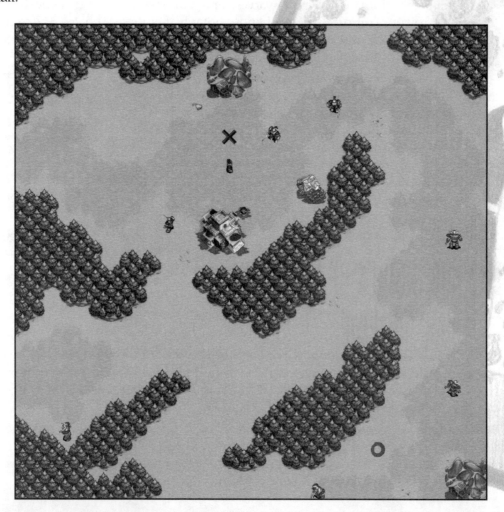

Carrying Out Our Orders: As soon as the workers had exhausted the mine's resources, we immediately began the construction of a Barracks. We received word of coming reinforcements, so all the local Peasants helped build the interior and exterior simultaneously in an effort to finish before the reinforcements' arrival. With that task completed, all that remained was to cut enough lumber for two more Farms. The workers are staying near the edge of the tree line; our troops continue to closely guard our efforts.

Securing the Area: Today the completion of the Farms heralded the arrival of reinforcements. They brought grim news of battles to the south and the presence of several bands of Orcs nearby. With our task completed and preparations for war begun, we decided to remain where we were and enjoy the quiet until we received new orders.

Mission Two: Ambush at Tarren Mill

Orders: The High Command has sent word that the Elves of Silvermoon have sent a contingent of Archers south to survey the Orcish threat. Unfortunately, our spies report that shortly after passing through the Alterac grasslands, the Elves were ambushed by Horde troops. It is believed that these Elves are now being held in a small prison camp near the northwest region of Tarren Mill.

Lord Terenas, hoping to enlist more Elves into the Alliance, has asked you to form a party to rescue the missing Elves. As a sign of good faith, the Elves have sent a cadre of Archers to assist you in your search. You will also be provided with plans to construct an Elven Lumber Mill and the sylvan craftsmen to operate it.

Objective: Find and rescue at least one Elven Archer and return him to the Circle of Power inside your base.

Opening Maneuvers: We arrived at Tarren Mill with a stalwart group of Footmen and were greeted by Elven Archers who had already prepared the village for war. They had also located our captured brethren to the northwest and were armed and ready to seek revenge. The enemy camp was too far inland for our warships to assist, so we made preparations to march. We briefly considered training more soldiers for the raid, but the Archers were eager to spill Orcish blood and convinced us to strike at dawn.

Carrying Out Our Orders: Still fatigued from yesterday's march, we gathered around the Circle of Power at first light and prepared our weapons. Spies reported that many of the Orcs had spread out to plunder the surrounding area, leaving a minimal guard at the unorganized outpost. We headed north and northwest in a tight group, wary of anything that moved. Startled Orcs and Trolls sent up war cries, but our force easily outnumbered them and slew them one at a time.

We then quickly returned through the village and headed west to approach the camp from the south, out of range of the Guard Tower. More foul beasts were felled on the way, and when we entered the clearing south of the camp, the guards came howling out after us as expected. We led them further south and killed those who did not turn back. This we repeated until all the guards had been dispatched; then we rushed the Tower as a group.

Before we had time to destroy it, a deep horn sounded an alarm, and we had very little time to break through a section of wall and get inside before the remaining Orcs returned. Once inside, our Archers tossed bows and quivers to the captives. We stood our ground inside until all was quiet.

Securing the Area: Cold and bleeding, our victorious group returned to Tarren Mill and immediately sent word of our success. Not a single Orc remained in the forest; enemy ships nearby were quickly sunk to prevent further problems. The reclusive Elves of Silvermoon bade us farewell to return home. I am not certain they will persuade their

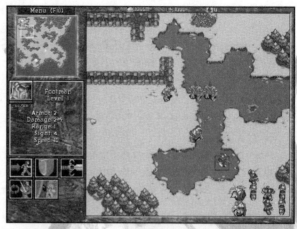

Lead bloodthirsty Orcs and Trolls from the safety of their defenses.

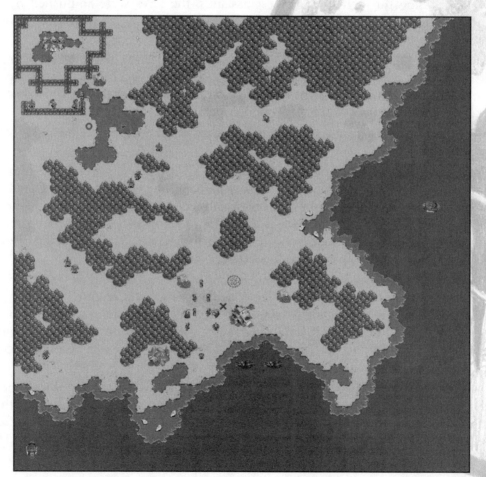

leaders to join the Alliance. We had but a single night's rest before an Elven Destroyer arrived with orders to board ship and sail to the south, where the sounds of war were becoming commonplace.

Mission Three: Southshore

Orders: With the safe return of the Elves, the Council of Silvermoon has resolved to combine the armies of Quel'thalas with those of the Alliance of Lordaeron. As a show of their support, they have sent a mighty fleet of Elven Destroyers to help safeguard the Lordaeron mainland.

In preparation for the arrival of these ships, Daelin Proudmoore–Lord of Kul Tiras and Grand Admiral of the Lordaeron Fleet–has ordered you to begin the construction of naval facilities near the township of Southshore. There is some suspicion that the Horde has constructed a secret base near the mainland, so it is imperative that you begin building your defense with haste.

Objective: Construct at least four Oil Platforms.

Opening Maneuvers: We began by using our troops and Destroyer to eliminate the four Orcs on land. Once our Peasants were safe from attack, we built another Farm to feed the large number of workers and sailors that would soon arrive. Next, we set the workers to collecting materials from the mine nearby and continued training new Peasants as fast as our resources permitted. The Destroyer on which we had arrived remained in place to guard the shoreline. The soldiers stayed near camp since spies had confirmed reports of an enemy base offshore. Rather than risk an encounter, we decided to build up as quickly and quietly as possible. Once we had five workers in the mines and a small amount of gold saved up, we constructed a Lumber Mill from the wood on hand and still had enough for another Farm. The troops were unhappy not to have a Barracks, but we were planning a naval assault and, therefore, trained still more workers to gather wood for processing in the new Mill. No enemies had been spotted yet, but we knew they were about.

Carrying Out Our Orders: After several days of gathering lumber, we began construction of the Shipyard on the shore to the east of our camp. On the night before it was completed, a small boat carrying shipwrights and sailors emerged from the mist above the waves. They were lucky to have come through alive. We gladly provided them with whatever building materials they needed, and soon they had christened their first Oil Tanker. It was a shoddy contraption, held together with pine tar and luck, but it managed to ferry enough supplies to build an Oil Platform nearby to the east. They built a second Tanker soon after, and a steady flow of black gold was soon filling our oak barrels as fast as we could make them. At the same time, more Farms were being built to feed the growing population of workers, who easily outnumbered the troops stationed here. We were all much relieved when construction of new Destroyers began, because we still had not enough time or resources to build a Barracks. With the surplus of workers gathering materials, we built five warships in a matter of weeks.

With this powerful fleet, we first swept along the coastline northeast and killed a Troll spy. Keeping this in mind, we then swept westward and secured the coast in that direction. At the western edge of the coast, we steered directly south toward the horizon and quickly spotted two enemy Destroyers guarding one of their own Platforms. These we sank effortlessly; we then destroyed their Platform. From there we sailed east and spotted more Destroyers around a small island. We sank those first; then we opened fire on the structures and enemies on the island. When the smoke from our cannons cleared, all that remained was scattered debris.

Structures close to shore are fair game for warships.

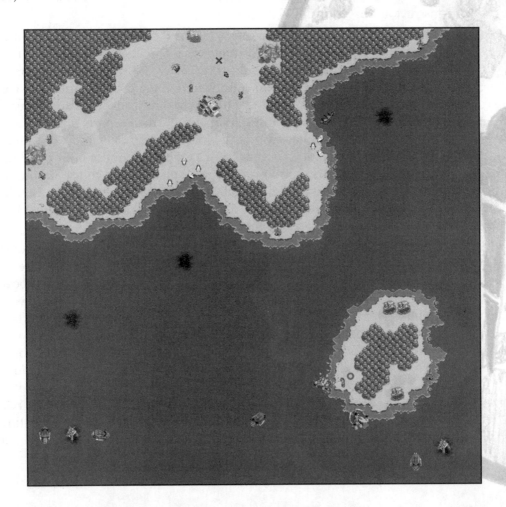

Securing the Area: The remaining Orcs on the mainland attempted a raid, but even the few troops guarding the camp were able to stop them. From there we quickly built three more Platforms–just in time for the approaching warships that would soon transform our camp into a busy seaport. We were not present to see it, however, since new orders took us elsewhere as usual.

Mission Four: Attack Zul'dare

Orders: Having established some order in the region with a display of naval power, Admiral Proudmoore advises that the time has come to seek out the secret lair of the Orcs. Scouts report that this base is located somewhere within the Zul'dare region of the Channel Islands, just southeast of Hillsbrad. Lordaeron artificers have completed designs for a Refinery to process oil with greater efficiency. With this new innovation, you are to construct Transport ships that can ferry your troops across large bodies of water. These vessels should provide great assistance in the completion of your task.

Objective: Seek out and demolish the Orc base.

Opening Maneuvers: Given the threat of enemy ships nearby, our first priority was to get a Shipyard into operation as soon as possible. First, we sent our worker into the mines to train more workers. At the same time, the two Destroyers that had brought us here were sent from the northern shore around to the south where an enemy Destroyer guarded an oil patch. After the enemy ship was obliterated, our Destroyers remained near the shore to guard the Shipyard site.

After training several more Peasants, we placed half of them in the mines and set the other half to collecting lumber. Soon we raised a Lumber Mill and, soon after, began constructing the Shipyard on the southern shore near camp. Taking no chances, we also constructed a Barracks to train a force of Archers for the coming amphibious assault. Though we were still training Peasants and building Farms, there was more than enough material and sufficient laborers to start the Refinery and Foundry. Meanwhile, new Tankers began exploiting the nearby patch of oil.

Carrying Out Our Orders: With all the necessary structures in place and operational, we next began preparations for war. We raised Guard Towers on the north shore to fend off landing raiders and spent time upgrading our arrows, ship cannons, and armor. More Destroyers were necessary to clear the way for our Transports, which were constructed only after we already had five Destroyers in the water. During this time, we continually trained new Archers until there were 10 units, which easily defended the camp until the Transports that would carry them were completed.

Our Destroyers began the operation by sailing south and southeast, directly into enemy territory. We kept them together and eliminated enemy craft one at a time. To make the invasion easier, we also set up a blockade around the southeastern Orc land, starving the Orcs for resources. Soon there was little opposition to our demolishing the platforms and coastal structures. With that completed, we anchored the Destroyers close to shore near the enemy camp and had them fire at Orcs while the Transports were being loaded with ten Archers and two Peasants. Once they had landed safely just west of our Destroyers, the Archers made sure our workers could construct two Guard Towers directly north of the Destroyers. We were very careful not to let our Archers wander into the camp, keeping them close to the Towers and Destroyers for defense. Once the Guard Towers were in place and upgraded, next came a Barracks, whose completion spelled doom for the vile Orcs.

Clear the way for an invasion with artillery support.

Securing the Area: While we were cleaning out the enemy camp, the remaining enemy ships in the area decided to try for our

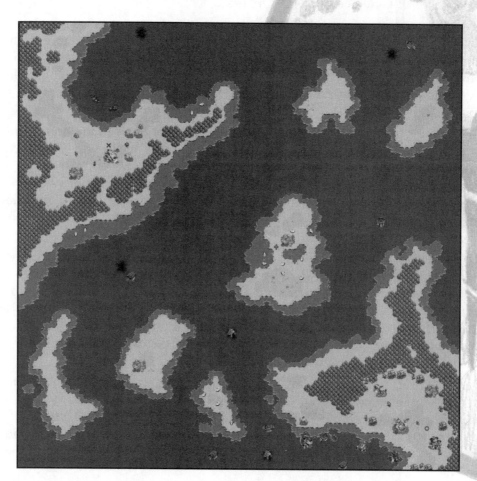

home base. They were soundly defeated by the Guard Towers we had constructed along the shore. We then sought out and killed the few remaining Orcs and celebrated our victory among the smoking ruins. Today was a great triumph for the Alliance; our skill in battle earned us a trip to the heart of the war on the mainland to the north.

ACT II: KHAZ MODAN
Mission Five: Tol Barad

Orders: Impressed by your series of victories against the Horde and by the destruction of the Zul'dare base, the High Command has decided to dispatch you and your troops to the main battleground. The forces of Stromgarde and Kul Tiras are currently stationed along the northern border of Khaz Modan, fighting to keep the Orcs from advancing into southern Lordaeron. An Orcish outpost, nestled near the ruins of the ancient Dwarven city of Dun Modr, has repeatedly beaten back Alliance troops and ravaged the surrounding farmlands. You must reclaim the nearby island Keep at Tol Barad and then launch an attack on the Horde outpost at Dun Modr.

Objective: Reclaim Tol Barad and destroy the Orc Base at Dun Modr.

Opening Maneuvers: As we rushed to board the waiting Transports, we could already see smoke rising from the nearby island. We sailed toward it, on the northeast side, and landed just in time to interrupt the demolition of a Barracks there. Several of our number died in the attack, but we were able to slaughter the Orcs and Trolls before they could finish their foul deed. Once we were safely inside the camp, the grateful inhabitants were eager to follow our orders, and soon the Barracks was repaired while we raised Cannon Towers behind it to prevent further destruction. With all the structures intact, we then built more Farms and trained workers to speed our efforts. On the western shore of the island we began a Shipyard. Meanwhile, the Tanker that accompanied us found an oil patch a short distance farther west and proceeded to build a Platform over it. We were soon ready to begin building Ballistae for our strike on the Orc-infested island to the northeast.

Carrying Out Our Orders: Within days, we had assembled our amphibious force near the Shipyard and had loaded the Transports with six Ballistae, five Archers, and one Peasant. Escorted by Destroyers, we sailed for the west side of the enemy base. We sank a single enemy Destroyer on the way while the rest of their fleet was busy guarding the other side. After landing, the worker we had brought quickly began a Tower on the closest patch of flat ground. With a line of trees obscuring the Orcs' view of our operation, we were able to construct two Cannon Towers and a makeshift Barracks unmolested. We then sent a single Archer to greet the Orcs and lead them back within range of our waiting forces. Shortly thereafter, we began the assault on the Orcs' base by land, a stratagem for which they were obviously unprepared.

Securing the Area: After leveling most of the Orcs' structures, we lined up our Ballistae along the shoreline and sank the majority of their ships. Those that remained were removed by a second group of our Destroyers. We finished the operation by hunting down and slaughtering all of the panicked Orcs that were left. News of our victory quickly spread to the mainland.

Land quickly to save the Barracks.

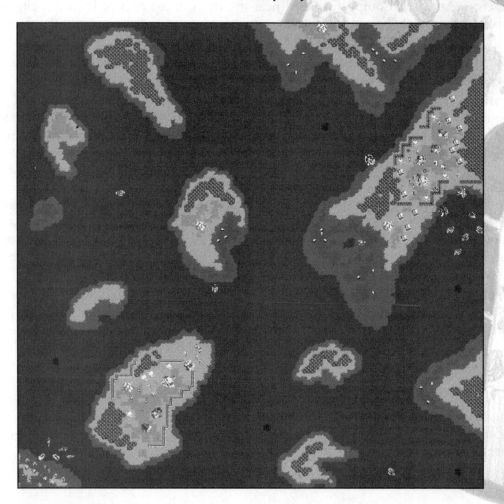

Mission Six: Dun Algaz

Orders: Following their defeat at Dun Modr, the Orcs were forced to retreat south, across the Thandol Valley to a secondary outpost at Dun Algaz. Lord Lothar, hoping to push the Orcs even farther back into Khaz Modan, has ordered you to destroy this newly discovered encampment. A small company of Knights has been placed under your command by Lothar to aid you in your mission.

Objective: Destroy Dun Algaz.

Opening Maneuvers: Our first task was to train more Peasants to plunder the nearby mine, for we would need its contents for the coming

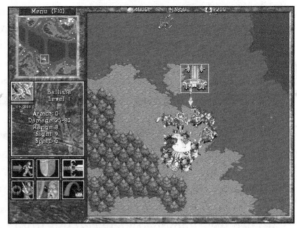

Destroy the enemy Barracks to make room for your own in enemy territory.

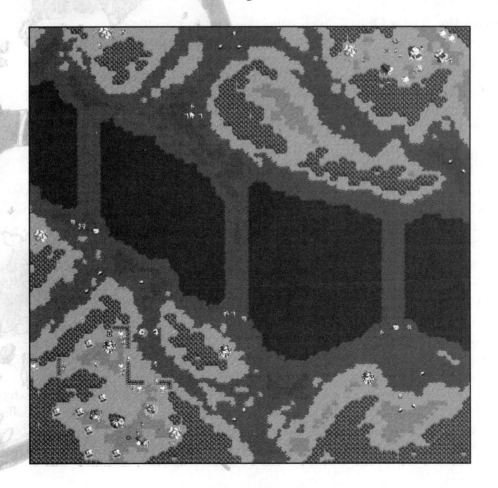

land raid. Our force would consist mostly of Knights and Ballistae, so a Blacksmith was required as well as a Keep. We also built Cannon Towers at the eastern and western openings of the base to fend off occasional raids by Orcs. Although we had the research and training available for Rangers, our commander was confident that Knights would be more suitable for the attack, and we spent much time and resources enhancing their weapons and armor.

Carrying Out Our Orders: The attacking force gathered just outside camp. It consisted of nine proud Knights and three Ballistae for heavy artillery. Scouts have located three narrow land bridges leading to the enemy; we chose the most direct route, down the center bridge. The Knights rode in front of the slower war machines, occasionally waiting for them. As we neared the end of the land bridge, a large party of mixed Horde monsters attacked, but they were no match for our great mounted warriors.

Close to the south, we spotted a makeshift enemy Barracks and promptly leveled it. Then we summoned a few Peasants from our home camp and set them to work on our own temporary Barracks on the same spot, while our Knights stood guard. For good measure, we also built Cannon Towers on both sides of the Barracks and, with those completed, sent the workers back home.

Securing the Area: One of our Knights was sent toward the enemies to lure them out; our Ballistae made quick work of their Towers after most of the defenders were dead. We made a point to concentrate fire on the Orc Catapults, as they were dangerous to our compact group of Knights. From this point, it was only a matter of demolition and slaughter as new Knights and Ballistae emerged from the makeshift Barracks to replace those lost in battle. For the first time in months, we were hopeful the Horde could be stopped, but the road to final victory would be long.

Mission Seven: Grim Batol

Orders: Advance scouts report that they have located Grim Batol—the primary base of the Horde's Refinery operations in Khaz Modan. Seeing a chance to strike a decisive blow against the Horde, Lord Lothar has ordered you to infiltrate Grim Batol and put an end to all Orcish activity there.

Lothar believes that once Grim Batol has been destroyed, the Orcs will have no further use for Khaz Modan and will therefore pull their forces back to the mainland of Azeroth. Victory could secure the shores of Lordaeron and greatly impede the Horde offensive.

Objective: Destroy five Oil Refineries.

Opening Maneuvers: We landed as close to Grim Batol as possible, and decided to sink our transports to yield more food for the army. From there we had to march south, leaving the workers behind for safety. As we proceeded, we were disturbed to discover two enemy Catapults, fortified behind a wall and guarded by several Orcs. We steeled ourselves and rushed directly toward them. Thankfully, the Catapults were unmanned, and after killing the guards, we broke through the wall and claimed the war machines for ourselves. Continuing south, we destroyed an enemy Tower and claimed yet another Catapult. Only then did we summon the Transports and Peasants south to join us, following which our force boarded ship to land on the other side of the river. This time we swept northward, careful to remove enemy Towers with the Catapults, and soon leveled all the foul Orcish structures so we could raise our own.

Carrying Out Our Orders: We quickly erected a Town Hall near a mine to the north and began collecting resources. Our commander was planning to build Battleships for the attack, so a Lumber Mill and a Shipyard were needed as soon as possible. While the Shipyard was being built, we decided to place a Refinery at the southeastern tip of a small penin-

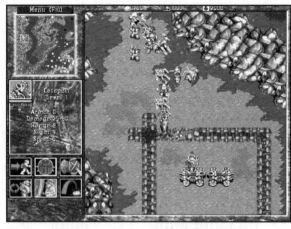

Capture unmanned enemy Catapults for your own use.

sula, conveniently near an oil patch. After Tankers had been built to exploit it, a Foundry was raised near the Shipyard, which provided the heavy cannons and armor for Battleships. Unfortunately, the mine was running dry, so we built a Transport to ferry workers across to

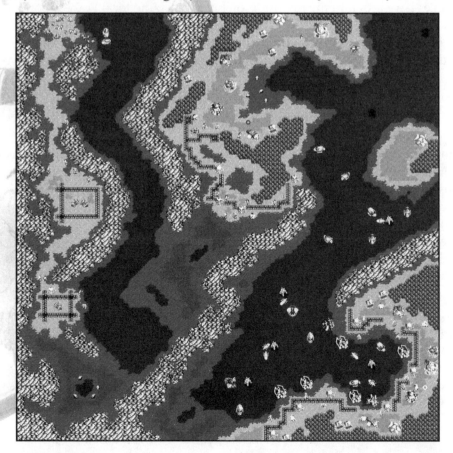

another nearby mine and built a temporary Town Hall near it to collect the resources. Finally, construction of the Battleships began; we spent our extra time and gold to develop better cannons and armor to ensure their success.

Securing the Area: At last we had six tall Battleships, and we sailed them south into enemy territory. They made quick work of the enemy vessels that tried to stop them. Ignoring the Oil Platforms and Refineries for a time, we concentrated on removing the Towers and Catapults that guarded them. As the Horde watched helplessly, we began pounding their structures; soon they were forced to surrender to our might.

ACT III: THE NORTHLANDS
Mission Eight: Tyr's Hand

Orders: With the destruction of Dun Modr and the downfall of the Oil Refinery at Grim Batol, the Orcs have completely withdrawn their armies from Khaz Modan. Although your victories have been notable, the menace of the Horde still hangs over the Alliance. Lord Lothar has stationed your troops in the northlands to protect the borders of Quel'thalas.

Troubles have arisen in the township of Tyr's Hand; the local Peasant population is in a state of minor revolt. You must quell this uprising and then summon the Knights of the Silver Hand to hearten and watch over the populace. Once peace has been restored, determine whether there is Orcish activity in the region. Any Horde forces are to be intercepted and routed.

Objective: Quell the peasant uprising in Tyr's Hand, construct a secondary Castle in the northwest to maintain order in the region, and destroy all enemy forces.

Opening Maneuvers: Slaughtering Human workers was unpleasant, but with the Horde nearby, this action was necessary to ensure our survival. Once the township was quiet, we had very little time to make preparations for war. We trained more Peasants to speed mining operations while our troops patrolled inside the town walls, ever vigilant for raiding Orcs. Barracks were constructed first, then a Lumber Mill near the forests on the east side of town. Next came the transformation of the Town Hall into a Keep. To protect our efforts, we constructed Farms to block the north and west entrances. Behind these we raised Cannon Towers, placing Archers near them for good measure. The remaining troops were gathered near the other entrances while Stables were prepared for the arriving Paladins.

Carrying Out Our Orders: Once the township had been properly fortified, we began training Knights and constructing Catapults for the coming battles. When resources were available, the Keep was fortified into a stalwart Castle, and a Church was constructed for the Paladins who invited our Knights to join them and learn their craft. To ensure their success, we spent much time and gold preparing better weapons, armor, and Ballista spears in the Smithy. Ten Paladins and four Ballistae gathered in the courtyard before sallying out, and the long process of cleaning out Orcs began in earnest.

Securing the Area: We sent a single Paladin northward to draw enemies toward a row of Ballistae defended by more Paladins. Though many of the creatures turned back, a few fell into the trap. We repeated this maneuver until the number of guards in the northern camp was greatly reduced. Only then did we roll in the Ballistae to help take out structures.

Several raids were made on our township, but our fortifications held nicely with Cannon Towers defending them. We then started destroying the camp to the west of town, replacing fallen warriors as needed. Finally, we assembled a large force of mixed units to remove the stronger threat to the northwest and, with

Build Farms and Towers to block entrances.

that task completed, constructed a second Castle on the ruins to prevent further problems here. The Horde was now on the defensive, and the ground was soaked with Orcish blood rather than our own.

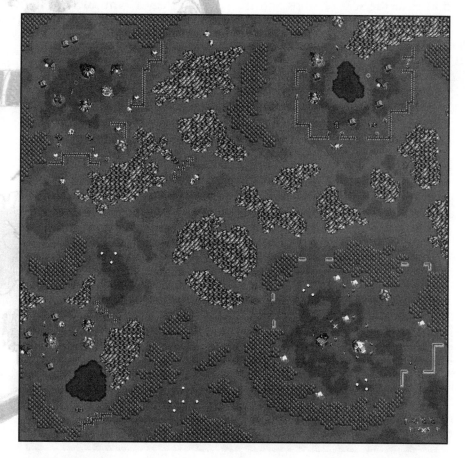

Mission Nine: The Battle at Darrowmere

Orders: With his Paladins keeping vigilant watch over the northlands, the Archbishop's assistant, Uther Lightbringer, has come to offer comfort to those who are suffering the misfortunes of war. Lord Lothar has entrusted to you the task of protecting Lightbringer and his entourage as they travel to the island township of Caer Darrow.

Objective: Escort Lightbringer to the Circle of Power at Caer Darrow.

Opening Maneuvers: Our Commander has decided to attempt a bold maneuver. Spies have reported that our land forces may not be able to deal with the heavily fortified Orcish settlement that separates us from Lightbringer, so we have

Towers can only fire at one target at a time.

endeavored to clear the seas of ships and trust Fate to deliver him safely to the Circle. Our first task was to assemble all our warships into a tight cluster; then we sent a single fast

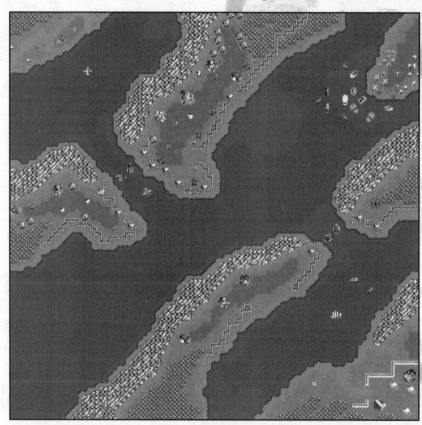

Destroyer south to draw out the enemy ships guarding the way to Caer Darrow. Once those had been eliminated, we decided not to risk doing the same with the traitorous Elven Destroyers beyond the gauntlet of Cannon Towers, for they are quite a bit smarter than Orcs and would perceive our trap. Instead, two more Horde destroyers were drawn out of the other passage to Uther and were sunk, leaving the sea lanes mostly open.

Carrying Out Our Orders: Our four Transports were then prepared for a dangerous mission. All unnecessary deck hands were invited to stay safely ashore with the troops. These four ships then set out unescorted toward Lightbringer. As they sailed quickly through the gauntlet, the Cannon Towers could not reload fast enough to hit them; and all four arrived, damaged but still seaworthy. Uther boarded the strongest of the four and prepared to sail back. His transport was placed in the middle in the hope that the lead and trailing ships would draw most of the cannon fire. The plan worked, but two of the four sank below the waves.

Securing the Area: With Uther safely among the warships, our entire flotilla set out directly for Caer Darrow. With so many targets, the second gauntlet could not possibly stop them all. Even the enemy Battleship near our goal was too busy with our warships to notice the Transports sneaking past. As soon as Uther's craft landed, he raced for the Circle of Power and stood with upraised hands. Boiling thunderheads soon filled the sky and unleashed bolts of lightning on the Elven craft, utterly destroying them. With the forces of nature on our side, the remaining Horde forces quickly abandoned their cause and retreated. Fate had smiled on us yet again, and the seed of hope had firmly taken root.

Mission Ten: The Prisoners

Orders: After the battle at Caer Darrow, a number of Orcish soldiers were captured, along with the infamous Warlock Gul'dan. A crew of Alterac sailors were caught assisting the Horde during the battle and have been placed under close guard. Under the edict of Lord Lothar, you are to restrain the prisoners until they can be escorted to the capital of Lordaeron for interrogation.

Objective: Guard the enemy prisoners, construct Transports, and escort at least four Alterac traitors to the Circle of Power at Stratholme.

Opening Maneuvers: Since we would need ships to carry out our orders, our first building priorities were a Lumber Mill, a Blacksmith, a Barracks, and, of course, a Shipyard. There was a plenitude of gold and lumber in the area, but we needed many workers to collect it. When the labor force had completed the Shipyard, we discovered that enemy Transports were unloading Orcs to the south of town. Although the few troops we had trained could deal with them for the time being, spies reported that they would soon arrive in increasing numbers. At the south edge of town, we erected several Cannon Towers and fortified these with Farms and Archers for good measure. Once the town was reasonably secure, we concentrated on a Foundry for the production of Battleships.

Carrying Out Our Orders: Getting to the captured sailors was no easy task. A small Horde village separated the main body of water from the river snaking toward the prisoners, so we prepared an amphibious group of three Battleships and two Transports loaded with

Footmen, Ballistae, and a couple of Peasants. First, we sent the Battleships in to take out the Tower and draw the Catapults closer to shore for their destruction. Once the coastline was clear, we moved our warships close to shore and landed the Transports. As soon as they unloaded, Ogres began pouring in from the settlement, but these monsters tried to concentrate on our Ballistae while Footmen and cannon fire cut them down. When the smoke had cleared somewhat, the Peasants built two Cannon Towers close to shore, and the remaining Ogres were drawn in to their deaths. The rest of the village fell quickly; the Ballistae made quick work of the enemy Juggernaught anchored on the river.

Clear the riverbank with Battleships before sending a Transport.

Securing the Area: In order to recover the prisoners, we first had to construct another Shipyard on the river. From here, we launched three more Battleships to deal with the numerous enemy Cannon Towers set up along the river. Only then did we launch a single Transport to pick up six of the captives. The rest were

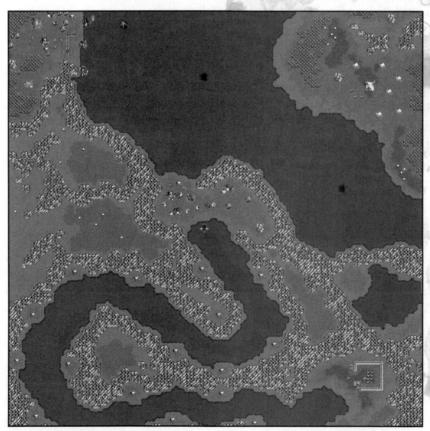

promised safe passage later, but at that time it was imperative that we get a few of them back to town. They were hurried from the river to the waiting flotilla on the sea and were escorted back. We then forced four of them to stand on the mysterious Circle, which glowed brightly for a time, then faded. The prisoners simply stood dumbfounded until they were locked up in the Town Hall. Later, we received word that their memories had been thoroughly inspected from afar, and what had been found was not to our liking. The traitor nation of Alterac was to be destroyed for its crimes. I am deeply ashamed and angered that those of my own race would betray the Alliance. I shall not mourn their demise.

Mission Eleven: Betrayal and the Destruction of Alterac

Orders: Having interrogated the treacherous warriors of Alterac, Lord Lothar sends word that the Alliance has been betrayed. Lord Perenolde, sovereign ruler of Alterac, has been working with the Horde since the beginning of the war. It was Perenolde who provided the Orcs with the travel routes of the Elven strike force passing through Tarren Mill. The rebellion at Tyr's Hand was also started by Alterac spies in the hope of concealing the Orcish mining facility located there.

By decree of the High Command, the nation of Alterac has committed treason against the Alliance, and its union with the Orcish Hordes must therefore be broken. Lord Lothar has ordered that you free those persons unjustly held by Perenolde and enlist their aid in launching an attack against Alterac's capital.

Objective: Rescue the imprisoned Peasants and Mages from the camp in the northwest and return them to your base to launch a full-scale assault against the traitorous Alterac.

Opening Maneuvers: Rescuing the captive Mages and Peasants was of paramount importance, for we had no workers and no gold to train them. We formed a standard land attack group of Knights and Ballistae, then set out on the north road leading to the compound. Getting in was troublesome, but not difficult, since our Ballistae had a slightly greater range than the enemy Towers. After breaking in and freeing the captives, we sent most of the force back to town, but not before destroying all we could.

Carrying Out Our Orders: With workers plundering the mines, we then began fortifying the town with Towers and Farms, closing off all the paths but one for our own troops to use. Next came the construction of Stables for our Knights, and soon after, the fortification of our Keep into a Castle. Since our attack plan required only Paladins and Ballistae, our final construction was a Church, and from then on, we concentrated on producing the necessary military units.

Time and gold were also spent on the Blacksmith to provide the best possible weapons and armor. When we had gathered nine Paladins and four Ballistae in the courtyard, our force was deemed ready to make the assault.

Securing the Area: Moving out to the northeast, our Paladins led the way for the slower Ballistae, occasionally stopping to wait for them. At first we met with only a few enemies, but as we drew near the walls of the foul capital, greater numbers of Horde and traitorous Human forces slowed our progress considerably. After we had leveled several towers and secured an open area within the walls, reinforcements were called and sent out while the Paladins healed the wounded. Following the advice of our spies, we decided to march north along the inside of the west wall, taking out Towers along the way and ignoring lesser structures until later. Soon we were inside the heart of the capital, but we had taken a great deal of punishment. Still more Paladins were called, and before long, we had our revenge on Lord Perenolde.

Bring Ballistae along to take out towers from a safe distance.

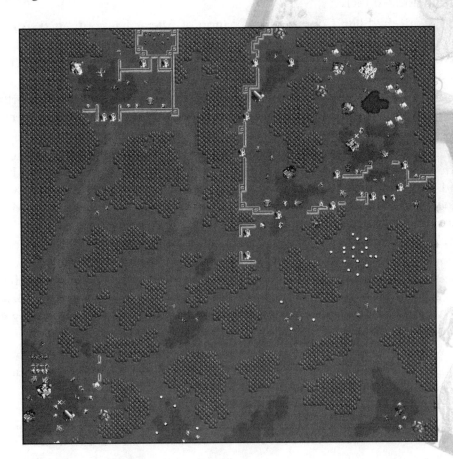

ACT IV: THE RETURN TO AZEROTH
Mission Twelve: The Battle at Crestfall

Orders: With the destruction of Alterac, the Orcish armies in the north have staged a massive retreat. Admiral Proudmoore sends word that Gnome Submarines have located the Horde's main naval base near Crestfall. Proudmoore believes that the Orcs plan to launch the remainder of their armada and retreat to the mainland of Azeroth. Lord Lothar has ordered you to destroy the base at Crestfall before the fleet can escape.

Objective: Destroy all Orc Transports, Oil Platforms, and Orc Shipyards.

Opening Maneuvers: Our first problem was feeding the large number of troops stationed inside the base, so the construction of two more Farms was necessary. These we placed at the northern opening to impede enemy landing parties. Then our workers went to work in the mine; the resulting flow of income went for the training of even more Peasants. During this time, we gathered all our forces safely inside the base and brought our ships close to shore with a Flying Machine overhead to watch for enemy Giant Turtles. With this new threat in mind, we raised a Gnomish Inventor laboratory for the construction of more Fliers, and eventually our own submersible craft. Preparations for defense were completed with several Towers along the northern perimeter of town.

Carrying Out Our Orders: The next task was to collect oil for a naval force. Fliers reported a barren island far to the north with a dark patch on its east side, so we loaded up a Transport with two Ballistae and a Peasant in preparation for building. By that time we had another Flier in the air, which escorted the Transport and two Oil Tankers to the island, approaching it from the west side to avoid detection. After they had landed, a Tower was quickly raised on a small patch of flat ground; this would allow Giant Turtles to be spotted

and sunk by the Ballistae. On the north end of the island, a Refinery was built at the same time as the Tankers constructed a Platform over the oil. When that task had been completed, a second Shipyard went up on the west side of the island, and we began constructing Submarines at both.

Securing the Area: While waiting for the Submarines, our ships sailed out to the northeast, escorted by a Flier, to remove an enemy Oil Platform and stop the flow of oil. This would help ensure that the sea remained clear after our Submarines had sunk the enemy ships and

Build a remote base near oil, and defend it well.

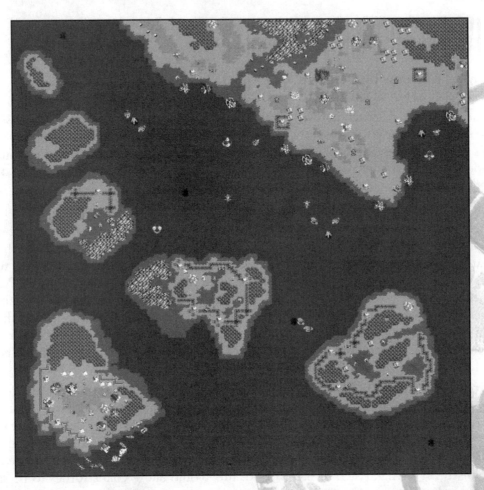

Turtles. More Fliers were constructed as spotters for the Subs, and once the enemy's naval power had been withered, a Foundry was built for the construction of Battleships. These vessels were then fitted with the best cannons and armor we could make, and a flotilla of six sailed out to pound the enemy coastline. They were very careful to draw the Horde's Catapults to shore, where they were much easier to destroy. Next went the Towers guarding the enemy's shoreline structures, and finally the structures themselves.

Mission Thirteen: Assault on Black Rock Spire

Orders: After the battle of Crestfall, the remnants of the routed Orcish fleet managed to reach the northern shores of Azeroth. Admiral Proudmoore believes that the Horde will attempt to reinforce their main Fortress at Black Rock Spire. Leading a large strike force of Lordaeron troops, Lord Lothar was sent to attempt a parley with the Orcish chieftain Orgrim Doomhammer. The war being all but finished, his intent was to accept the unconditional surrender of the Orcish Hordes. No word has been heard from Lothar or his strike force in days.

Assuming the worst, Admiral Proudmoore and King Terenas agree that it falls to you to stage a final siege against Black Rock Spire. The feral Dwarves of the Northeron wildlands have offered the service of their Gryphon Riders to assist in the decimation of the foul Orcs.

Objective: Destroy Black Rock Spire and eradicate any and all enemy forces.

Opening Maneuvers: On our arrival, we found only workers and injured soldiers hiding in the few structures they had managed to defend. The town had been sacked once already, meaning Lord Lothar was likely dead. When the survivors described the landing of enemy Transports, we decided to cripple the enemy's navy before concentrating on a major land assault. We immediately boarded our few warships and, escorted by a Gryphon, set out westward to follow the trail of the Transports.

Two enemy Destroyers were sunk before turning north, and near the mainland we spotted an Oil Platform being built. Not wanting to let them collect oil, we waited for the slower Battleship and planned an attack. Two enemy Juggernaughts waited to the southeast, while a Cannon Tower on land was judged able to strike targets only on the west side of the platform. First, we sent our Gryphon to chase and sink the Juggernaughts, while the warships sailed to the east side of the Platform to begin demolition. By the time the Gryphon had done its work, the Platform had fallen and was replaced with a Destroyer to prevent rebuilding. To complete the task, we then sent the Battleship and Gryphon north to sink the landed Transports, and thus prevented the Orcs under the orange standard from using them ever again.

Carrying Out Our Orders: Next on the list was the oil production of the red standard Orcs. For this we sailed our Battleship eastward, followed closely by the remaining Destroyer and the Gryphon. We sailed directly into the harbor toward another newly built Platform, and again sent the Gryphon to remove a Catapult from the southeast shoreline near it. Then, while the ships pounded the Platform, our faithful Gryphon started on the landed Transports north of it to prevent them from making any deliveries. Next went the Cannon Tower west of the enemy Shipyard, and by then the Platform had been removed and replaced by a Destroyer. Waiting until the Tower was out of the way, the Battleship then went to work on the Shipyard, and its destruction ended the enemy attacks by sea.

Securing the Area: A third and final threat to our base was the Dragon Roost on the central island, but this would require a bit more effort. While the Orcish navy was being neutralized, our workers built a few Guard Towers for minimal defense, then concentrated on all the structures and upgrades required to launch more Gryphons into the air. We also built a Foundry and a Refinery to produce more Battleships, but the mine was starting to run dry.

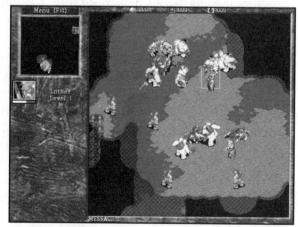

Sir Lothar betrayed!

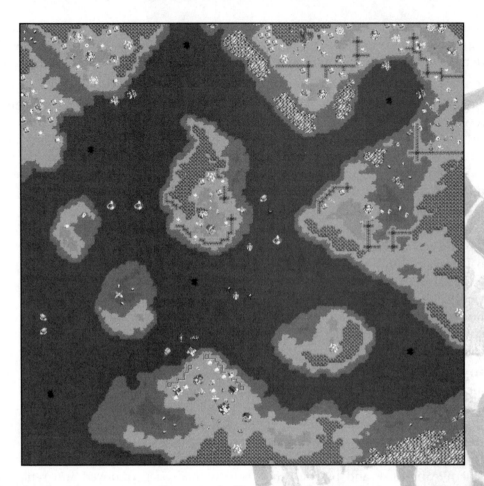

To solve this problem temporarily, a single Transport was launched to ferry some workers east. There, the workers built a secondary Hall on a small island with another mine. This extra income allowed us to assemble a flotilla of four Battleships, four Destroyers, and three Transports with which to land a mixed force of Rangers and Knights on the central island.

First, the warships removed as many enemy Towers as possible, with the Destroyers concentrating on any Dragons that threatened. The land units came ashore on the north side and quickly swept into the village, slaughtering the defenders and finishing Towers before removing the rest of the foul structures. More workers were ferried in, and a third Hall was set up to plunder the rich mine there. From this point, the Horde was defenseless against the mobs of Gryphons we launched from four Aviaries. Standard landing parties of Knights and Ballistae made slow but steady work of anything remotely Orchish, while Gryphons circled overhead. Black Rock Spire was last to fall, and soon the Great Portal would receive the same treatment.

Mission Fourteen: The Great Portal

Orders: The Orcs have been driven from the Northlands as the hulking remains of Black Rock Spire lay silent among the freed lands of Azeroth. The battered remnants of the once-mighty Horde have rallied to protect their last bastion of hope—the Great Portal. With Lord Lothar dead, you have been given the duty of leading the forces of Lordaeron to ultimate victory over the Horde—a victory that proceeds from the destruction of the Great Portal itself.

Objective: Destroy the Great Portal.

Opening Maneuvers: Before we could make the final assault on the Great Portal, we needed to find flat ground to build a village. Predictably, there were strong defenses at the closest available land, so the first task was to clear the way for a landing with our few warships. Knights, Footmen, and Archers were loaded onto Transports and soon followed westward, for we would need to build quickly. A single Destroyer swept past the shoreline to the west to draw out the Catapults, then all three regrouped to attack single targets and retreat. This was repeated until all but one Tower remained on the shoreline; however, the Destroyers had been sunk, and the Battleship was taking on much water when we decided to make a landing. Knights and Footmen hit the north beach first and engaged the waiting Ogres, and as soon as there was room, the Archers came next to speed the slaughter with missile weapons. A few Knights were sent south to take out the Tower, and soon the area was secure enough to fetch the remaining units.

Carrying Out Our Orders: While building a Hall near the mine, our Archers were lined up to bring down marauding Dragons, and our two Mages stayed safely behind to launch Fireballs at the beasts as well. With this in mind, our next building priorities were Farms, a Barracks, and a Lumber Mill to train more Archers. These would ensure that Dragons were no longer a problem once we had a small army. The mine was quickly running out of resources, so we would soon need to claim another in the Ogre village close by to the north. To clear the way, our growing number of Archers were lined up behind Farms and better-armored soldiers, and a single Knight rode forth to bring the Ogres into our arrow trap. Spies reported that three more Dragons far to the east were watching for smoke on the horizon, so we ordered our troops not to level the foul Orcish structures until we were fully prepared to greet the Dragons. A second Hall went up near the new mine to speed the collection of the great wealth within. This would ensure our survival against the next enemy village to the east, for soon we could afford to call on the skills of elite Elven Rangers to train our existing Archers. With these at our disposal, we began destroying the rest of the Horde structures and easily defeated the Dragons that came too late.

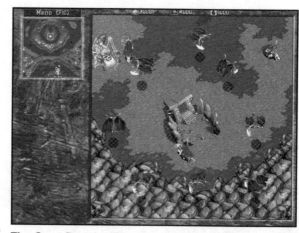

The Great Portal will not be easily destroyed.

It was not long before we had two more Barracks, a Blacksmith, and a Stable to add more muscle to our forces. The muscle came in the form of many Knights and two Ballistae, all with the best weapons and armor we could make for them. Several Rangers and the Mages were left behind for defense, while a stalwart army marched eastward to begin clearing out the Orcs once more. We ordered them to stand their ground just outside in a standard formation of Knights first, Rangers behind, and Ballistae in the rear. Our greatest danger was the Death Knights that cast horrible plagues in our midst, so our forces were spread out to minimize

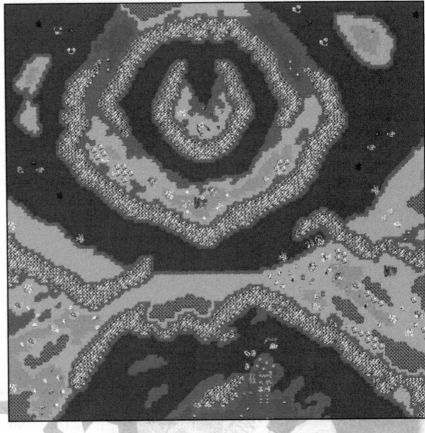

their damage, and several Knights were kept moving to ride them down on sight.

Once the defenders were mostly gone, demolition began once again while we hunted down any remaining enemies hiding nearby.

Securing the Area: With a third mine and Hall to collect gold, we then built four Gryphon Aviaries to claim the skies for ourselves. Once we had a flight of eight in the air, these were sent out to wreak havoc on all the enemy ships in the waters surrounding the central island. In the meantime, a Gnomish Inventor supplied fearless Dwarves with explosives to bomb a path through the narrow line of mountains north of the third mine. This was done to place a Shipyard much closer to a supply of oil, and with the accompanying Foundry and Refinery, we could then produce Transports for the assault on the island. Our growing mob of Gryphon Riders then concentrated on drawing the defending Dragons and Demons away from their Guard Towers. Meanwhile, transports were loaded with Knights and Ballistae to do most of the demolition and slaughter on the island while the Gryphons kept the skies clear. Workers were brought to set up a second Shipyard on the inner ring of water, and by then the fate of the Orcish Horde was sealed. The glorious destruction of the Portal was followed with weeks of celebration worldwide.

Chapter 4
The Domination of Lordaeron

I am Utok Scratcher, apprentice shaman and chief advisor to a ruthless new commander of the Blackrock clan. I am called Scratcher for my habit of scribbling rather than mindlessly killing. For too long my people have ignored the need to record our methods. However, I am confident that these chronicles will benefit those who recognize this need.

As a follower of mystic arts, I am aware that the devouring of a world is the highest possible honor in the eyes of our dark Gods. The Great Portal has allowed us the opportunity to do just that, and it is my intention to arm the Orc, Troll, Ogre, and Goblin allies of our clan with knowledge in addition to power. Bloodlust is our nature, but the passion for destruction requires direction. Therefore, I am compiling maps from our scouting reports, accompanied by descriptions of our orders and military tactics for clarification. These pages will be the weapons with which our clan ascends above all others, to claim the honor of annihilating this new world and its inhabitants.

ACT I: SEAS OF BLOOD
Mission One: Zul'dare

Orders: The Horde is preparing to launch an assault against the mainland of Lordaeron. Orgrim Doomhammer, war chief of the Orcish Hordes and ruler of the Blackrock clan, has ordered you to establish a small outpost on Lordaeron's southern shores. To secure the Zul'dare region, as Doomhammer demands, you must construct a Barracks and several Pig Farms to feed your troops. Your success may help us determine the extent of the pathetic Human defenses and the resistance they can offer against our forces.

Objective: Build four Farms and a Barracks.

Preparations for Battle: My commander has been given a pitiful number of troops and workers with whom to carry out our orders, yet we have managed to easily overtake a Human outpost and convert it to our cause.

We needed new food sources after the long voyage across the Great Sea. Therefore, we beat an injured soldier into submission, made him a worker, and began fencing in new Pig Farms.

Attack in groups to weigh the odds in your favor.

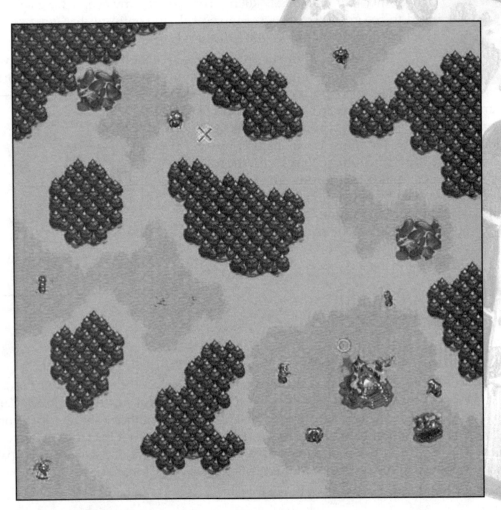

Methods of Destruction: Those who were not building were sent to labor in a nearby mine, for we needed mineral resources in addition to food. Bored with standing about, our troops banded together in a tight group and began patrolling the area; they managed to find a few scattered Humans to quench their thirst for blood. Only one of them returned, but by then we had begun construction of a new Barracks. This we needed for the coming reinforcements, so all available workers were whipped into helping.

Completion of Orders: With the Barracks completed, we needed only a bit more farmland to raise pigs, and soon the promised reinforcements arrived.

After a short time, all the Human spies in the area had provided skulls to adorn our standard. With the area secure, we waited impatiently for new orders.

Mission Two: Raid at Hillsbrad

Orders: Our spies report that a band of Human soldiers has captured a war party led by Troll commander Zuljin and has taken them to the township of Hillsbrad. Seeing an opportunity to place these captives in debt to the Horde, Doomhammer sends you to ransom Zuljin and his Trolls. The war chief believes that this raid on the unsuspecting settlement will strike terror into the hearts of those who would dare resist the Horde.

Objective: Rescue Zuljin and at least one other Troll, then return them to the Circle of Power.

Preparations for Battle: Our Grunts had gathered in the courtyard of the village; they were quite eager to seek carnage.

In fact, every soldier in the village marched north, shouting war cries, and left the Peons standing alone scratching their heads. The war party encountered feeble resistance and swept forward toward the enemy prison camp, leaving the village unattended.

Methods of Destruction: On reaching the camp, our troops first massacred the weaklings guarding it, then patrolled about looking for more before venting their frustration on the walls.

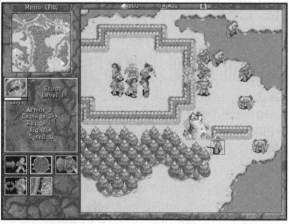

Rescue allies behind enemy lines to add to your forces.

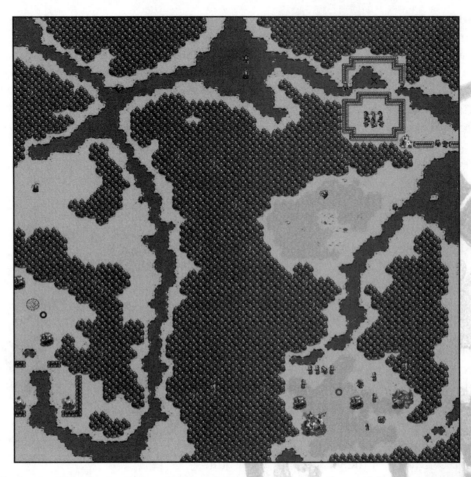

Completion of Orders: As we followed the frozen river west and then south, a few more Humans were found and slaughtered–hardly worth the trouble–before we continued south to the abandoned village near Hillsbrad. This we claimed for ourselves.

Mission Three: Southshore

Orders: In preparation for a final strike on Hillsbrad, the war chief directs you to begin construction of facilities for the Orcish armada near the Southshore region. Zuljin and his Trolls, eager to take revenge on the Humans who imprisoned them, have agreed to aid the Horde by supplying Axethrowers and Destroyers to assist in the defense of your Southshore operation.

A Shipyard must be constructed, and you will need much oil to build your fleet. The seas are rich with this substance; your Oil Tankers must build Platforms where it is thick. The Tankers will bring this oil back to the mainland to power our ships of war. Our assault on Hillsbrad cannot begin until your task has been completed.

Objective: Construct four Oil Platforms.

Preparations for Battle: The training of more workers and the construction of Pig Farms came first to build up resources for a Lumber Mill. This we needed to process boards and masts for new ships and to supply the materials needed for a Shipyard.

Pelt enemies on land with Destroyers.

Methods of Destruction: Once construction of the Shipyard had commenced, we sent the Destroyer, which had brought us, to survey the rest of the island. It found several Human spies hiding in the tree line east of the camp and easily blew them to bits before returning to the Shipyards. We also spotted several enemy ships and structures around a smaller island to the northeast. With a growing number of workers and Farms to feed our sailors, we soon launched our first Oil Tanker to build a Platform over

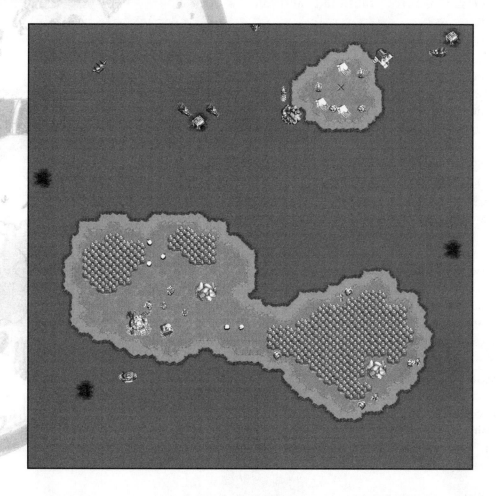

a convenient patch of dark sludge nearby to the southwest. With this, we could also begin building more Destroyers to clear the way for more Platforms.

Completion of Orders: Four Tankers quickly provided the oil required to launch four more Destroyers; we sent these northward in a tight flotilla. The Humans were completely unprepared, having no spies left to report to them, and we laid waste to their work. With five warships against no more than two enemy ships at a time, the task of clearing the seas was disappointingly easy. Our Tankers then moved in to replace the Human Platforms we had obliterated. Plans were made to conduct a final amphibious raid on Hillsbrad.

Mission Four: Assault on Hillsbrad

Orders: Now that the armada is well supplied with the oil your Tankers have amassed, Doomhammer feels it is time to make a gruesome example of Hillsbrad. With the aid of new Refinery sites, you can build Transports to deliver your forces across the channel to the cowering Human settlement. All who oppose the Horde must be taught a lesson. Leave no one alive!

Objective: Destroy Hillsbrad and all its defenders.

Preparations for Battle: We needed a large number of workers and Pig Farms to support this operation. Much time was spent making preparations and gathering resources before constructing the Lumber Mill and Shipyard required to begin the first stage. We kept the Destroyer close to the shore north of town. With eight workers at our disposal, the Shipyard went up near where the Destroyer was anchored.

Methods of Destruction: Soon we had both a Shipyard and a Refinery on the north shore, with several Tankers gathering oil from a nearby patch. Four Destroyers were launched to

Sink enemy Transports before they have a chance to make deliveries.

clear the seas, then all five were sent far to the northeast where an enemy Platform needed removal. From there, we swept westward to the coastline near Hillsbrad, sinking a Transport that had managed to make a single delivery of Humans to our base. To prevent further annoyances of this sort, our warships made quick work of the enemy's coastal structures, leaving the nearby enemy Tower standing so its inhabitants could watch. The Destroyers remained near their shore; soon we would prepare to land our own force.

Completion of Orders: While a new Barracks provided training for six Grunts and six Trolls, we constructed two Transports for them, and the Lumber Mill cut new, nicely balanced throwing axes for the raid. Once the Transports had been loaded and delivered to the waiting Destroyers, we placed a single warship close enough to shore to pound the enemy Tower. This panicked the enemy soldiers into thinking they could stop us at the shoreline; as

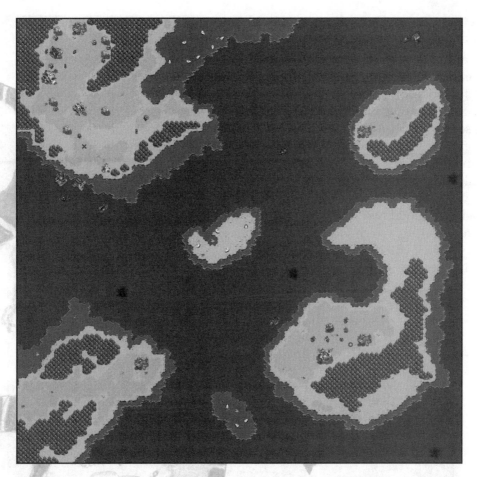

they came, our other warships opened fire. With the coast reasonably clear, the Transports landed and released our Hordes to level the town. All the defenders were slaughtered first; then their structures fell like straw huts. Soon word of our victory reached Doomhammer, who shortly thereafter rewarded us with an opportunity for more destruction near the mainland to the north.

ACT II: KHAZ MODAN
Mission Five: Tol Barad

Orders: The township of Hillsbrad has been decimated, and throughout the Human kingdoms the rumors of impending doom spread like wildfire. Doomhammer is pleased with your success and has deemed you worthy of a more difficult task. Troubles have arisen in the Dwarven lands of Khaz Modan. A task force of Stromgarde warriors has lain siege to Dun Modr, a vital staging area for Horde troops. You are to retake Dun Modr, then bring your forces to bear against Stromgarde's nearby island citadel of Tol Barad.

Objective: Retake Dun Modr and assault the citadel of Tol Barad.

Preparations for Battle: After unloading our forces, the Destroyers immediately sailed south to look for enemy Oil Platforms and reduce enemy naval power, while we established a base south of the landing point. All our troops swept into the village of Dun Modr and slaughtered the inhabitants before we brought in the Catapult to work on their structures. Once the village was secure, we summoned the workers and had them build two Pig Farms north of the mine in a clearing, which would serve to block enemies from entering from that direction. While lumber was gathered to the east, a Great

Catapults make quick work of structures, but are vulnerable to mobile enemies.

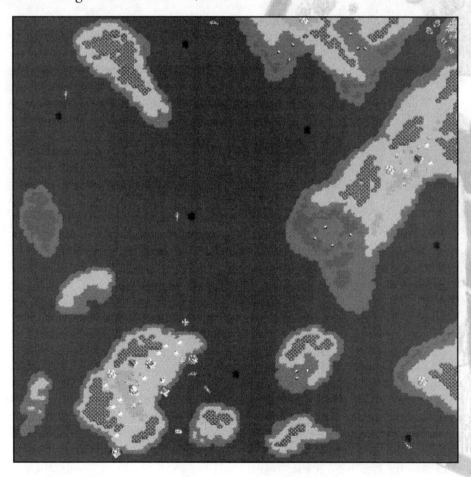

Hall was constructed just northeast of the mine, and more Farms were constructed in a defensive east-west line just south of the mine. During this time, we trained as many slaves as possible to work, for we needed to build up quickly.

Methods of Destruction: Our amphibious force needed many structures to produce the necessary warships and troops. Therefore, a Lumber Mill, a Blacksmith, and a Barracks headed the list. With these completed, a Shipyard was built on the east shore near an oil patch, and Tankers were launched to exploit it. Our starting Destroyers had managed to prevent enemy Tankers from installing another Platform by resting on the oil, which prevented the enemy from producing more ships. Soon, we had a flotilla of six Destroyers and two Transports with which to make the assault.

Completion of Orders: We loaded eight Grunts and four Catapults onto the Transports and set out for the west side of the enemy city, behind the mine there. It was only a matter of time before the town was in ruins. The Destroyers went out to clear the seas of any remaining enemy ships. Our Gods were pleased that day; our ascension to power was well under way.

Mission Six: The Badlands

Orders: Doomhammer has sent word that the Ogre-Mage Cho'gall, chieftain of the Twilight's Hammer clan, is personally inspecting the Refinery at Grim Batol. Cho'gall and his convoy will be traveling through the badlands of Khaz Modan; an ambush by Stromgarde warriors is expected. The war chief expects you to escort Cho'gall and his minions through this region. Should he die, your life will be forfeit as well.

Objective: Escort Cho'gall to the borders of Grim Batol.

Preparations for Battle: The importance of this mission earned us the use of a powerful army, which we assembled before setting out southward along the coastline. Cho'gall and the Catapults remained in the rear; the other troops led the way for them. Occasionally, Cho'gall created floating Eyes to inspect ahead of us. Soon, we came to the first Human defensive wall.

Methods of Destruction: The Catapults were brought to the front and trained on the enemy Ballista behind the wall. With that threat removed, the troops set about knocking down a section of wall to slaughter the other defenders. We constantly ordered them to return to the main group, for their bloodlust kept leading them inland to alarm more enemies. Continuing south along the coast, we encountered a second group of enemies with Destroyers close by, so we gutted the Humans before sinking the ships with our Catapults.

Completion of Orders: With our goal in view to the east, we ripped apart a final, large group of Humans before we marched in and claimed the village for ourselves. After Cho'gall had made contact with higher powers on the Circle, our bloodthirsty and frustrated troops were released to wreak havoc wherever they wished. Many did not return.

The Eye of Kilrogg safely reveals hidden dangers.

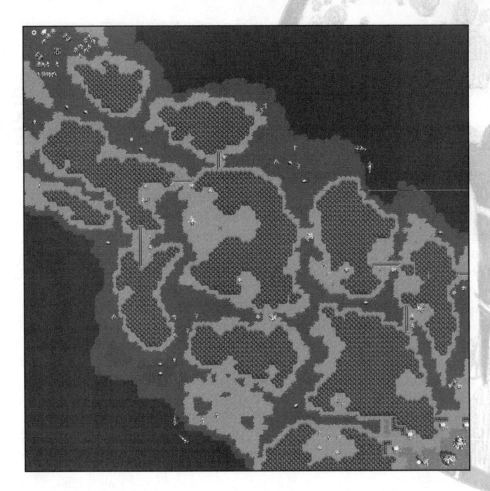

Mission Seven: The Fall of Stromgarde

Orders: Cho'gall reports that the Khaz Modan Refineries are well maintained and fulfilling their quotas. The Horde now has more than enough oil to mount a fierce campaign in the lands far to the north. Only the troublesome Human defenders of Stromgarde remain to be dealt with before sending the Horde on its next journey.

The Human fleet has captured a group of our Transports just south of Stromgarde's capital. Recapture these vessels and then lay waste the capital.

Objective: Recapture the Orc Transports and destroy Stromgarde.

Preparations for Battle: First we called in the Destroyers from the west, gathering them together before concentrating on the two approaching enemy Destroyers. With all four intact, they sailed into the harbor and quickly loaded troops aboard the Transports, reclaiming them. The inland troops then marched north, leaving the workers behind, and fought a path to the waiting Transports. Meanwhile, the Destroyers lingered near shore for cannon support. With all units safely aboard, the flotilla sailed north and landed on the east side of a large island, killing the defenders there and bringing down a Tower that guarded a mine. The Destroyers continued north and west around the tip of the island, heading for an enemy Oil Platform to destroy it.

Enemy Destroyers attempted to stop us, but our tight formation eliminated them one at a time with combined fire. The Platform was removed, and a Destroyer sat directly on the oil to prevent construction of a new one. The enemy's naval power was crippled, leaving us plenty of time to build up safely on the island.

Methods of Destruction: While we were removing the wall around the mine to make room for the workers, a Great Hall went up as close as possible to it. Then we began cutting lumber on the south side of the western forest. Pig Farms were next for the training of more slaves, and a Lumber Mill was constructed near the forest with all available workers helping. With a growing force of laborers, soon we also had a Blacksmith and a Barracks in operation. To fortify our base, Farms were constructed on the north side, with Cannon Towers behind them to fend off occasional raids. Next, we fortified the Hall with stone and iron, then built a Shipyard on the east shore near some oil. Preparations for our invasion continued with an Ogre Mound; then a Foundry and a Refinery allowed construction of more ships. With all necessary structures in place, we spent extra time and gold to upgrade our weapons and armor for soldier and ship alike and gathered our forces to make the assault.

Make a run for your Transports to avoid fighting.

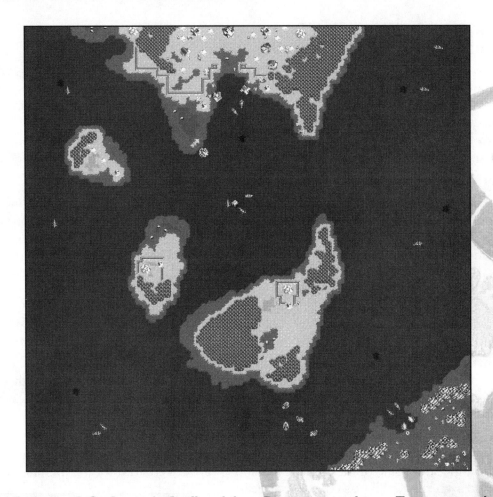

Completion of Orders: A flotilla of four Destroyers and two Transports sailed out, carrying seven Ogres, four Catapults, and a Peon. The Destroyers cleared the way for a landing on the west side of the enemy; the worker set up a makeshift Barracks on enemy soil while the army stood guard. When the attack commenced, the Catapults removed defensive structures from a distance; the troops were constantly ordered to stay near them.

Slowly we leveled the city from west to east, replacing fallen Ogres as necessary. The enemy's Shipyards, as well as the ships anchored in the harbor, fell last to the Catapults. Had we not placed a Barracks on the island, it would have been much harder to ferry replacements in. The invasion was deemed a major success. Fear and honor were heaped on the name of our commander. The tide of war was slowly turning in our favor.

ACT III: QUEL'THALAS
Mission Eight: The Runestone at Caer Darrow

Orders: Your forces have been assigned to an area along the southern border of the Elven kingdom of Quel'thalas. Gul'dan, hoping to sow the seeds of chaos among the Human and Elven allies, has located a mysterious Elven artifact near the Keep of Caer Darrow. This huge, monolithic Runestone is guarded by a Human Castle on the small island located in the middle of Darrowmere Lake. You must destroy the forces that guard this relic and gain control of the Runestone for the Horde.

Objective: Destroy the Human Castle and secure the Runestone.

Preparations for Battle: Since many of the necessary structures were already in place, our first task was the collection of resources for the invasion. Pig Farms and slaves were created at a dizzying pace; Tankers set out southward to install a Platform and collect oil. Our warships stayed close to shore with a Zeppelin overhead; our Stronghold and Towers were upgraded as soon as our supply of resources permitted. Construction continued with a Foundry, a Refinery, and a Goblin Alchemist to produce more Fliers for the invasion. A second Shipyard was erected to double our Juggernaught production, and soon we had a powerful flotilla in the bay.

Danger lurks beneath the waves.

Methods of Destruction: Six massive Juggernaughts sailed out with a Zeppelin overhead to spot enemy submersibles, and we began the slow process of pounding the defenses on the central island. Keeping the ships together, we made constant strikes on single targets, then sailed back out of range to regroup. Enemy Ballistae were drawn out to shore for their destruction. With most of the Towers removed, we started on their Shipyards at both villages. Many of our Juggernaughts were sunk in the process, but more were constantly produced to replace them. Once their naval power was decimated, the Juggers moved in close to shore and removed most of the land structures to make way for a landing.

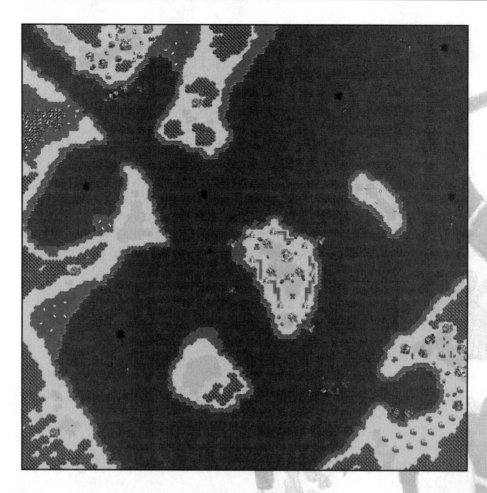

Completion of Orders: While the island was being pounded, an Ogre Mound went up within our base, and 12 Ogres were loaded on Transports to assault the island. Resistance was minimal, and soon the Runestone was ours. This sent a clear signal to the remaining Humans in the other village, who beat a hasty retreat. Our might was growing daily, and our morale was higher than it had ever been, even during the destruction of Azeroth.

Mission Nine: The Razing of Tyr's Hand

Orders: With the capture of the Elven Runestone, Gul'dan has been able to warp its power to mutate an entire legion of his Ogres into wielders of arcane magicks. This transformation has granted these Ogre-Magi deadly magicks and a malicious cunning rivaling that of Gul'dan himself. You are to employ the Ogre-Magi in the creation and defense of a Fortress at the mouth of Tyr's Bay, cutting off the Human supply lines into Quel'thalas.

Objective: Construct a Fortress and a Shipyard on the island at the mouth of Tyr's Bay.

Preparations for Battle: As usual, we needed scores of slaves to build and collect material. Training began in earnest while our warships sailed out with a Flier to quickly eliminate an enemy Platform to the northeast. This cut enemy oil production in half. Our own oil production started with the launching of a Tanker. A Foundry went up next to produce Juggernaughts. Towers were erected to guard the coastline against submersibles and landing raiders. A large labor force was amassing wealth to build the necessary warships.

Overzealous Juggernauts are easily sunk by Cannon Towers.

While the bay filled with our ships, we upgraded our Hall into a Stronghold, built an Ogre Mound, and provided an Alchemist lab for more Zeppelins.

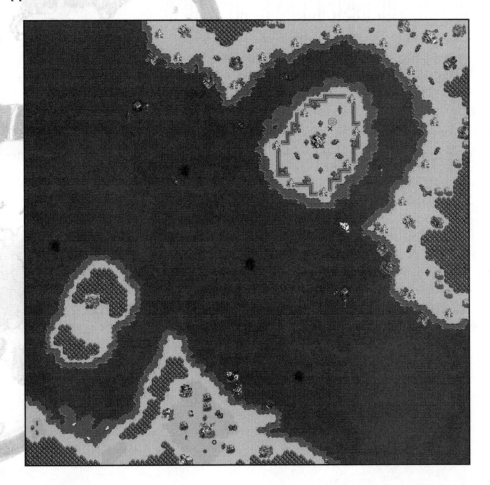

Methods of Destruction: Once we had six or seven Juggers at our disposal, we sent them out with Fliers and began pounding the coastline, concentrating on the enemy's Shipyards to put an end to its naval force. During this time, we again fortified our Stronghold into a Fortress; we also erected an Altar of Storms to instruct our Ogres in the dark arts. A constant stream of Juggers sailed out to replace those we had lost. A second Barracks went up to double the training of Ogre-Magi.

Completion of Orders: After the enemy Shipyards had been removed, we began assembling an amphibious force of two Transports loaded with three Catapults, eight Ogre-Magi, and a single worker. Our Juggers then began carefully taking out Towers and Ballistae on the central island while avoiding those on the mainland. When the Transports arrived and landed, supported by cannon fire from nearby Juggers, the Ogre-Magi quickly cast Bloodlust on themselves and set to work demolishing the remaining forces on the island, staying near the Catapults until they could remove the rest of the Towers from a safe distance. All that remained was to build the necessary Fortress and Shipyard on the island, sealing the fate of the Alliance forces on the mainland.

Mission Ten: The Destruction of Stratholme

Orders: Stratholme, the chief source of the Alliance's oil in the north, is preparing to deliver massive amounts to the kingdoms in western Lordaeron. You must sabotage their Refineries and Oil Platforms to halt this shipment. Once Stratholme's ability to gather and process oil is removed, proceed to crush any and all resistance offered by the Alliance.

Objective: Destroy all Oil Platforms and Refineries; destroy Stratholme.

Preparations for Battle: First, our Sappers had to blow a path inland for our troops. Our plan was to take the city by land first, then to build ships to finish the job, so our forces prepared to march farther north after slaughtering the Alliance forces to the east. One of our slaves remained to build a Hall to the north of the gold mine nearby; the rest headed out to set up closer to the enemy city. Again we gutted any enemies we encountered but avoided the large clearing at the city entrance, not wishing to draw attention before we could build. We built a second Hall as close to the other mine as possible, and we quickly built Farms to the west, for food and to impede enemy forces coming from that direction. With supplementary income from the southern mine and more workers from both Halls, resources piled up quickly and we could build as fast as possible.

Methods of Destruction: We had to erect several structures before building up for the land assault. First was a Barracks to start the training of Grunts, for we needed all the forces we could muster to defend the settlement. A Lumber Mill and a Blacksmith went up next, then a second Barracks to double our troop production. We were careful not to cut lumber near the Hall, instead sending the slaves further north so that the tree line remained a good natural barrier. Many Cannon Towers were erected behind the Farms to the west; these pounded enemies as they tried to break through. Catapults were placed near these Towers to make sure enemy Ballistae did not attack them. The Hall was upgraded to a Fortress but building an Ogre Mound, an Alchemist, and an Altar of Storms was our final task; the buildup had begun in earnest.

Completion of Orders: We assembled a huge group of Ogre-Magi and Catapults for the first wave of the attack, armed with the best possible weapons, armor, and spells. We then moved northeast to assault the city from the rear. After we had killed the pitiful forces outside the city walls, Catapults rolled up and smashed a path through to the inside. Enemy units began pouring through, but our Magi with Bloodlust made quick work of them. After briefly entering the walls to draw out defenders, we began producing Sappers back in our settlement, which

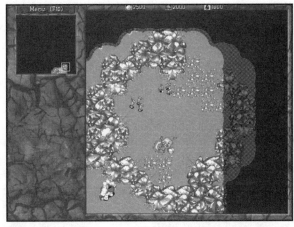

Sappers can blow up mountains as well as enemies.

now had a clear path to enter and demolish structures at will with Ogre escorts. Slowly we worked our way westward, removing Towers and Ballistae first and defending our Catapults

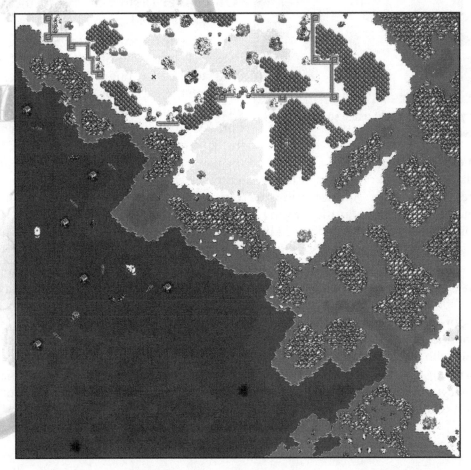

with troops. Within a short time, the city lay in ruins. At our leisure, we built a Shipyard to take care of any targets beyond the range of our Catapults. The Alliance knew my commander's name now, and soon they would know their Maker as well.

Mission Eleven: The Dead Rise as Quel'thalas Falls

Orders: With the destruction of Stratholme, the Alliance's supply lines to Quel'thalas have been severed. Only a handful of Human and Elven defenders remain to safeguard the ancient Elf kingdom from the onslaught of the Horde. The enchanted domain of the Elves has inspired Gul'dan to unleash his most perverted creation—the Death Knights. Formed from

Set Runes for your enemies, but make sure to remember where they are.

the corpses of the fallen Knights of Azeroth, these once-proud defenders of Humanity now serve the Horde in a blasphemous state of eternal undeath. Unleashing dark spells of necromantic horror on their terrified foes, these Death Knights seek to loose their wrath on any foolish enough to stand in their way.

Objective: Destroy the last of the remaining Elven Strongholds.

Preparations for Battle: Since our objective was to remove the Stronghold itself, our plan was to raise a huge force and beat a path through the back door as we had at Stratholme. First we needed to secure our base for construction. A group of Alliance troops were already inside our walls, so the Sappers were quickly moved out of the way for our Ogres to do their work. When all was quiet again, the Ogres immediately marched out through the west entrance and circled around to the other side of the forest, where more Alliance troops were trying to gather. From that point onward, we continued to keep forces in the clearing to eliminate enemies before they had a chance to gather in force there. We then plugged the west entrance with two Farms and began building an army of workers to prepare for the assault.

Methods of Destruction: Soon we had our Hall built up into a Fortress complemented with an Ogre Mound, an Altar of Storms, and three Barracks. It was then necessary to send workers south to raise another Town Hall near a second mine. A constant stream of Ogre-Magi poured out of our Barracks; a group of them was sent to guard the new Hall while the rest continued to guard the clearing. Sappers were also built in large numbers, for these were the tools with which the enemy Stronghold would easily be demolished. At last we had a huge army of twenty Ogre-Magi, four Catapults, and ten Sappers to begin the final assault. Other Magi stayed in the clearing to defend the base. Our army marched off in force to the southeast corner of the area.

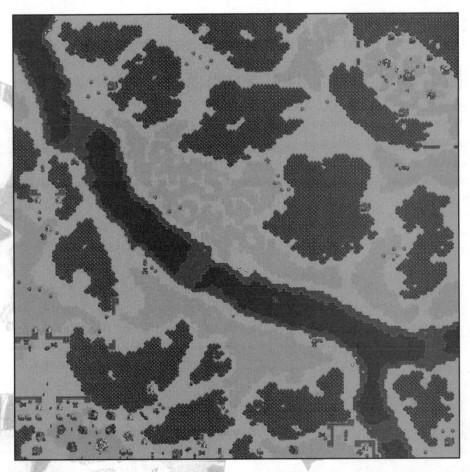

Completion of Orders: After slaughtering the few defenders around a third mine directly east of the city, our Magi gathered west of it near an ice bridge but did not cross. Floating Eyes were summoned to look to the west, where a Tower and Ballistae awaited our arrival. The Magi then cast multiple Runes just north of the tower and brought in Catapults to start on it. The first barrage prompted the Alliance guards to rush us; they exploded nicely on the Runes we had set for them. Having cleaned up the remaining units, we continued west and demolished a Lumber Mill and a Farm. While we waited for our magic to build up again, the Sappers were brought up. They remained in the rear, however, as we removed another emplacement of Towers and defenders in the same fashion as the last, with Runes doing most of the work for us. From there we made the final push through the back door of the city, pausing to build up magic again, and set Runes to draw city guards to their deaths.

Finally we allowed the Runes that had not gone off to dissipate, cast Bloodlust on our Magi, targeted Towers with our Catapults, and poured into the city to create as much chaos as possible. This cleared the way for our Sappers, who rushed in and leveled the Stronghold. The rest of the Elves soon retreated, knowing that the Horde could not be stopped. Today, once again, our Gods were pleased.

ACT IV: THE TIDES OF DARKNESS
Mission Twelve: The Tomb of Sargeras

Orders: The Northlands have fallen. Now only the western regions of Lordaeron stand defiant before the irresistible might of the Horde. As the Orc clans prepare for their final, massive campaign against the weakening Alliance, Doomhammer sends you ill tidings.

Gul'dan and his Stormreaver clan have betrayed the Horde and coerced the Twilight's Hammer clan to set sail and seek an ancient tomb said to be buried beneath the waves. An infiltrator under the direction of Doomhammer reports that Gul'dan has indeed raised volcanic islands from the ocean floor and has thus opened a hidden vault. Though it is unknown what the great Warlock has released from this tomb, Doomhammer has issued this command: Destroy the renegade clans and return with the head of Gul'dan.

Stop the treacherous Gul'dan from unleashing Daemons on his former allies.

Objective: Destroy the Stormreaver and Twilight's Hammer clans; slay the Warlock Gul'dan.

Preparations for Battle: First, we had to establish a city on the largest of the islands to the east and north. For this purpose, we sent our warships with a Flier to clear the way. Two enemy ships and a submersible had to be sunk first, then a Tower. Finally, the inland Catapult was drawn to shore with a fast Destroyer and disassembled. While the warships waited, the Transports were loaded with all but Sappers and Peons to make a landing; soon the island was ours. While the existing structures were removed, the Transports went back for the rest of the units and brought them safely to shore.

From that point, it was a matter of building a city from scratch, starting with a Hall as close to the mine as possible without being too close to shore. With the threat of enemy Juggernaughts coming soon, all units were moved as far inland as possible, and the ships were sent to anchor at the southern tip of the island.

Methods of Destruction: As soon as a Barracks, a Lumber Mill, and a Blacksmith had been built, we concentrated on producing Catapults. These we used to sink any enemy ships foolish enough to wander too close to shore. We did this by directing all of them to attack at once, then moving them safely back inland. Cannon Towers helped somewhat, but their lack of mobility got them destroyed almost as fast as they could be built. Once we had a fair-sized group of Catapults to fend off ships, construction of the Shipyard and accompanying structures began on the southeast side of the island, as far from enemy eyes as possible. To carry

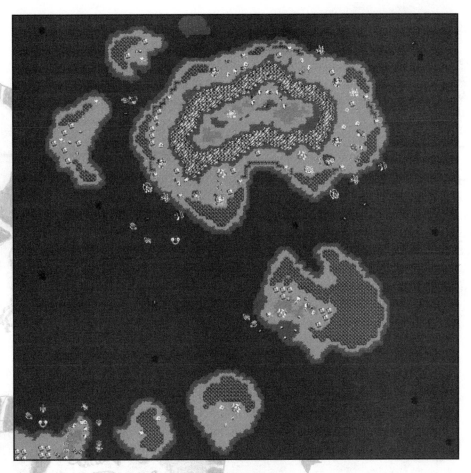

out our plan of invasion, we needed only two Juggers and three Transports to make a landing on the main island. We loaded them with five Trolls (to give them a chance against flying Demons), a single Worker, six Ogres, and six Catapults.

Completion of Orders: Escorted by a Zeppelin to spot enemy submersibles, the flotilla sailed west to the edge of the area before turning north and quietly passing the main island. Then it headed east to find a good landing spot south of a small barren island. The Juggernaughts were sent in first to clear the shore of a Tower and a Catapult before the troops were unloaded behind a small stand of trees.

We were careful to unload the Ogres first, with Catapults behind, and Trolls on the other side, since the enemies on shore would come to us once the Catapults started on the enemy Barracks nearby. When things quieted down a bit, we erected our own Barracks and began pouring troops and Catapults through it to slowly take over the island. Later we finished Gul'dan and Cho'gall by blowing a path through the rock with Sappers, and we claimed both of their heads as a clear signal to all who would oppose the Horde.

Mission Thirteen: The Siege of Dalaran

Orders: The hour of judgment is close at hand as the Orcish Hordes stand ready to sweep across this domain and seize the capital of Lordaeron. Standing vigilant above the plains is the Violet Citadel of Dalaran. The Citadel—serving as sanctum and haven to the Mages of Lordaeron—is the last barrier between the Orcs and their subjugation of Humanity. Manifested in the combined magical prowess of all Mages within the Alliance, this place must fall for the Horde to conquer Lordaeron.

Very little can stop a pack of Dragons.

Fortunately, Orgrim Doomhammer has saved his greatest weapons, the Dragons, and stands ready to unleash them on the unsuspecting Alliance at just this moment.

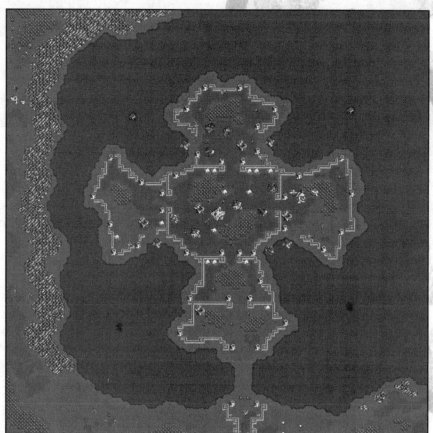

Objective: Destroy Dalaran and all its defenders.

Preparations for Battle: Dragons indeed would be our main weapon in the conquest of the island, but first we had to raise a city to support their production. All our military units swept quickly southward and removed all defenders near the mine; the construction of the necessary buildings was begun in earnest. During this time, we erected many Guard Towers to deal with the constant harassment by enemy Gryphons; a Shipyard went up to produce Tankers and Destroyers for the same purpose.

Methods of Destruction: When we started running out of gold, we needed to assault the southern outpost to get Peons beyond it to another mine. The first step of this operation was to send a single Sapper to blow up the western Tower. With this task out of the way, we rolled in Catapults to remove the rest, escorted by more troops. The way was then cleared to start another Hall and plunder its resources. Another Shipyard went up near it, to launch more Destroyers on that side of the land bridge for defense against Gryphons. By that time, we had four Dragon Roosts started. Soon the skies would belong to us.

Completion of Orders: The assault on the island required the combined efforts of Dragons, Catapults, and Ogres. The Dragons could do most of the destructive work, but Catapults with Ogre escorts were required to take out enemy Guard Towers, which could fire on the Dragons. Sappers also came in handy, but most structures fell to the Catapults while the Dragons worked on mobile targets. With careful and constant strikes on single targets, each followed by a brief retreat, the island was quickly ours. Very soon now, we would be able to say the same for the rest of this world.

Mission Fourteen: The Fall of Lordaeron

Orders: The alabaster parapets of Lordaeron's capital loom before you in the distance. The proud, defiant armies of the Alliance stand resolute in their final moments. All that remains is the shrill clarion call to battle and the fulfillment of our destiny. The tides of darkness are now at hand!

Objective: Destroy all that you behold in the name of the Horde!

Preparations for Battle: Once again, we would rely on Dragons to sack most of the capital. The most suitable site for the Roosts was on the island where our troops had already made a successful landing. Though we already had a base started, it was doomed to fall to a constant stream of raiders soon, so new construction began near the mine on the island. This site was also far enough inland that only Gryphons could harass us, and these would be taken care of by numerous Guard Towers and Trolls.

Methods of Destruction: All the structures necessary to develop Dragon Roosts were built first. Four Roosts were soon launching the terrible beasts into the air. Once we had about eight of them flying, their first targets were the numerous enemy troops stationed near the center of the island. It was odd that they never organized a land attack; perhaps they were savoring the last hours before their inevitable destruction. Next came their navy, which never stood a chance against so many firebreathers flying together. Though their Destroyers managed to bring down a few, these were replaced quickly. The assault continued with the removal of their Shipyards. A protective circle of Guard Towers made attacks on the center of the capital prohibitively expensive, but little was left to hinder an amphibious landing.

Completion of Orders: While the Dragons incinerated Towers and cleared a wide section of coastline for a landing, we constructed a Shipyard and accompanying structures to produce two Transports. These made a standard assault on the mainland with four Catapults, seven Ogres, and a single Peon to raise a Barracks. The Dragons then concentrated on mobile units, while the Catapults methodically removed stationary targets near shore and later focused on the Guard Towers so our reptiles could start on the interior.

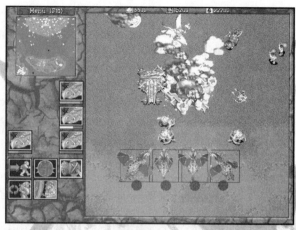

The fall of Lordaeron's capital.

It was all too easy. I now believe that it is our right and destiny to devour this world.

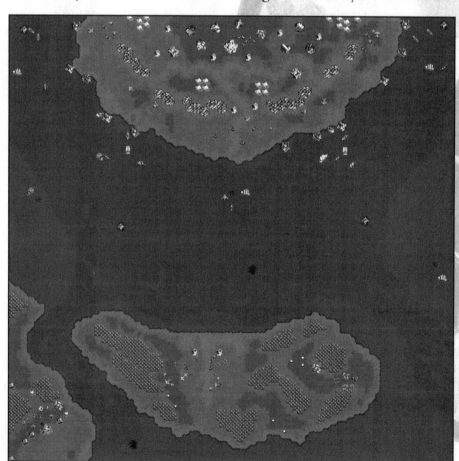

Chapter 5
Methods of Madness

The leadership of any army, great or small, determines whether or not the army will live to fight another day. This chapter not only describes the simple and effective deployment of troops, but also the secret tactics that immortalize great generals in song and legend.

Standard Tactics

These strategies are designed to work in almost any situation, and they encompass the majority of effective operations in both single- and multiplayer games. Used as a foundation, this advice ensures that you will survive long enough to apply the more advanced tricks in the latter section.

Gathering Resources

The first and most important key to quickly gathering gold is to keep a clear path between the Hall and the mine. Placing structures directly beside or even one space away from either of these causes the workers to emerge on the wrong side, or stop altogether if they walk into a bottleneck. Worse still is a situation that forces them to choose a longer route, often taking them outside the town where they become fair game for enemies lingering out of range of your defenses. Players busy with military concerns cannot afford to spend time making sure their workers are doing their job, because the smooth and constant flow of gold is vital to an effective buildup.

Since there are usually several mines on any given map, try sending a lone worker and a few combat units to set up a secondary Hall close to another mine. Assuming it remains unmolested for a time, new workers can be trained on the spot and begin gathering gold to double or triple your rate of income. If the mine has a large amount of gold in it, consider building Towers or another Barracks nearby to ensure the survival of your workers. This also provides a backup plan if your primary village gets sacked.

When gathering lumber, pay close attention to exactly where your workers are getting it. A line of trees is a very effective natural barrier, and cutting holes in it only allows more enemies to pour through. Since workers are dim and will start cutting wherever it is convenient after their initial orders, send them to forests without any strategic significance, even if it means doing so outside of town. In this case, send soldiers to help defend them while they work. Losing a few workers is far less damaging than an assault on your structures because you can always train more if the remainder concentrates on gold instead. Finally, whenever possible, build Lumber Mills as close to the cutting as possible to greatly speed the gathering process.

Building Cities

The city *must* be able to defend itself from enemy raids as soon as possible. Quickly inspect the surrounding territory and determine where enemies are most likely to invade from. At these spots, first build Farms to block passage, or start a defensive line of Farms that form a wall. Farms have considerably more hit points than Towers or walls and will take much more time to get through. Directly behind these Farms, place one or two Towers or several Archers/Trolls to pelt enemies lined up before the barrier. After that, you need not worry about invasions from that particular direction. Often, only Farms are necessary to cause enemies to take a longer path, since the computer chooses the shortest open path to its destination, and Farms are usually not a primary target.

Next, decide which units are needed to accomplish your goals, and build only the structures required to produce them. As previously mentioned, the most effective attacks are conducted with large numbers of basic units. The more resources you have available to devote to them, the greater the number of active units. Building a second or third Barracks is also highly recommended because players often have more gold than time available. Spending huge amounts of effort to get Dragons into the air might all be in vain if the city gets overrun in the process. Establish a strong city and army before devoting attention to specialized units.

Land Attacks

Safety in numbers is the key to success in any situation, and the ability to issue orders to nine units at a time allows them to decimate single opponents. Always assign a portion of your forces to concentrate on one enemy at a time, because half-dead adversaries still do the same amount of damage as perfectly healthy ones. The computer makes a habit of engaging either the closest convenient target or one that attacked first, then pounding it to death before moving on to the next. Keep your units tagged and gathered together, so they don't run off chasing retreating foes and end up getting killed when they separate from the pack.

When commanding a mixed group of units, always keep those with one-space attacks in front of those with missile weapons. One of the most effective coordinated assaults involves the use of many Knights or Ogres in front of a few Ballistae or Catapults. Mobile computer enemies often target more powerful units if given a choice. When they come calling, your fighters can easily cut them down while the war wagons launch missiles at stationary structures. When taking out Towers, order all of your Catapults/Ballistae to attack from a distance so they stop at their maximum range before firing. Although out of range of even Cannon Towers, your faster units are subject to bombardment if they wander just one space ahead. Therefore, order them to stand their ground on either side, and let advancing defenders get a few hits in until the Tower falls first.

Marine Tactics

A quick inspection of cost-versus-firepower of warships shows a decided advantage in building Juggernaughts and Battleships rather than Destroyers. (However, keep in mind that only Destroyers can target flying units such as Dragons.) Submersibles are also nice, but they're too easy to sink once detected. A flotilla of tall warships escorted by a flier can not only decimate all other vessels, but their extended cannon range allows heavy bombardment of many land targets as well.

However, having at least one fast Destroyer does come in handy for leading enemy Catapults/Ballistae closer to shore. Meanwhile, the main group waits safely out of range before attacking all at once. For that matter, even a Transport or a Tanker can serve the purpose of baiting mobile enemies to shore, as long as you do not need them for more important tasks.

Amphibious landings should always utilize at least two fully loaded Transports, escorted by as many warships as possible to clear the beach head. A standard landing party should consist mostly of melee units, supported by two or three Catapults/Ballistae for long-range fire. Where an extended campaign on foreign soil is expected, bring along at least one worker to immediately throw a Barracks up. Enemies will concentrate on the new structure, which has considerably more armor and hit points than any single combat unit, letting your own forces concentrate on the attackers. After an initial cost of resources, the Barracks continually "heals" itself without further cost. Even if enemies manage to destroy it before construction is complete, it at least draws fire away from your armies.

An Elemental Relationship

One key strategy to keep in mind is the relationship between land, sea, and air units.

Archers/Axethrowers, Mages/Death Knights, and Guard Towers are the only land units that can attack air units.

The Destroyer is the only ship that can attack air units.

Only flying units, Subs/Turtles, and Towers can spot Submarines.

For example, a group of Battleships with a Flying Machine will completely annihilate anything that sails the seas or runs along the coast. But even a single Dragon will wreak havoc because none of the mighty ships can fire back.

TIPS, TACTICS, AND SECRETS

Whether you are playing custom scenarios or any of the campaign missions delineated in chapters 3 and 4, certain strategies remain constant. In the paragraphs that follow, you will be given many tools to enhance your command abilities. Use them well and wisely to mold an unstoppable force.

- If you have Peasants/Peons repair a building under construction, it gets completed much faster. A second Peasant makes the completion twice as fast, three Peasants are three times as fast, and so on.

- Casting Invisibility on Transports makes them quite effective. Unfortunately, if you select a Transport and tell it to unload all its troops, it becomes visible. However, if you select the individual unit's portrait to unload it, the Transport remains invisible. This allows for great covert operations on the enemy's shoreline where your units just seem to appear out of nowhere—try this with Bombers.

- If you are being attacked by a clump of units, cast a Flame Shield on the center unit. This begins to cause damage to all units around that one. It also causes your opponent to spend time moving his units away from the flamed one instead of attacking you.

- Bomber and Sapper units can be used to clear terrain. Tell them to detonate a forest or rock hex; when they explode, they remove a hefty chunk. This is useful for craftily creating a pathway into enemy territory.

- Cast Invisibility and Flame Shield on a Destroyer and wreak havoc on your enemy's naval fleets. Destroyers are exceptionally quick and cannot be hit since they never become visible (the Flame Shield is doing the damage, not the invisible unit).

- Build Towers in an opponent's city to create a great deal of chaos. If you can get them up and upgraded quickly, they start to open up on everything within range.

- Exorcism damages both Skeletons and Death Knights.

- Cast Unholy Armor on a Death Knight, then cast Death and Decay on that Death Knight. This is a tremendously effective way to kill a large number of enemies who come to kill the Death Knight.

- Cast Runes on the ground between a gold mine and the enemy's Town Hall; this greatly disrupts his economy.

- Use your Catapults to take out Towers. The Catapults' range is slightly greater than the Towers'.

- To get the first shot on a Tower with a Destroyer or Battleship, order the ship to move toward the Tower. The Tower fires and generally misses the moving target. Then immediately order the ship to attack the Tower. It stops and fires, thus giving you the first hit.

- Have your flying units follow your Destroyers and Battleships so they can easily spot any Submarines or Giant Turtles. This saves you from having to group them with the ships, thus allowing you to move even more than nine units.

- If you are attacked and have only Peons, make sure to group them and have them attack a single opponent. The damage they do is small, but it does add up.

- Use your Death Knight to cast Death Coil on a group of enemy units. When they come after the Death Knight, immediately cast Death and Decay between them and you. If you can bring up a second Death Knight, he can cast Death and Decay immediately behind the advancing enemy, cutting them off from their usual safe retreat.

- Sending your Bombers and Sappers into large groups can kill several enemies at one time. Also, telling your Bombers or Sappers to detonate between two buildings damages both. This is very effective for taking out Farms.

- Destroying enemy Farms can cripple their ability to produce more units in a siege.

- Do not group select Bombers and Sappers and give them one target. They arrive at the same time, and the first to detonate kills the target before the others can damage it.

- Keep Dragons and Gryphons spaced apart, or they risk hitting each other and damaging themselves. A good tactic is to send a single Dragon or Gryphon in among a large group of enemy Dragons or Gryphons and watch them damage each other.

- If your opponent seems to build a great number of sea vessels, start concentrating on Dragons or Gryphons. Not only can they damage ships, but your opponent's land defenses are probably not as well developed if he has been concentrating on the seas.

- In a narrow river area, you can use a Peon to create a Shipyard and then immediately cancel the build. He pops out of the canceled building on the opposite shore. This is a quick way to get across to enemy territory or to flee from enemies so you can start up another Town Hall. Also, you can put a Transport in a narrow area and use it as a bridge for units (having them get on and off). Try choosing different places to build Shipyards and different ways to best use the terrain as a natural defense.

- Move a Sub or a Turtle under an untapped oil patch. When the enemy's Oil Tanker comes exploring, it's in for a surprise!

- Whenever you ally yourself with another player, put either a unit you can afford to lose or a Tower in his town. If he chooses to remove you as an ally, you have advance warning immediately when your unit is attacked.

- Slow is a great counter against Bomber squads—it gives your units the ability to get to them before they can do damage. Similarly, casting Haste on your Sappers gets them in much faster than your opponent expects.

- In a two- or three-player game with medium or high resources selected, build a Farm, Barracks, and as many Grunts as possible without building a Town Hall. Then send out your troops and find the enemy before he can get an economy going. This works only in a two- or three-player game—with more players than that, you may get the quick kill, but you're soon fodder.

- Casting Speed on Catapults makes for a very fast and fierce attack squad.

- Whirlwinds and Runes are great for killing Peasants or Peons. Whirlwinds are very effective when cast on Barracks because they immediately damage any unit being produced. Multiple Whirlwinds can be devastating to a town and its Tower defenses.

- Troll Berserkers with Regenerate are great for tactical battles where rotating your troops is a strategy. Their ability to heal themselves is a great benefit in running battles.

- Raise Dead is effective when you are planning an assault on Peasants or Peons. Not only do you destroy your opponent's economy, but you then use his own people against him.

- Peons and Peasants are effective when you are scouting an enemy's lands. If you are attacked or approached, they can immediately build Barracks or a Tower, making them as strong as the building. This assumes that you have enough resources, of course.

- Although the time and effort to develop Rangers is costly, upgrading their arrows to their maximum strength allows them to inflict as much or more average damage as a Guard Tower. A row of Rangers set to receive a charge can decimate anything that steps within its range (which is also longer with the appropriate training).

Chapter 6
Warcraft II Multiplayer Strategies

One of the praiseworthy attributes of *Warcraft II* is that the game allows multiple players to wage war against each other. This presents *Warcraft II* players with myriad strategic options other than simply striving to defeat the computer. This chapter details strategies that are the difference between victory and defeat on the sometimes crowded and evermore competitive multiplayer battlefield.

While many of the strategies outlined in this chapter may also apply to players pitting their wits against the computer, they are mainly intended to facilitate multiplayer efforts.

ALLIES
Choose Your Allies

Before you begin the game, discuss who you plan to ally with. Make sure that both you and your allies select each other in the Ally menu as soon as possible so no accidental contact occurs between you that could result in an attack. You also have the option to Share Vision, which will allow you to see exactly what your ally is looking at! (You cannot see your ally's units that have invisibility cast on them.)

Pick Different Races

If there are two or more allies on the same side, they should pick opposing races (one Human and one Orc, etc.). This ensures that the allied parties have the widest selection of spells available to them. If they choose the same race, they both have the exact same benefits—and weaknesses. When mixed, the allied parties can help defend one another, diluting their combined weaknesses and supporting their strengths.

Allied Victory?

Discuss with your ally what your goals are. Will you share the spoils of victory, or battle each other for ultimate supremacy? For instance, if you plan on clobbering all of your opponents en route to a *team victory,* but your ally plans to fight you for the ultimate prize, your strategies will conflict.

Communication

Another benefit of having allies is that, through communication, you can discover more about territory in a mission map than you could on your own. This helps you decide the best locations to place your buildings. For instance, if you know that your ally is east of you, and the only other significant opening for attacking your forces is to the west, you can focus all defenses on the west side. (Of course, that's assuming you can trust your ally.)

Coordinating an Attack

Continuously communicate with your allies. Knowing that your ally has sent four Paladins to aid your Death Knights in a raid could very well decide whether you launch the attack. Furthermore, when coordinating an attack, let your ally know what you are sending, and where. This allows your ally to send some troops for support. And don't forget to reciprocate the favor when the time comes—unless you have your own dark plans.

OPTIONS

Race

Although each race can hold its own against another, choosing one race leads to a slightly different mode of play. A real-life player has the ability to accentuate the differences (see below) and develop unique gameplay with each one.

Humans

The healing abilities of the Human Paladin are very beneficial in siege attacks. Send units forward; then retreat, heal, and send again, rotating different lines of attack with plenty of Paladins to sustain healing power. Also, the Exorcism (for Paladins) and Polymorph (for Human Mages) spells are very effective, the latter even from a distance. Both spells are especially useful against the more powerful creatures of the Horde. Even when the God cheat is enabled, these spells can cause mass destruction. Also, Blizzard and Flame Shield are very useful ambush spells for the Human Mage.

Orcs

The Ogre-Magi spell called Runes is highly effective at guarding entrances and/or exits. It is also a great spell to use to begin an ambush. Death Knights also have a solid set of spells, with Death and Decay allowing them to inflict destruction on multiple units at a one time. In fact, Death and Decay works well in conjunction with the Ogre-Magi's Runes spell. Draw other players into attacking you and, when they trigger the Runes spell, quickly lay a Death and Decay spell behind them, forcing them forward into, hopefully, an onslaught of devastating Runes spells.

Resources

A beginning player may want to select High resources to make life a little easier. This allows you to build more units and buildings at the onset when your mining operation is at its lowest level of production. By the time you run out of gold, your mining operation should be running fairly smoothly.

Cheats Enabled

Whether you enable cheats depends on how much experience you have at *Warcraft II*. You should probably leave cheats disabled until you have learned how to operate the game's controls efficiently. Enabled cheats affect everyone, and a more seasoned player, or the computer, can make much better use of the cheats than a beginner. You definitely should *not* use the God cheat, but the Harvest cheat *can* come in handy at times.

Tileset

Other than aesthetics, there isn't much difference in gameplay here. One neat thing to point out is that critters change between the tilesets.

Units

For multiplayer games with beginners, use the default mode for units. Some of the scenarios have buildings premade for you, so you can develop certain more advanced units more quickly. However, if you have experienced players, starting with only one peon gives you more flexibility with your game development.

Fog of War

This is an option you should definitely leave on. A lot of the new features in *Warcraft II*, such as Flying Machines/Zeppelins, lose something of their value and most of their fun when this feature is left off. Also, the range of sight via these flying devices is less valuable if you have Fog of War off. It makes the game easier, as you can develop one flying machine and easily send it across an entire map, but you lose a little excitement without it.

Starting Locations

If you start at a random location, you may or may not land anywhere near a decent starting point. Conversely, starting at a fixed location generally lands you within a few steps of a mine. Until you are confident enough in your ability to locate a decent place to mine, you should begin at a fixed location.

However, if you begin the game with High resources, you don't necessarily have to start at a fixed location to succeed early. You can actually create a town that is nowhere near a mine, protect it, send your peon (along with a few guards) to find a good mine, and begin developing a second town. This strategy can be beneficial if you are playing with allies and aim to link your cities together quickly. (You both have a longer line to defend, however.) If fairly close to your ally in proximity, this strategy also gives you both a greater area of protection in which to develop units and buildings.

COMBAT
Offensive Tactics
Know the Layout of the Land

Before you can mount a decent attack, you need to know the lay of the land before you. Unless you are the gung-ho type who charges directly into battle, you'd probably like to save as many of your units as you can. Learning the lay of the land you're about to wage war on can accomplish this.

Performing advanced scouting on the land awaiting you can be done easily with a Flying Machine/Zeppelin, or by sending out cheap scouts like Peasants, who can draw deadly fire away from your actual fighting forces. For instance, send Peasants to build a Scout Tower right in the middle of the enemy camp (or as close as you can get). The Scout Tower doesn't last as long as a Farm or Barracks, but once built, the visual range it provides you is invaluable in determining how many nearby reinforcements the enemies have. And if it gets upgraded to a Guard or Cannon Tower, it not only allows you to see the enemy, but it also can initiate an attack upon them as well.

Coordinated Attacks

Once you locate an enemy, let your allies know immediately. Then, plan an attack formation best suited for your combined protection as well as the destruction of your enemy.

For example, if planning to attack an island fortress, both you and your ally should load a Transport or two with Archers/Axe Throwers, Paladins/Ogre-Magi, and Mages/Death Knights. Follow by sending a Destroyer and Battleship to protect the Transport(s). (If you can supply more protection, do it.) Next, send a Flying Machine/Zeppelin ahead to search out your enemy's location. Set a trap or two and see if you can bait the enemy into following you. The computer falls for traps regularly, but a human opponent may not, so you probably have to be the aggressor. Lay down some cover fire with your Archers, Axe Throwers, and ships; then send the Paladins and Ogre-Magi to engage the enemy hand-to-hand. If you brought Catapults or Ballistae as well, let them assist in providing cover.

Concentrate on the enemy's more powerful units and magic-users, and keep your Mages and Death Knights busy casting spells such as Slow and Haste. (You can cast these cheaper spells many times before needing rest.) This helps your melee fighters get in many more attacks per round than their opponents. Also, have your Ogre-Magi cast Bloodlust on each other and the Paladins just before they actually engage the enemy. Finally, if you are a good distance away, a nice Blizzard can help destroy a large number of enemies.

Using Control Groups and Attack Moves

Warcraft Battle.net Edition has many new features, including Control Grouping, which allows you to bring a group of 9 units onto the battle with a click of a button. Organizing your troops in squads of 9 and control grouping them can be the difference when waging an all-out war on your opponent!

Attack Moving is also a good tactic to use. Instead of selecting a unit to fight one at a time, simply grab a squad of units and click the attack button near your enemies. The new Attack Move selection enables your troops to fight intelligently, ensuring your victory on the battlefield.

Defensive Tactics

Create a Lifeline

If possible, create a lifeline to your allies as early as you can. Line the pathway with Footmen and Archers (or their equivalents). Have your ally do the same, and you meet twice as quickly. Once you have met up with each other, begin developing more powerful units and lining the lifeline with both units and Towers (Guard and Cannon, if financially possible). With both you and your Ally responsible for maintaining the lifeline, it should require only minimal upkeep.

Ally-Aid

Often times, your allies need aid when you can't afford to send it—at the very beginning of the game. Nonetheless, sending any units you can spare is usually enough for your ally to survive. Most allies do remember your efforts too.

Here's something else to keep in mind—sending even a lone Footman to the aid of your ally allows you to view many portions of the particular mission map you're playing. You often run into another gold mine en route to your ally. If you happen to have sent a Peasant along, you can build a new Town Hall even closer to your ally, while still reaping all the benefits of having already completed one Town Hall.

Buildings

Town Hall

Build this first. Place it as close (unobstructed) to the mine as possible. Don't worry about the forest; place a lumber mill close to it. The mill produces more lumber (+25) and can be placed away from the hall and mine, not obstructing the path of miners.

Farms

You need one of these second (assuming you started with only a Peasant). Develop as many Farms as you can quickly. They are great for defense, and with excess food, you can develop armies at will, as opposed to needing to build a Farm in the middle of a battle to create reinforcements. This can be the difference between winning and losing a battle.

Towers

Set these up to block key areas, and upgrade them as soon as possible. Setting them *behind* farms tends to work the best, but be prepared to devote units to repairs in the heat of battle.

Lumber Mills

Place your Lumber Mill right up against the trees if you can. This gives your Peasants a shorter distance to travel to process lumber. Keep the Mill away from your Town Hall, however, because the continual traffic between the mine and the forest could cause congestion and leave several Peasants carrying their loads and not going anywhere.

Barracks

These structures should be placed near your main exit (they require the least amount of time to move, if the need arises). They need to be built quickly so you can begin producing Footmen and Archers to protect your budding city before it is capable of producing heavier artillery.

Blacksmiths

Blacksmiths are the benefactors of the whole army. They are capable of upgrading most of the basic units, making them much more powerful. The upgrades are permanent at a one-time cost, so a Blacksmith is well worth the investment. One of the best aspects about the upgrades is that oftentimes your opponent is busy building a large army to conquer you, but you have spent your money on upgrading the few units you have. With just a little luck, you can overpower your enemies quickly enough to bring them down before they grow enough in size to do you in.

Gnomish Inventors

These little guys are great for both land and sea campaigns. They allow you to construct Submarines and Flying Machines. A great Submarine tactic is to send the vessel along the coasts of enemy islands, steering clear of enemy Towers. The Submarine is all but invisible to most units, except airborne units and Towers, so it can attack from the sea from relative safety. Remember that Submarines cannot attack land or air units.

Stables

Stables are necessary if you are planning a major land-based attack. They allow the production of Knights, the honorable and powerful cavalry of your army. However, if you are planning on making the most of your attacks at sea, concentrate your efforts on erecting another building.

Foundries and Refineries

Both are necessary if you plan on seafaring. Without Refineries, your Oil Tankers process slightly slower, making you wait longer to add units to your army. Foundries also allow you to upgrade the weapons and armor of your armada, essentially making a smaller, waterborne force more effective and less visible than a larger, unmodified one.

Church

The Paladin is researched here. Known for their healing abilities, Paladins are the epitome of honor and courage. They ride into battle to lay their healing hands on fellow soldiers, often absorbing enemy attacks in the process.

Additionally, you should not overlook the Paladin if you are building a fleet of ships or an air force. With a Transport to ferry him where he needs to go, a Paladin can often extend the life of a Gryphon Rider who has had the bad luck to meet with several Axe Throwers.

Mage Tower

The Mages are costly to summon, but once they have been upgraded with a full contingent of spells, they can be the most devastating of all the units. With their Polymorph spell, they can transform even the most powerful units to passive seals or sheep. In a siege on a town, their Blizzard spell can cause chaos, especially for units left in the open. Your opponent often sends a large party to find and attack you after being hit with a Blizzard, so be ready with an ambush.

Gryphon Aviary

The most expensive unit to summon, the Gryphon Aviary is also one of the most versatile. However, the 2,500 gold pieces price tag can often make people shy away from building it, especially when the route to making an Aviary available is also very expensive and fairly slow. For this reason alone, you may want to reconsider having a full air force as opposed to just a couple of Gryphons to back up your naval fleet.

If you are lucky, your opponent will concentrate all available resources on producing Gryphons. If so, produce a lot of Rangers and Guard Towers—they are both cheaper and can damage an air force. If you notice your opponents not producing a lot of units, they may be saving to produce Gryphons, so you may want to get to their land first. Also, Gryphons damage anything in their path when they fire, and you can sometimes trick them into killing their own people by maneuvering your men between them.

MULTIPLAYER CUSTOM SCENARIOS

One of the greatest things about *Warcraft II* is the ability to create your own scenarios. You can edit everything from the map, to the unit values and sounds. It does take a significant amount of time and effort to create a quality scenario, but when it is finished, it is well worth the effort. By editing the units, you can simulate features such as low morale (by making the units slower and weaker), and even make units superhumanly powerful.

Playing Custom .PUD Files

Single-player *.PUD* files:

- Go to single-player
- Select Custom Scenario
- Choose Select Scenario
- Set Scenario type to Custom
- Choose the *.PUD* file you wish to play.

  When you create a custom *.PUD* file, make sure it is saved in the *Warcraft II* directory (i.e., *C:\WAR2*). This is the default directory for the map editor.

  Multiplayer *.PUD* files (from the multiplayer setup screen):

- Select Custom Scenario
- Choose Select Scenario
- Set Scenario type to Custom
- Choose the *.PUD* file you wish to play.
- If you have included computer players in your .PUD file, be sure to remember which players (i.e., Player One–Red, Player Two–Blue, etc.) you set up as computer enemies so that you can set them up as computer opponents in the multiplayer setup screen.

Playing Custom .PUD.BNE Maps or "Bennys"

- When you create a custom *.PUD.BNE* Map, make sure it is saved in the *Warcraft II BNE* directory *(C:\WarII BNE\Maps)*. This is the default directory for the map editor.

First Contact Scenario

Here's an example of a custom scenario to tackle, when the Horde forces are just coming through the Portal. The Orcs are powerful and bloodthirsty, and they have prepared for attack by praying to their dark gods for unholy strength. The Humans are caught off guard, but not completely unaware. Raise the Orcish units' damage and hit points, but give them limited resources. Give the Humans plenty of resources and structures, but a limited amount of starting units. This gives the game a whole new level of play for both teams, as they both have to deal with severe shortcomings. There should be an equal number of players on both sides, with no more than two people allied together (to simulate the arrogance of each kingdom and the chaotic nature of the Orcs). Try it out.

PLAYING WARCRAFT II OVER BATTLE.NET

Battle.net is Blizzard Entertainment's Internet gaming service. It allows players from around the world to battle against each other. Battle.net also supports a world-wide ranking system, enabling you to test your *Warcraft* skills against comparable opponents.

When creating a game on Battle.net, you have the option of playing several game types:

Melee	The standard game type where up to eight players start with one Peon only, have random starting locations and are free to ally at any time.
One on One	Two players are pitted against each other for the ultimate heads-up match. No allying and no computer opponents are allowed.
Free for All	An all-out brawl where **no** allying is allowed—even computer players will fight each other!
Use Map Settings	Playing like a campaign or scenario, these games often include changes to resources or units, the addition of Heroes, rescueable units and specific attack settings for the computer AI.
Top vs. Bottom	Players are divided into two distinct forces for team battles, matching the first set of players on the map with the second set. There can be four-on-four, two-on-two, or any other combination of teams based on the number of starting locations on the map. The "Top vs. Bottom" game type, when using the "fixed order" option, works the same as "Use Map Settings," allowing you to design four-on-four maps with preset towers or units! Computer players cannot be used with this game type.
Ladder	Players with 10 or more wins are eligible to compete in Ladder Games that are open challenges on special Blizzard-approved maps. While you have the option to select starting resources, the game speed is preset at "FASTER" and you always start with only one Peon.
IronMan Ladder	Ladder players who achieve a ranking of 1200 or higher are then eligible to compete in this special Ladder where the competition gets even tougher because the maps are random and you always start with low resources!

Game Options:

One Peon Only	This is a special option used for Top vs. Bottom games that enables you to start with only one Peon. "One Peon Only" is automatically used for all other game types, except those utilizing the Use Map Settings option.
Fixed Order	This disables the ability for players to start into a Random location. If you are creator of the game, for example, you will start in the first set position on the map every time.

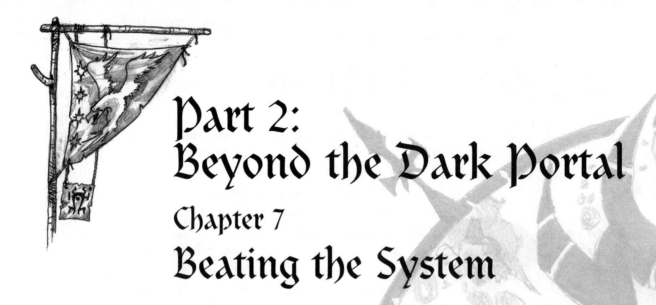

Part 2:
Beyond the Dark Portal
Chapter 7
Beating the System

There's more to winning *Warcraft II: Beyond the Dark Portal* than learning where the mines are. Blizzard took the time to create units with complex interactions. Understanding the general strategies that take advantage of this complex system is critical to winning, whether you face the CPU or an opponent from across the world.

THE ARTILLERY BARRAGE

Frequently, the enemy must approach your village through a narrow passage. Setting two or three Catapults or Ballistae to bombard the area of approach can seriously weaken, if not kill, approaching bad guys. Plus, they work on "autopilot" so you can focus your attention elsewhere.

THE WALL OF STEEL

Placing a couple of Guard and Cannon Towers in a narrow passage can shut it down quickly (because of their range advantage, place the Cannon Towers behind the Guard Towers). This is most effective when used with the artillery barrage, deadly when coupled with the working party described below, and impregnable with a couple of Grunts or Footmen at the base.

THE WOODEN BAND-AID

Your enemies do their level best to take out your Towers. If the going gets dicey, detail two or three Peons/Peasants to repair each Tower. As long as they stay on the opposite side of the attack, the computer won't bother them. The Towers stand up to brutal punishment because the workers repair them as fast as they're damaged. If you place the Towers so each can cover the others' bases, they can pick off any attackers hacking at their Tower counterparts. Please note that this does not work against Catapults and Ballistae.

LUMBER MILLS AS TOWN HALLS

In many scenarios, you must erect the Town Hall or Great Hall at some distance from the nearest lumber. Do not be dismayed: Lumber may also be dropped off at Lumber Mills. To accumulate it faster, merely build a Lumber Mill near the woods.

Catapults bring down a deadly rain of fire.

DEATH KNIGHTS AS RECRUITERS

When the computer runs out of gold, it sends Peasants to the closest active mine—even if you own it. Place a three-Grunts, one-Death-Knight reception committee at the mine in question. As Peasants arrive, the Grunts kill them, and the Knight raises them from the dead—effectively recruiting them into the Orcish Horde.

STRENGTH IN NUMBERS

Subtle tactics rarely work in *Warcraft II*. Don't be bashful about ganging up on the enemy. It's not like he wouldn't do it to you. Mobs of Grunts or Footmen backed up by Axethrowers or Archers can devastate almost anything in their path. The game allows you to group together up to nine units. It's usually a darned good idea. We group eight, then right-click on a ninth, ordering the group to follow it. Make this "ninth" a distinct unit if you can. For example, place an Ogre in charge of a group of fully upgraded Grunts and Axethrowers.

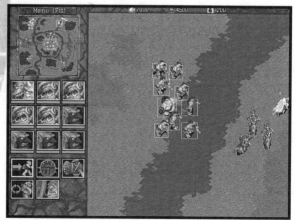

An Ogre-led assault force.

THE TRIPWIRE DEFENSE

Several *Dark Portal* missions require a 360 degree village defense with limited resources. Try placing a light outer ring of Guard Towers and Footmen/Grunt types, with a strong counterattack force (Ogres and the like) in the center of the village. When the enemy hits the outer ring, counterattack and crush them with the Ogres. Of course, if the bad guys attack two places at once, you're screwed.

THE OFFENSIVE DEFENSE

You'll never win a *Dark Portal* scenario by defending a base. If constant attacks threaten to overwhelm your encampment, it's time either to start over or to take the offense. Frequently, the only way to get the computer off your back is to get on its back. Form a reserve and start hitting one of the computer's villages. This usually forces the motherboard to concentrate its resources on defense, removing some of the pressure from you.

THE DEFENSIVE OFFENSE

Try this neat trick when attacking. Stop your formation just out of enemy range. Place Footmen/Grunts in front, Archers/Axethrowers immediately behind. Now bombard, cast a spell on, or send someone to taunt the opposing line. When the enemy reacts by charging the threat to their front, they march into the teeth of your prepared defenses.

THE RED BEAST BURGER

You didn't know these guys were good for something besides blocking construction and emitting excellent screams when slaughtered, did you? Well, they are. If a Death Knight utilizing Death Coil kills a Red Beast, he gains three health points. Not a big deal, but in some scenarios—"The Slayer of The Shadowmoon," for instance—this may be what keeps these creepy guys creeping.

COMBAT FARM HOUSES

Buildings can assist you in defending your village. Let's say the Alliance is streaming into your settlement from two directions. One of these avenues of approach is through a narrow valley bordered by woods and rocks. Let's say the valley is about as wide as a Pig

Dining at the Beast Burger Inn.

Farm. Are you starting to get the picture? Building a Pig Farm in the valley blocks the Humans, and their Elf cousins, from gaining easy access to the village. This is great used in conjunction with the tripwire defense.

What's Up with Those Upgrades, Anyway?

After you buy and research an upgrade, it affects *all* units—those currently in play as well as future purchases. Subsequently destroying the building used for the improvement (for example, Elven Lumber Mill, Blacksmith) does *not* cancel the upgrade.

What's Up with All This Basic, Piercing, and Effective Damage Stuff?

This is how combat works in *Warcraft II:* To get the attacker's Effective Damage (what is actually applied to the defender each time the attacker strikes), a defender's Armor rating is subtracted from the attacker's Basic Damage rating (this value can never be less than zero), and then Piercing Damage is applied (Piercing is unaffected by Armor). After this is figured, there is a random chance that only half the damage is inflicted (it's all or half). For example, Ogre (Basic Damage eight, Piercing Damage four) attacks an Alliance Footman (Armor two). The Ogre's Effective Damage would be his Basic Damage (eight) minus the Footman's Armor (two), plus the Ogre's Piercing Damage (four).

$$8 - 2 + 4 = 10$$

The Ogre's Effective Damage when attacking the Footman equals ten (with the exception of the random "half damage" calculation cutting the attack to five). So Effective Damage is five or ten.

You Can Never Have Too Much Money——Or Can You?

The two rules of thumb when it comes to money are: If you don't have enough, you'll probably lose, and if you have too much, you'll probably lose. On one hand, you need a constant cash flow to finance builds, upgrades, and training. That's why training Peons/Peasants should be on the top of your scenario "to do" list. On the other hand, too much money is a sure sign you're not building, upgrading, or training quickly enough. Look at the situation. Are you waiting on construction? Then assign more workers to repair each building. Always a Footman short? Then build a couple more Barracks and train two or three at once. The perfect situation is enough cash to do what you want but not much more.

Chapter 8
The Alliance…of Dwarves, Elves, and Men

MISSION ONE: ALLERIA'S JOURNEY

Lord Khadgar, Keeper of the Eternal Watch and master of the mystic Citadel of Nethergarde, has sensed a dark power gathering around the remnants of the rift that lies within the Black Morass. He believes that a new Orcish invasion is imminent, and he has urged the Alliance to act. The Elven Ranger Alleria, and a small band of her elite guard, have been sent as escorts so that you may gather reinforcements to counter this threat.

Your travels to the Castle of New Stormwind will lead you across the paths of both the Paladin Turalyon and a mercenary captain known as Danath. Engage their aid during your journey, as their leadership may be needed by the Alliance in the dark days ahead.

Marching Orders

- **Objectives:** Find Turalyon. Find Danath. Bring the Heroes Alleria, Turalyon, and Danath to the Circle of Power at New Stormwind.
- **Starting Location:** Southeast corner.
- **Enemy Location:** Distributed in small clusters.
- **Resources:** One Lumber Mill in the lower center of map.

Courtesy Calls

Gather your band and move north along the eastern map border. Reverse a short distance past the first intersection and dispatch three Knights to destroy the trailing Catapult.

Continue north and recruit the Ballista. March to the river village and liberate all you find there. Return with your entourage to the previously passed clearing. Walk southwest to an intersection bordered by mountains. Follow the foothills, kill the Ogres, stop at the pass, and array your troops in a defensive formation.

Be careful. Some greenskins, supported by a Catapult, wait on the other side.

Have your Knights charge the gap and draw the Catapult's fire. The accompanying Grunts should follow the horsemen onto your troops' waiting swords. Once you've massacred the Orcs, you can make kindling of the Catapult.

> **TIP**
>
> The Knights move too fast for the Catapult to target. It tracks and slaughters slower units. If you don't go far enough beyond the fork, the Catapult will be supported by a Grunt and a Troll stationed just beyond the intersection.

The Alliance troops wait at the pass.

After the battle for the pass, move northeast to the Lumber Mill and put the Peasants to work. You find a new recruit just north to assist them. Keep your guard up; powerful Orc forces—including a Juggernaught—roam the area. Destroy the greenskin infantry; then sink the Juggernaught. If you can, try to hole the Transport as well, although it leaves the scene quickly.

> **TIP**
>
> Use the Knights to draw the Juggernaught's fire. Move your Ballista into range and let loose. You need Archers to support the Ballista, otherwise the Juggernaught might get a shot off that could seriously hurt the Archers. If you feel exceptionally cunning, have the Knights exit from the Juggernaught's view after drawing its fire. The Juggernaught will then bombard the closest Farm while you sink the imperceptive behemoth.

Return to the gap. You can rescue Danath two ways:

- **Choice A:** The safest approach is to continue following the eastern ridge until the forest thins. When you spot a farmhouse on the wood's far side, use the Peasants to deforest the area and move through the hole. Next to the abode waits Danath. This is tedious but necessary if you've lost most of your troops.

- **Choice B:** From the gap in the mountains, follow the western path. You meet a Death Knight who casts Whirlwind on your troops and then runs north. Pursue, overtake, and slay the Death Knight and his undead cronies. Follow the southern path. Danath waits a short way down this trail.

After recruiting Danath, send your military units back to the Shipyard and Foundry settlement. Keep the Peasants harvesting lumber. Build a Transport and upgrade the arrows.

The Ballistae turn the Tower to rubble.

Before boarding the waiting Transport, creep west along the river to ambush the Troll Destroyer waiting there. The Ballista does a good job on this fellow. Now, cross the river, journey west, kill some undead, and head north up their path. You find Turalyon at the Church. Say a prayer, upgrade your Knights, reboard the ferry, and sail west. Unload on the north bank, west of the mountains. After you chop up the undead guards, use your Ballista to take out the Guard Towers.

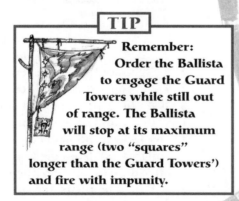

TIP

Remember: Order the Ballista to engage the Guard Towers while still out of range. The Ballista will stop at its maximum range (two "squares" longer than the Guard Towers') and fire with impunity.

Move northwest, annihilate remaining enemy forces, run your heroes through the Circle of Power and *voila*—we have a winner!

MISSION TWO: THE BATTLE FOR NETHERGARDE

A great host of Orcs has reconstructed the Dark Portal and now lays siege to the Citadel of Nethergarde. The Horde still maintains its hold over the great winged Dragons of Azeroth. Some of these creatures, seeming to have grown to crave the taste of battle, have become willing allies with the Orcs under the leadership of a great Black Dragon known only as Deathwing.

Danath has been asked to raise an army from New Stormwind to relieve the beleaguered forces at Nethergarde and drive the Horde back toward the Portal. You must lead the forces of Azeroth in an attempt to break the vanguard of the invading Horde, for unless their assault is stopped, they will gain dominion over the Black Morass.

Marching Orders

- **Objectives:** Destroy all enemy forces. Danath must survive.
- **Starting Location:** Southwest corner.
- **Enemy Location:** Shadowmoon clan–center; Warsong clan–northwest corner; Laughing Skull clan–southeast corner.
- **Resources:** Six gold mines–northwest, southeast (two), northeast corner, northeast-center, west-center.

Fight the Good Fight

Trudge northeast, scouting ahead with the Gnomish Flying Machine and brushing aside the pitiful Orc warriors in your path. Set up camp near the Mine, constructing a Town Hall and Lumber Mill. Watch your back! An Ogre trio creeps up the trail. After butchering the Ogres, head north and scout out a river crossing. Don't cross right away–the far bank boasts some serious firepower.

Back at the Nethergarde ranch, things look pretty green. Don't sweat it. Not much can be done to prevent the township's capture. Instead, focus your attention on the upcoming battle for the river crossing.

Move your Ballista to the stream and engage the southern Guard Tower. Move Knights, one at a time, over the water and gallop south until they're out of the Tower's range. Hopefully, these guys will draw the Orcs' attention from their Tower. Your Ballista should destroy it in short order. Next step, take out the

Placement of units when attacking the crossing.

northern Tower. Keep Knights by the Ballista—but out of the Guard Tower's range—to pummel any Ogres who show their gruesome heads.

On the economic front, expand your village and commence liberating Nethergarde. Send a squad of units to the city's south wall. Place your Footmen and Archers in a good defensive formation just inside the east gate. Order them to stand and bring up a Ballista to pound the Orc barracks.

The Alliance reenters Nethergarde.

The red-eyes reply piecemeal, presenting little more than mobile targets to the Alliance veterans. Once you've neutralized their military, slaughter the Peons and have the Peasants construct a Cannon Tower (it immediately opens up on all in sight).

Don't forget your own town. The persistent greenskins mount numerous small-scale raids. An ounce of preventive Guard Tower construction is better than a pound of rebuilding after a couple of Dragon fly-bys. Keep Danath in the center of your village from now on. You don't need him, and losing him means another saved game down the drain.

Focus most of your efforts on economics during the middle to late game. Build a second Town Hall in Nethergarde and a third northeast of it. Research and purchase all the upgrades you can afford.

Once the research is complete, and you're churning out full-blown Ballistae, Footmen, and Paladins, take two Ballistae, a couple of Paladins, and a few Footmen, and head northwest. You see a gap in the mountains overlooked by two Guard Towers. Attack with the Ballistae. A high-level Grunt or Troll seeks revenge, and you can axe him with your Knights. Be careful to spring the ambush outside the Towers' range. Once you've weeded out the Orcish foot soldiers, let your Ballistae blast away.

Having silenced the Towers, you're free to sack the Orc village. Let the Ballistae handle any remaining Towers while your troops destroy the buildings. You find no enemy soldiers past the mountain gap.

TIP

Try to take out the Dragon Roost in the Laughing Skull village as soon as possible. It is located in the southeast corner of the map.

After leveling the northwest village, send a similar force to the southeastern Orc encampment. This village is even more lightly defended than the last. Again, use your Ballista to destroy the Towers. There shouldn't be more than one or two other Orc warriors. Build a couple of Cannon Towers, destroy everything in sight, and gain victory.

MISSION THREE: ONCE MORE UNTO THE BREACH

Having broken the momentum of the Horde offensive at Nethergarde, the time is ripe for a decisive counterattack. The High Command agrees that a strong assault upon the Fortress that the Orcs have raised near the Dark Portal may end the conflict before it begins.

The Arch-Wizard Khadgar, however, believes that the Orcish Hordes may not be here for the sake of mere conquest. He believes that if the Portal can be captured and not destroyed, he can uncover the purpose for the Horde's present invasion into Azeroth.

Marching Orders

- **Objectives:** Destroy all Strongholds and Fortresses. Turalyon must reach the Dark Portal alive.
- **Starting Location:** Southwest-center.
- **Enemy Location:** Bleeding Hollow clan—southeast corner; Warsong clan—center, midwest; Thunderlord clan—north-center, upper islands.
- **Resources:** Five gold mines—mid-north, center, east-center, southwest, southeast. Four oil splotches—west-center, east-center, south-center, southeast.

Everything but the Kitchen Sink

First off, put those Peasants to work. Next, upgrade your Scout Towers to Guard status. Third, stand by for incoming rounds. A small force of Ogre-lead greenskins attacks. Position your Footmen across the gateway with a "Stand" order. Have your Archers back them up with the Ballista. These units, in addition to your Guard Towers, make quick work of the bad guys.

Continue training Peasants and a couple more Footmen, and begin funding research and upgrades. Watch your food supply and build Farms as you need them.

Send your Knights, a Peasant, Turalyon, the Ballista, and two Footmen over the river crossing. March northwest until you come to a couple of Orcish Towers under construction. Destroy them. Proceed to the gap in the mountains and attack the Guard Tower. Watch out for counterattacks from Orcs who have recently ferried across the river.

Once the Ballista has collapsed the Tower, turn its awesome arrows on the Temple to the north. Have the other soldiers destroy the Lumber Mill while the Peasant builds a Town Hall near the mine. Leave at least one unit outside the mountain pass to guard against Orc landings.

Pump up the economy with more Peasants gathering lumber and gold. Use the money to finish outfitting your army and construct a solid defense for the second village, which receives the brunt of the Orc attacks. This defense should include at least four Guard Towers and several Archers to meet the inevitable Dragon attacks. Meanwhile, upgrade your Keep in the main village to a Castle; then build a Church, Gryphon Aviary, and Mage Hall.

Once your production is going nicely, and you can fight off the incessant raids, prepare for your assault on the large concentration of Orcs in the southeast corner.

You want two Ballistae, two Gryphons, two Paladins, four Rangers, four Footmen, and a pair of Mages. After crossing the stream just north of your main village, head for the gap in the mountains. This is the entrance to the first Orc settlement. Place the Gryphons, the Archers, a Footman, a Paladin, and a Mage as backup in a defensive perimeter, west-northwest of your position. They defend your backside from Dragons or a roving band of Orcs.

A wall of arrows and steel, the human defense of the second village.

Assault the village with the standard fire-the-Ballista-and-draw-them-out-to-their-death tactic. Keep a close rein on your ambushers so they don't follow retreating units through the gap and become the *ambushees*. Keep your Mage and Paladin on hand to counter the inevitable Death Knight.

As you subdue the village, kill off Peons whenever possible. These seemingly innocent Orcs repair buildings you want to destroy and harvest resources that could be yours. With the Towers destroyed, it's safe to bring Peasants in to erect a Town Hall. When the Hall is complete, build a couple of Towers and a Barracks to ward off those irksome Dragons.

Dive into an aggressive shipbuilding program and explore the rest of the map with the Gnomish Flying Machine. A river cuts the map in half. In the center, you see an island shaped like a smile, another frown-like island above it, and a small circular island in the middle where the Portal stands.

Conquer the southern island first. Use Ballistae to hit the enemy Oil Platforms and replace them with your own. The Cannon Towers along much of the Orc shoreline make good target practice for the Gryphon Riders and Mages. Build a couple of Battleships to destroy Refineries, Shipyards, and the occasional Foundry. Once the sea lanes are clear, load a Transport with Ballistae and ground troops. Hit the beach. Resistance is usually light. Once the island is secure, build a Barracks.

If the Orcs are being aggressive, however, they build throngs of Dragons, Juggernaughts, and Destroyers. Use Guard Towers and Destroyers to kill the Dragons. Have decoys lure the Dragons to the friendly Guard Towers—the winged lizards don't seem to have a sense of self-preservation. Use Ballistae and Gryphons against the greenskin Juggernaughts.

Next in line is the center island. You need at least two Ballistae and a pair of Paladins for the job. Exorcise the Death Knights using the Paladins, and use the Ballistae to take down the northern Guard Towers. Collapse the walls surrounding the Circle of Power and run Turalyon through it.

Finally, destroy the Fortress on the northern island—easier said than done. The island often contains numerous Catapults, Death Knights, and Ogres. Land on an edge of the island, behind the forests. This limits the Orcs' avenues of approach to the coastline. Use your ships to hit any units moving down the coast.

The Alliance takes up positions on the center isle.

Gradually move your forces up the coast toward the center. If Dragons are out, build Towers. At this point, you outproduce the Orc commander, so he should run out of units far faster than you. Take your time, wear him down, and victory is yours.

MISSION FOUR: BEYOND THE DARK PORTAL

Elven scouts bring chilling news from Azeroth. A tearing of shadows heralded the arrival of the mighty Orc Shaman Ner'zhul and his guard of Death Knights within the Royal Library of New Stormwind. Unleashing their black magicks, they slaughtered all who opposed them and then fled into the night with their prize—the Book of Medivh.

This serves to confirm what Khadgar has gleaned from the Battle of Nethergarde. He is convinced that the Horde is attempting to learn how the great sorcerer opened the rift between our world and that of the Horde known in the Book of Medivh as Draenor.

With countless domains to plunder, the Horde would become an unstoppable power. The High Command believes that our only recourse is to venture through the Portal—both to reclaim the Book of Medivh and to ensure that the Horde can never again threaten Azeroth.

Marching Orders

- **Objectives:** Erect a Castle to protect lands near the Portal. Destroy all enemy forces.
- **Starting Location:** Center of map.
- **Enemy Location:** Shattered Hand clan–south-center; Warsong clan–west-center; Shadowmoon clan–northeast; Laughing Skull clan–scattered about.
- **Resources:** Four gold mines–two south, one west-center, one northeast.

Kickin' Green Butt

Your first objective is the Shattered Hand village. Use the Gnomish Flying Machine to scout the southern area for possible ambushes while your Gryphon Rider eliminates the Cannon Towers guarding the Portal's eastern passes. You should be able to capture this village rather easily. Have one of your Peasants begin building a Town Hall midway between the two gold mines in the area. Have the others build plenty of Farms and a Barracks.

An effective AD (anti-Dragon) defensive line.

The other clans waste no time badgering your new settlement. Move most of your troops to cover the western approaches, but keep several Archers and your Gryphon Rider to the northeast to protect against Dragon attacks.

As soon as possible, build a string of Guard Towers north of your town and position Archers between each. Three or four Towers should do the trick.

As your settlement grows, form a hammer to smash the greenskins.

Your next target is the Warsong clan to the northwest. Divide your force and attack through the two southern passes. Lead with Ballistae, covering them with your foot soldiers and Archers. Take out the Towers first. This fight can be tough, so be sure to have reserves ready. After leveling the village, build a Town Hall and start collecting gold. A small garrison might be a good idea too. Orcs have a sneaky habit of rebuilding their villages after the destroying armies leave.

The last city is a pretty tough nut to crack. Train two armies. Position one at north-center of the map and the other east-center. Slowly advance within Ballista range of the Towers and eliminate them. Gryphon Riders also work well against Cannon Towers (or just about anything, for that matter). As the Orcs pour forth to defend their village, bring up the troops. Once you've thinned the ranks of green, use your Ballistae and Gryphons to take out the Dragon Roosts, severely throttling the Orcish air support. The rest of the battle is just a matter of sacking the village.

Gryphons raid the Dragon Roosts.

MISSION FIVE: THE SHADOWED SEAS

Having fortified your position on the Hellfire peninsula where the Portal is located, the time has come to establish a fleet to attack the surrounding clans. The Orcish shipyards of Zeth'kur lie nearby. Destroy them and the ships of war that are stationed there.

While the Horde has been stunned by the ferocity of your attack, our presence here has driven the clans to new heights of fury. You won't maintain this foothold for long against their numbers, so your victories must be daring and swift.

Marching Orders

- **Objectives:** Build three Shipyards. Destroy the Orcish Shipyards of Zeth'kur.
- **Starting Location:** Northwest corner of map.
- **Enemy Location:** Bonechewer clan–northwest; Bleeding Hollow clan–center; Thunderlord clan–southwest; Laughing Skull clan–southeast.
- **Resources:** Eight gold mines–four on the north side of the sea located northwest, north-center, center, and northeast; two on the southwestern islands; one south-center; one southeast. Six oil patches–west-center, center, east-center, south-center, southwest, and southeast.

Sweeping the Seas

A straightforward scenario, just remember the objectives and stick to them. Start by assaulting the Bonechewer village south of your starting position. The Bonechewers are a weak clan and present little resistance. Immediately begin building a base of operations on the ruins of the Bone-head settlement. Position your forces to defend against attacks from the east.

Pump up your army; then send out a reconnaissance in force. You may want to leave the Ballistae behind in case a quick retreat is necessary. Once you discover the Bleeding Hollow clan (to the east), build up your forces and make a direct assault. They're closely allied with the Laughing Skulls to the south, so prepare for sea-borne reinforcements. Raze the village, build a Town Hall and commence digging for gold.

Scout the remainder of the north shore, using Knights. Next you must construct Shipyards, Oil Tankers, five Destroyers (to hunt drilling sites), a Gnomish Inventor, and a Foundry.

Fabricate an undersea armada to use against the Thunderlord clan's navy. These greenskins, from islands in the map's southwestern quadrant, own an impressive force of Juggernauts and Destroyers—impressive against *surface* combatants, that is. Little more than targets for Gnomish Submarines. While this battle rages, build Battleships to bombard the Orc coastal Cannon Towers.

Don't lose sight of the undersea war. The Thunderlords get plenty tricky, employing Death Knights to cast Whirlwind spells powerful enough to sink your Subs.

Shore bombardment.

Your newly constructed Battleships can lend a hand, bombarding the coastal Towers and Death Knights who wait on the shore.

The southern isle.

From now on, this is an engagement for Admirals. Pound the Orcs with your navy while the Alliance's army guards the northern shore. Once you've destroyed the Thunderlord navy and Shipyards, move east to take out the Laughing Skulls. Their navy is smaller than the Thunderlords', but their coastal defenses, studded with Catapults, can be wicked. It's possible to win the battle without Transports, but you may want to land a force of Marines to assist in the Laughing Skulls' destruction. Remember, you need not destroy all enemy forces, only their Shipyards.

MISSION SIX: THE FALL OF AUCHINDOUN

Kurdran—Gryphon Rider of Northeron—has returned from his patrol with vital news. He has located the hidden Fortress of Auchindoun and the battlements that serve as Stronghold to the Bleeding Hollow clan. Alleria's Rangers also report that they have seen a massive force moving towards the North, and suspect that these troops are staging another attack upon Azeroth.

Although the Orcish army is too large for your forces to battle alone, you may be able to launch a raid against Auchindoun. Should your strike succeed, you would force their army to retreat—or be cut off and destroyed.

Raze the Fortress of Auchindoun and retreat before their forces can rally against you.

Marching Orders

- **Objectives:** Destroy Auchindoun. Return the Heroes Turalyon and Danath to the Circle of Power.
- **Starting Location:** Northeast corner of the map.
- **Enemy Location:** Bonechewer clan—northwest; Warsong clan—east-center; Bleeding Hollow clan—southwest; Shadowmoon clan—south-center.
- **Resources:** Six gold mines—three along the eastern map edge in the north, center and south; one northwest, one southwest; one south-center. Four oil patches—all in the center.

From the Jaws of Defeat

This scenario is difficult even *with* this guide. If you fail to stick to the objectives, the last thing you see is the business end of an Orc battleaxe. First off, establish a base. Use your Gnomish Flying Machines to scout the land mass directly south of your starting position. Ferry your forces across the water, landing just south of the village.

At this point, you have two options. The best is to capture the Warsong village. This is arduous duty, but it's better for the Alliance in the long run. Nevertheless, if you desire, you may base near the gold mine in the east-central edge of the map and defeat the Warsongs after you build up your forces. The Warsongs won't just sit and wait for your attack, however. Count on them doing all they can to disrupt your plans for economic force enhancement.

If you decide to take the village at the start, position your Destroyers and Battleships along the shore, near the pass leading to the village. Then move your Ballistae forward to engage one of the Towers. When the Orcs counterattack, withdraw your Ballistae toward your ships and remaining soldiers. Repeat this drill several times, eliminating most of this Orcish Horde. Now you can concentrate on destroying the Towers and sacking the village.

This is a great spot to build your base. You find a prolific gold mine and an oil patch nearby. The mountains provide natural protection from land attack.

Right off, build Guard Towers to protect against Shawdowmoon Dragon raids. The Towers also come in handy against the amphibious incursions of the Bonechewer clan. Archers with Ranger training and upgraded arrows help round out your defenses.

Lure enemy units from the Towers into range of your naval guns.

Beef up your forces and eventually upgrade your Town Hall to a Castle. Three or four Gryphon Riders are excellent not only for defending your base, but for attacking enemy ships and Cannon Towers. Hammer out a few Submarines to help sink enemy ships as well.

As in all things, stick to your guns. Protect Turalyon and Danath and don't worry about much aside from the destruction of Auchindoun. Once your force is large enough to fill four Transports, send a force of Gryphon Riders south to take out any remaining Bleeding Hollow Cannon Towers. Bring along a few Battleships for shore bombardment.

Use Gryphon Riders to eliminate Cannon Towers.

The fight for Auchindoun is bloody and requires constant attention. Ignore attacks on your home base—that distraction could cost you the battle. The Archers and Guard Towers should be sufficient, in any case. Leave Turalyon and Danath at the base with a small bodyguard. As soon as you destroy the last Bleeding Hollow unit in Auchindoun, rush them across to the Circle of Power and to victory.

MISSION SEVEN: DEATHWING

The arcane powers that surround the blazing ruins of Auchindoun have made urgent the summoning of Khadgar to the dark lands of the Orcs. The destruction of the Bleeding Hollow clan was not without great price, however, for both Kurdran and his mount Sky'ree were captured by the Horde.

While examining the remains of the great Fortress, the Arch-Wizard has learned not only the location of the Book of Medivh, but also that another artifact is needed for Ner'zhul's plans to reach fruition—the Skull of Gul'dan. Khadgar believes it possible to destroy the Portal and permanently seal the rift created by Medivh if he can acquire these artifacts.

A great mountain isle lies to the northeast, atop which the Black Dragon Deathwing dwells. The Skull of Gul'dan lies within his lair. Alleria and Khadgar have agreed to aid you in stealing away the Skull and—if possible—destroy the great Dragon. It is rumored that Orcish tribes live on this island and offer captives from the Great War as sacrifices to Deathwing. If you can rescue the captives, they may know of some weakness in the creature.

Marching Orders

- **Objectives:** Destroy Deathwing and his lair. Khadgar, Alleria, and Kurdan must survive.
- **Starting Location:** Southwest corner of the map.
- **Enemy Location:** Bonechewer clan—southeast corner; Shattered Hand clan—northwest quadrant; Warsong clan—northeast quadrant; Deathwing and his lair—east of center.
- **Resources:** Three gold mines—southeast, northwest, and mideast. Two oil patches—south-center and southeast corner.

Lizards to Go

This battle allows you to get up close and personal with your charge, since what you start with is all you get. Warm up by destroying the Bonechewer village east of your starting position. Here's how: Load your troops in the Transport and head for the village, Destroyers in the lead. Have the Elven ships bombard the shore while the troops disembark. This engagement goes quickly, but be careful not to lose anyone. Don't let your wounded die—use your Paladins to heal them.

After you free the captives, have the Peasants build a Town Hall, several Farms, a Lumber Mill, Oil Refinery, and Shipyard. Divide your forces to protect the Transports and village from Dragon attacks. Have the Shipyard crank out a few Tankers and all the Destroyers your coin will allow. While you expand your navy, the Gnomish Flying Machine can scout the map to locate other captives.

Once the gold mine collapses, load up your troops and set sail for the northwestern map edge. You pass the western shore of Shattered Hand Island. Don't trade shots with the locals. Their Giant Turtles wait beneath the surface to sink your forces. Above all, protect the Transports.

After passing by the island, head east and land your troops. Use the Destroyers to exterminate the red-eyes' nasty welcoming committee. Once your troops are ashore, advance east to rescue the captured Paladin and his compatriots. Take care—although resistance is light, you can't afford to lose a single sword.

A little magic in the air—use Blizzard to take out Towers.

The trap springs on Deathwing.

Two Cannon Towers and several undead guard the entrance to the final POW camp. First, lure the Undead outside the Towers and destroy them. Then send Khadgar to unleash a Blizzard on the Towers. If the first spell doesn't crumble them both, wait until Khadgar's power is recharged and let the ice fall once again. After destroying the Towers, advance cautiously, taking out the remaining undead and Catapult.

The mountains southeast of this final POW camp harbor Deathwing and his lair. Kurdran is the only figure capable of reaching it, but he can't defeat this powerful Dragon alone. Position your Archers in a line near the pass leading to the lair. Keep the Paladins nearby to heal their wounds. Once this trap is ready, have Kurdran attack Deathwing. As soon as the Dragon responds, withdraw Kurdran through the line of Archers. When Deathwing comes in range, have Khadgar cast a Slow spell on the Dragon. This gives your Archers time to defeat this great menace. Afterward, send Kurdran in to destroy the lair.

MISSION EIGHT: COAST OF BONES

By seeking the artifacts you need to seal the rift, you've given the Horde time to mount a strike against you. A great Orcish armada threatens your captured coasts, and Alliance armies are pressed hard on many fronts.

Your only chance for victory lies in obtaining the Book of Medivh. All knowledge of the Portal rests in the keeping of Ner'zhul and his Order of Death Knights at the Fortress of Shadowmoon. You must storm and raze the Strongholds that guard the coastline of his lands so you may bring your forces to bear and isolate and destroy his cursed sanctuary.

Marching Orders

- **Objective:** Destroy all enemy forces.
- **Starting Location:** Central northern map edge.
- **Enemy Location:** Shattered Hand clan—northwest; Thunderlord clan—southwest; Laughing Skull clan—southeast.
- **Resources:** Five gold mines—southwest, center, southeast, and two northwest. Four oil patches—west-center, southeast corner, and two center.

Wipe 'Em Slick

An interesting encounter, this battle allows you to use some slightly unconventional strategies. Your first objective is to destroy the Shattered Hand village west of your starting position. Use your Battleship to pulverize the Cannon Tower, then rush the village with your troops. Casualties may be high.

While the survivors sack the Shattered Hand encampment, put your Peasants to work building a base. Don't worry about a Shipyard until you have a Keep (or perhaps a Castle). Your first priority is expanding infrastructure. Immediately upgrade arrows and use Archers, backed by a couple of Guard Towers, to shoot down the occasional Dragon raider.

Gold is abundant (two mines) on this peninsula, so build only the best units and max out the weapons upgrades. Gryphon Riders are the unit of choice. They fly anywhere and are invulnerable to most units.

Gryphons and Mages on a rampage.

While your Peasants erect the Shipyard and accompanying maritime buildings, capture the oil patch southeast of your base. Bypass the patch just south of your base—it's within range of Catapults and the Death Knights' Whirlwind.

As your Gryphon force grows, use it to secure a clear beach on the land mass just south of your base. Land at least two Transports full of ground forces there (including Mages). Once you've destroyed the Orc's Towers, send the Gryphons after enemy units.

Use the Mages' Blizzard on enemy concentrations and Polymorph on the truly dangerous animals.

> ### TIP
>
> Peasants are an invaluable addition to your landing force. Use them to build Guard or Cannon Towers in the middle of the enemy village. Not only do the Towers give you a position on which to fall back, they destroy the village as well. Also, to shorten the training pipeline, it helps to build another, on-scene, Barracks.

Clearing the island for a Town Hall.

By the time you capture and sack the Thunderlord village, your gold mines are close to depleted. The island between you and the Laughing Skulls contains a good mine. Send a boatload of Peasants to clear the forest on the isle's northeastern end and build a Town Hall. Next, clear the wood from around the Mine and get yourself some gold.

While you gather a force to assault the Laughing Skull village, flesh out your navy with several Battleships. Together with a force of Gryphons, these vessels can destroy the green-skin armada and their defending Towers. Once you eliminate these obstacles to invasion, use this combined air–sea force to soften up the enemy so you can land your troops with little difficulty. By this time, the Laughing Skulls have exhausted their gold supply and can't reinforce themselves. The battle now becomes a matter of leveling the village and mopping up.

MISSION NINE: HEART OF EVIL

The towering spires of Shadowmoon reach upward as obsidian blades to cleave the hostile amber skies above. The corrupt heart of the mighty shaman's power is within reach. Press your attack and wipe the bane of Ner'zuhl and his Order of Death Knights from the face of Draenor forever.

By destroying this dark Fortress and claiming the Book of Medivh, Khadgar can close the rift and rid Azeroth of the Orcish Hordes forever!

Marching Orders

- **Objectives:** Destroy the Fortress of Shadowmoon. Raze the Mystic Runestones of Gul'dan.
- **Starting Location:** Central northern edge of the map.
- **Enemy Location:** Shattered Hand clan—northwest; Laughing Skull clan—southeast.
- **Resources:** Five gold mines—southwest, center, southeast, and two northwest.

Daemons to Sheep

Initially, this is a tough battle. Your first objective is to move your forces east toward the Bonechewer village. Don't attack yet, however. Parade your forces past its northeastern Guard Tower and release the captives in the POW camp. *Now* you may attack. Use the Catapult to take out the Towers; use the Archers and foot soldiers to protect the Catapult.

Once you've taken the village, destroy the enemy buildings and begin fabricating your own base. Surround the encampment with Guard Towers to defend against Dragons and raiding Death Knights. Train enough forces to garrison the camp, and use the rest of your coin to build up base infrastructure. Upgrade all weapons and soldiers. Build a few Gnomish Flying Machines to scout the map, especially the central northern section, to locate your objectives. Make sure the Alliance army you train includes Gryphon Riders, Mages, several Ballistae, and the like. Leave some Archers and a few Gryphon Riders at home and take the rest of the entourage to ravage the Shattered Hand village.

Once again, lead with your Ballistae and take out the Towers guarding the village entrance. Use your Mages to either Polymorph the defenders or cast Blizzard in their midst. If you brought a sizable force, this township should fall without difficulty. Bring along Peasants to build a Barracks while your army sacks the village. For the next stage, you need several Rangers, so train them and task the Paladins with healing your wounded.

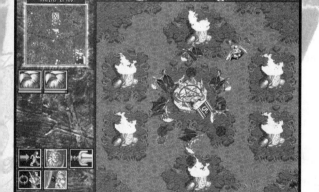

The Mystic Runestones of Gul'dan and their keepers.

You can begin your advance on the village of the Bleeding Hollow and Shadowmoon clans by taking out the undead guarding the entrance. Make a line of Rangers and Ballistae just south of the entrance Cannon Tower and crumble the structure with a hail of arrows.

Your Gnomish Flying Machines should already have found your main objective–the Mystic Sanctum of Ner'zhul. Six Daemons protect it.

Send in a Gryphon Rider to attack the Daemons and then retreat across your line of Rangers. While they let loose with deadly volleys of arrows, your Mages can Polymorph the Daemons into harmless beasts.

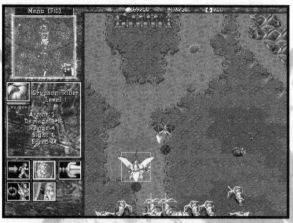

Rangers turn the Daemons into flying pincushions.

You may need to repeat this a couple of times to get all the enemies. Once you've eliminated them, take out Ner'zhul and plunder the village. Stay alert–the Warsong Clan counterattacks from the east. Merely shield the units destroying the village to achieve success.

MISSION TEN: THE BATTLE OF HELLFIRE

Although the Fortress of Ner'zuhl has been destroyed and the Death Knights scattered, neither the shaman nor the Book of Medivh has been found. As Khadgar and Turalyon use their magicks to search the ruins for some clue as to the location of the mystic tome, a Gnomish Flying Machine descends, bringing news from the Hellfire peninsula and the Portal.

A multitude of Orcs have laid siege to the fortifications at Hellfire. Although the attacking warriors are not well equipped, their sheer numbers may spell the downfall of our forces there.

You must take command of the Alliance armies at Hellfire and break the siege before our troops are pushed back through the Dark Portal. We must withstand their charge long enough for the Book of Medivh to be recovered and the rift forever sealed.

Marching Orders

- **Objectives:** Outlast the besieging Orcs until lack of supplies forces them to retreat. All your Heroes must survive the siege.
- **Starting Location:** Southeast corner of the map.
- **Enemy Location:** Shattered Hand clan–southwest; Thunderlord clan–north-center; Bonechewer clan–west-center.
- **Resources:** Five gold mines–north-center, two west-center, one south-center, and one southeast. One oil patch northeast.

Creative Slaughter

This battle takes some creativity to win. Right from the beginning, you're under attack by three clans. The Shattered Hand clan primarily sends Ogres and Catapults with a few assorted Orcs or an occasional Death Knight. The Bonechewers raid from the north with Grunts and Axethrowers. The Thunderlord clan, located north of your position, sends only Dragons.

Your first priority is to expand your army. Quickly upgrade your Keep to a Castle and train Paladins, Gryphon Riders, Mages, and Dwarven Demolition Squads. These are your mainstay for victory. Use Gryphon Riders to attack Catapults and lower-grade units at a distance from the base. Position Mages near the outer walls so they can quickly Polymorph Ogres and Dragons that venture too near. Your Cannon and Guard Towers should take care of the rest with a minimal complement of lesser units. Use Paladins either to attack enemy units that break though or, more importantly, to heal the wounded. Gold is limited, and the winner is the commander who best conserves his resources.

As your defenses stiffen, and you can create extra units for offensive operations, target the Shattered Hand village. Gather six Demolition Squads, six Mages, four Paladins, and eight Gryphon Riders. Group each type of unit separately. Stop them beyond range of the village defenses. The Gryphons act as your air cover. The Paladins are the medics and last-resort support. Use the Dwarves to blow up the outer Towers.

Now send one Mage at a time to Polymorph an Ogre or other powerful enemy and quickly return to the Mage group. If enemy units follow, attack them with the Gryphons or other Mages. As the Mages clear the Orc units, send in more Dwarves to demolish the

Dwarves rush in under cover of Gryphon Riders.

remaining Towers. Because they can attack your Gryphons, Guard Towers should be the priority. If units sustain damage, heal them between these short raids. After destroying their defenses, move in to raze the village.

After you destroy the first village, you may need to bring up reinforcements, particularly Dwarven Demolition Squads. The Bonechewer village is next on the agenda. Use the same tactics and you should have no trouble. If there's still a gold mine, bring Peasants over, build a Town Hall, and mine away.

Your final objective is the Thunderlord village across the water. Their defenses are mainly Towers with a sprinkling of support units. They spent most of their resources on Dragons to raid your base. By this time, they're probably out of gold. To get across the water, build a Shipyard, Foundry, and a Transport or two. Use your Gryphon Riders to secure a small beachhead, then send over a load of Demolition Squads. Use them to fell the Guard, Cannon Towers, and Catapults. The next load is your Mages and Paladins. Polymorph the defenders and then level the village.

Mission Eleven: Dance of the Laughing Skull

The perfect team for storming an Orc village.

Y ou have proven your strength in battle, but none can stand against the combined might of the Horde. We of the Laughing Skull clan, however, seek advantage within the turmoil of this war. With the aid of your strongest warriors, our clan can gain dominance over the northern clans of Draenor.

Do not show surprise, Human—only the strongest survive within the Horde. You must secure the passes across the Blade's Edge Mountains and destroy the Stronghold of the Thunderlord clan that dwells there. We will supply you with warriors and supplies culled from our villages. In return, we will give you the Book of Medivh, which we seized from Ner'zhul's Stronghold before your armies could destroy it.

Marching Orders

- **Objective:** Destroy all enemy forces. All your Heroes must survive.
- **Starting Location:** Southeast and northeast corners.
- **Enemy Location:** Bonechewer clan—northwest corner; Thunderlord clan—south-center; Laughing Skull clan—northeast corner.
- **Resources:** Five gold mines—north-west corner, southwest corner, south-center, center, northeast corner.

Brother Against Brother

The challenge here is developing a strong defense while expanding your economic base. Your opponents, located west and south of you, usually conduct closely concurrent attacks. The fellows in the west favor Catapults, while the southerners pitch in a couple of Death Knights

A sturdy defense at the Western Gap.

for flavor. Coordinated attacks are a major headache in *Warcraft II*. You may be able to outthink the computer, but "out-mousing" it is a bit more dicey. Just when one front stabilizes, you realize all the units on the other front are dead.

The *good* news, though, is that a mountain range running roughly north–south down the entire map separates you from the greenskins. This range has only three gaps, and the enemy never seems to use the middle one. Furthermore, your opponent doesn't use Dragons.

At the scenario's start, head north as fast as possible. Recruit the Orc village you enter and defeat a minor counterattack from the west. Build a wall of Farms across your side of the gap. These huts take a lot of damage and occasionally attract the attentions of opposing units. Behind these, erect two or three Cannon Towers to keep the attackers honest. Finally, form a reserve to attack Catapults when they trudge to the front.

Once you've stabilized this area, turn your attentions to the southern gap. After you defeat an attack by four Ogres, build two Guard Towers here and back them up with a few Knights. If you can get this stuff together you'll have no more worries from the south.

Once your defenses are ready, focus on the economics of expansion. Upgrade your troops and build a Fortress when possible. Your gold mine doesn't contain an infinite amount of gold, so send an expedition to plunder the gold mine south of the mountain's middle pass. Clear the area; build a Great Hall and Barracks. Both buildings drastically reduce transit times for your units, both to get to the front and to drop off resources.

Having stabilized the defense and economy, it's time to hit the offensive highway. The western Orc settlement should be the first to feel your wrath. Head out with two Ballistae, two Grunts, two Ogres, a pair of Death Knights, and Khadgar. Work the Death Knights (employing Death and Decay) and the Ballistae to break down enemy defenses. Destroy the city, erect a Great Hall, and reap the spoils of victory.

Southern hospitality?

This leaves the southern greenskins. Going directly south of the western village you find three Towers and a similar number of Ogres. Use your Ballista and Dragons to terminate this threat. Only the Tower in the center can touch the Dragons, so use the Ballista on this one. Watch out for Death Knights lurking in the shadows.

Once past the gates, you don't encounter much organized resistance. However, exercise caution when mopping up this last village. A Death Knight might surprise you and assassinate one of your all-important Heroes. I hate it when that happens.

MISSION TWELVE: THE BITTER TASTE OF VICTORY

Khadgar has discovered that although the Book of Medivh was stolen from Ner'zhul, the ancient shaman has learned enough of its secrets to conjure his darkest spell. Over the blood red skies of Draenor, huge dimensional rifts appear, crackling with the cosmic energy of the Twisting Nether. Alleria's scouts report that Ner'zhul and his followers escaped through the largest of the new rifts as Draenor felt the first of its death throes. The tremendous energies emitted from the converging rifts have succeeded in breaking down the fabric of reality on Draenor, unleashing massive earthquakes and tidal waves upon its shores.

Unless the Dark Portal is closed on both worlds, Azeroth will be subject to an enormous backlash of energy.

Using the combined powers of the Book of Medivh and the Skull of Gul'dan, you must return Khadgar to the Dark Portal and seal the rift between Azeroth and the doomed world of Draenor, forever.

Marching Orders

- **Objectives:** Destroy the Dark Portal. (Only Khadgar can destroy the Dark Portal.) Khadgar must survive.
- **Starting Location:** North-center, southeast-center, and center (briefly).
- **Enemy Location:** Warsong clan—east-center; Bonechewer clan—center; Shadowmoon clan—northwest corner; Shattered Hand clan—south-center.
- **Resources:** Five gold mines—northwest, east-center, south-center, southeast corner, center.

The Final Frontier

March your northern forces to safety in the southeastern village. Have your Dwarves blow a hole in the mountains directly south of your position. Race through it to the village, ignoring all else.

As you run through the mountain pass, send your units south and a little east. When you get to the north–south mountain range, travel south down its east side. Once you reach the end, head southwest along another ridge until *it* ends. Make a U-turn and rush behind the comforting walls of your village. You pass three Peasants near this last mountain range; bring them along.

Take a breather as the Orcs destroy the rest of your center township. Start mining and cutting lumber. Build a Ballista and research upgrades at the Lumber Mill/Blacksmith. Get your troops in order to face the unwashed masses.

Make sure you have Footmen at the gate and the northern entrance to your encampment. Order them to Stand. As the first Orcs arrive, have Khadgar unleash a Blizzard on their approach path. This is great stuff—10 to 15 Orcs die without ever touching you. As the Blizzard fades, send your Gryphon to kill the Catapult moving up to pound your tightly packed units. This should blunt the Orc offensive.

Now develop your Portal assault and building strategy. The Portal is in the town west of your position. Have Khadgar destroy it and you've won. Because of this, there's no need for a 30-year plan. Focus on immediate unit improvements and building Guard Towers to counter periodic Dragon attacks.

The assault party should advance in an organized fashion. Move forward until you can anchor your Footmen between the forest and the Orc's Blacksmith. Have your Knights set up across the north side of this line connecting the Blacksmith to the mountains. Your Archers should fill in behind the Footmen and Knights. Bring the Mages and Ballista through the center. Command all units to Stand.

A chilling defense.

Once this position is set, roll the Ballista around to attack the first Tower south of the Portal. Extend your defensive line to cover the Ballista. Cast Blizzard on the Peons attempting to rebuild the Tower you're destroying. Use these techniques to level the other Towers in the village and fight off the constant Orc counterattacks.

By now, there isn't much armed resistance left, just a group of Peons.

Set up a defensive perimeter and order Khadgar to destroy the Portal. Unfortunately, this takes darn-near forever. Bring a couple of Peasants over to build a Town Hall, Barracks, and several Towers to assist in your perimeter defense.

That's it. Now it's just a waiting game. Eventually the Portal falls, and you can sleep soundly, knowing you saved the world.

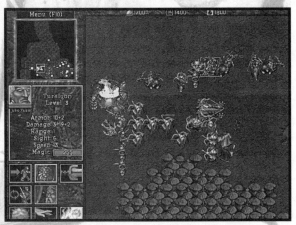

The Alliance arrayed in front of the Orcs' village.

Chapter 9
The Orcish Hordes

MISSION ONE: SLAYER OF THE SHADOWMOON

Though the elder shaman Ner'zhul holds the rank of war chief of Draenor, your position as slayer to the Shadowmoon clan gives you the duty of leading its army into battle.

Ner'zhul has discovered how the rift was first formed and now wishes not only to reopen the gateway into Azeroth, but to create new portals and seek out even more worlds to control.

You must subjugate an order of Death Knights. The renegade Ogre-Mage called Mogor, of the Laughing Skull clan, has taken control of these dark soldiers and is seeking to create a powerful spell with the aid of their necromantic magic. His life is also forfeit.

Although we have no Dragons to command, we have learned that Grom Hellscream, leader of the Warsong clan, has been captured by the Laughing Skulls and is being held prisoner. Free him and he will surely aid in your battles.

Marching Orders

- **Objectives:** Destroy the Death Knights and their Temple. Grom Hellscream must survive.
- **Starting Location:** Southeast corner.
- **Enemy Location:** Various. Temple of the Damned and Ogre-Mage Mogor are located in the northern center of the map.
- **Resources:** There are no gold mines in this scenario.

To Kill an Ogre

Although the scenario provides no mines, what you initially see is not what you get. As you travel, you find new forces to strengthen your army. Nevertheless, conserving strength is important. The starting forces are tough enough to deal with most encounters, but the casualties taken in doing so directly affect the outcome of the battle for the Temple.

Keeping this in mind, set out on your quest. Place the Death Knight in the rear of your party to prevent his untimely demise at the hands of undead ambushers. Proceed to the mid-southwest area of the map and free the Trolls residing there.

Leaving the Axethrowers' small village, head northwest, killing the undead as you go. Soon you bump into Grom Hellscream, eager to join up and ready to fight. Continue toward the top of the map until you stumble on a small village containing a Lumber Mill. Use the Lumber Mill to upgrade the Trolls' axes—you'll need a sharp blade soon. Another stash of Trolls and some Goblin Sappers wait just north of the Lumber Mill.

Heading out with the Death Knight in tow.

Before you press on to the Temple, heal the Death Knight. Remember, when Death Coil is cast on living entities, the Knight gets stronger. These beings don't have to be enemies, but they can't be your own troops. This leaves the Red Beasts. For each of these the Knight zaps, he receives three health points, so take time to kill any you find grazing the pastures of Draenor.

You can tackle the end game and gain access to the Death Knight's Temple in either of two ways: (1) Use the Sappers to blast through the rock formation to the east of the Lumber Mill. (2) Bypass the rock formation and attack the Temple from the east.

Certainly the first option is the most direct. If most of your initial force remains alive, this is the preferred method. If your Horde looks a little sickly, continue south of the formation. The scenario's biggest brawl happens here, but it's winnable. Keep the Sappers and Death Knight to the rear and wade in with Grunts, Ogres, and Axethrowers. Use the Death Knight's Death Coil to assist the frontline troopers—particularly Grom Hellscream. Once you defeat the enemy Orcs and Trolls, free the prisoners in the corral to the right of the rocks.

The sappers prepare to breach the wall.

131

Advance west toward the Death Knight Temple. Use the Sappers to breach the wall. Zap Mogor's Knights with your own, and when they come at you, kill them with your Ogres, Trolls, and Hellscream. Grom is one hell of a fighter, but he *can* be killed, so keep an eye on him. If his health bar falls into the yellowish range, pull him back.

After you slay the Death Knights, tiptoe into the compound, Knight to the rear, remaining Ogres in front. Ogre-Mage Mogor comes forth ready to rumble. Occupy him with your Ogres (or whatever infantry is left) and use the Death Knight for the kill. Now it's merely a matter of destroying the Temple, and victory is yours.

Mission Two: The Skull of Gul'dan

The Skull of Gul'dan is a powerful artifact and essential for resurrecting the Dark Portal. A pathetic Orc captain of the Bonechewer clan wears the Skull as a symbol of his station and does not know of its true power.

Ner'zhul has sent the Ogre hero, Dentarg, to influence warriors from the Thunderlord clan to join in the battle against the Bonechewers. The warriors of the Shattered Hand, and their leader Korgath Bladefist, are also ready to assist.

Move quickly to the Thunderlord village and raise an army to crush the Bonechewer captain and win the Skull of Gul'dan.

Marching Orders

- **Objective:** Capture the village controlled by the Thunderlord clan. Destroy the Bonechewer captain and his encampment.
- **Starting Location:** Northwest corner of the map.
- **Enemy Location:** Mideastern edge.
- **Resources:** Gold—four mines—northwest, southwest, northeast, mideast.

Victory to the Bold

This one is a tad tougher than "Slayer of the Shadowmoon." The Orc starts with Dentarg and one Grunt. He must build his forces rapidly and raze the enemy settlement.

The key is aggression. You'll go bankrupt attempting to slow down the persistent Bonechewer raids. However, season the aggression with a dash of prudence. Headlong assaults don't work. Instead, you must defeat the enemy little by little.

One way to do this is to split up Dentarg and the Grunt. Send the Ogre to the southwest corner of the map to recruit the Thunderlords living there. Meanwhile, walk the Grunt southeast to enlist Korgath Bladefist (located at the Blacksmith east of the mine at the western map edge) and his Axethrowers.

Divvy up your newfound allies to guard the north and east entrances of the southern village. Immediately train 10 to 12 Peons. Eight should mine while the remainder work on the woods in the northeast corner of the settlement. Keep an eye on these guys—cutting completely through the woods opens an avenue of attack for the bad guys.

Build two Barracks. Place one next to each village entrance to cut down the time reinforcements take to reach the "gates." When gold allows, start churning out troops. Build a Lumber Mill and upgrade the Scout Towers to Guard or Cannon Towers. As soon as it's practical, erect a Stronghold and Ogre Mound.

By now—usually before the Stronghold or Ogre Mound are fashioned—the bad guys have come calling. Don't panic. Your Cannon Towers, aided by three Grunts and a couple of Axethrowers, can usually buy time to assemble a counterattack force. Once a small force of Grunts, Ogres (if you have them), Peons, and Axethrowers, supported by a catapult, has been assembled, exit the east village entrance and attack northeast.

The initial north gate defense.

The Bonechewers react strongly. The path runs thick with green blood. Hopefully, you can make it to the lower reaches of their settlement and lay waste to a couple of Farms. Don't push it! Plenty of Ogres and Guard Towers remain, waiting to liquidate your troops.

When the attack loses momentum, call it off. Use the Peons to build a new Barracks near your spearhead and start training replacements for the depleted attack force.

Meanwhile, gold may be running short. Before it gets critical, send a Peon task force, escorted by Grunts, to the mine at the western map edge. Build a Great Hall and commence gathering loot. If you keep the pressure up on the southern front, the bad guys will probably leave this little mining expedition alone.

Now winning is just a matter of chipping away at the Bonechewer village. Build plenty of Catapults and Ogres. The Catapults are great for taking out Guard and Cannon Towers, enjoying a slight range advantage over both. Ogres are great for taking out anything else. Continue to use the attack–regroup strategy. Capture the southern enemy gold mine as soon as you find it, limiting the enemy's ability to replace its forces. Once the large east-northeastern settlement has been raised, send your Hordes to the southeast corner to eliminate the last vestiges of the enemy clan.

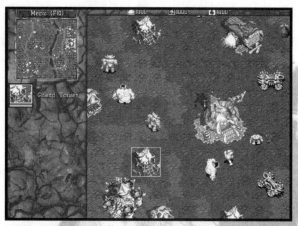

Initial bad guys defense.

A final note: It isn't necessary to upgrade the Stronghold to Fortress and construct a Temple of the Damned or Altar of Storms. You may, however, want to give it a try as an alternative.

MISSION THREE: THUNDERLORD AND BONECHEWER

Ner'zhul has met with opposition to his plans from the leaders of both the Thunderlord and Bonechewer clans. They desire to journey to Azeroth and have their clans triumph where Doomhammer had failed. This is a vision not shared by your war chief.

You are to lead the forces of Shadowmoon against the strongholds of both Bonechewer and Thunderlord. Once these weak fools and their clans are removed, no others will dare to interfere with the dark schemes of Ner'zhul.

Marching Orders

- **Objectives:** Destroy the Thunderlord clan. Destroy the Bonechewer clan.
- **Starting Location:** Just east of center map (and a little north).
- **Enemy Location:** Everywhere (specifically northwest, southwest, northeast, and southeast). Bonechewer clan—south, Thunderlord clan—north.
- **Resources:** Five gold mines—northwest, southwest, northeast, southeast, and just east of center map (and a little north—in your camp).

Lookin' for Green Blood

Obviously any scenario, in any game, has its key elements. "Thunderlord and Bonechewer" is no different. Remember three things to defeat the Thunderlords—build Cannon Towers, build Catapults, and train Ogres. The Ogres and Catapults are the mainstays of any assault force you send out. The Cannon Towers are the mainstay of your survival.

You start surrounded by your rival Orcish brethren. These guys are all lookin' for your blood. Discourage them by rapidly constructing a Lumber Mill and upgrading the Scout Towers to Guard status. As the cash flow increases, build another Guard Tower to protect the encampment's northern entrance. This should hold back the enemy for a while.

With the base saved from destruction, and currency in the coffers, it's time to build a Blacksmith and a Cannon Tower next to the Great Hall. The Cannon Tower, with its longer range, serves as a suitable backup to the previously placed Guard Towers.

The initial base camp defense.

Next, upgrade the Hall, pile up a mound of Ogres, and use any pocket change for weapon improvements. This lays the foundation for the next phase.

The push north: Catapults in the lead, protected by Ogres.

Handle the constant Bonechewer raids with the least possible force, preferably Grunts and Axethrowers. Despite this constant pressure, train a counterattack force of five to seven Ogres, two Catapults, and a pair of Axethrowers.

Send these guys northeast toward the mine located in that map quadrant. Lead with the Catapults and screen them with foot soldiers.

Secure the mine and set up shop. This camp should include a Barracks, Great Hall, and two Cannon Towers. Once the Towers are operational, send the Catapults home. You need them to raze the southeastern Orc village.

Of course, while you've been off leveling the neighborhood, things haven't been quiet at home. The raids continue. However, if you have enough structures heaving spears and spitting cannonballs at the intruders, you're probably OK.

Take time to groom another strike force. Send these greenskins southeast, kill the Orcs, flatten their buildings, and steal the gold. In addition to the normal camp accoutrements (Great Hall, Barracks, etc.) you need a Goblin Alchemist for the coming end game.

Here's how that tune plays. Train a Horde at the initial village and one in the southeast. Recruit three Goblin Sapper squads and move them, with the southeastern troops, to the east edge of the north–south woods separating the camp from the Bonechewer city. Blow a path through the forest. As the last trees are cleared, roll south with the base camp Horde. They hit the Bonechewers about the same time as the eastern gaggle pours out of the woods.

135

After the majority of the Bonechewers' Towers falls silent, let the Peons build a couple of Cannon Towers to demolish the rest of the city while you commence refitting the army.

The final portion of this encounter is simple. Take your time; by now the Thunderlords' last mine has collapsed, and they aren't getting any stronger. Lead a force thick with Catapults and Ogres north, chipping away at Thunderlord defenses. Again, construct Cannon Towers to handle mop-up.

MISSION FOUR: THE RIFT AWAKENED

From the ranks of the Death Knights comes Teron Gorefiend. The death of Gul'dan places the dark horsemen under the authority of no clan, but Gorefiend shares Ner'zhul's desire to open numerous portals. He offers his influence over the Death Knights of Draenor in exchange for a world the Death Knights can claim as their own.

Using both the knowledge gained at the defeat of Mogor and the necromantic powers of the Death Knights, Ner'zhul successfully awakens the arcane energies of the mystic rift. As you lead the forces of Shadowmoon into Azeroth, a Human battlement, constructed to keep the Portal closed, stands before you. Destroy this Citadel and claim the lands surrounding the rift.

Marching Orders

- **Objectives:** Destroy the Humans. Teron must survive.
- **Starting Location:** North-center.
- **Enemy Location:** Northwest, southwest, and center.
- **Resources:** Five gold mines–northwest, midwestern map edge, southwest, center, and southeast.

The Three Nations of Man

As the Orc Leader, you're faced with destroying three Human settlements. One, the nation of Azeroth, is far too powerful to engage at the beginning of the scenario. The second, the nation of Dalaran, is way too far away. The third is perfect. These unfortunate men belong to the nation of Kul Tiras and are ripe for the plucking.

The opening moves are easy: Get the Goblin Zeppelin away from the Elven Archers and attack those same Archers (and their attendant city). Make five groups from the initial war party: Catapults, Axethrowers, Ogres, Grunts, Teron Gorefiend, and Peons. Don't forget to lead with your Catapults. This may sound odd, but they have the greatest weapon and sight range (excluding the Zeppelin).

> **TIP**
>
> Catapults hold a slight range advantage over both Guard and Cannon Towers. Direct the Catapults to attack these Towers from max range—outdistancing the Towers. Use the foot soldiers to protect the Catapults from Alliance infantry and cavalry.

After securing the Kul Tiras village, build five Pig Farms and a Great Hall. Place the Pig Farms to partially block the passage between patches of woods to the south-southeast. A lot of action takes place there, and the less area you must defend, the better. Once you build the Farms, build a Lumber Mill—put it next to the southeast woods—and a Blacksmith. Now you're set to build three Cannon Towers (two guarding the southeast approach, one sighted directly down the throat of the southern approach).

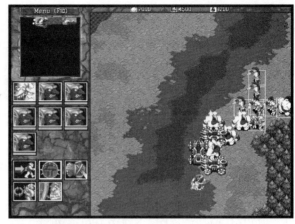

An assault on the Northwest Village—the Catapults lead the way.

After basic village-tending, upgrade the weapons and Great Hall. Build an Ogre Mound, Ogres, and, if you have the money, a Temple of the Damned. Don't sit around and wait for the money to accumulate, however. As soon as you can amass an eight- to twelve-unit task force of Ogres, Axethrowers, and Catapults, move south. Capture the mine midway down, build another Great Hall, and start some serious gold reaping.

Next stop is the Dalaranian village due south. There are plenty of Guard and Cannon Towers from here on in, so you may want to have at least five Catapults in the assault force. A good mix is five Catapults, five Ogres, four Axethrowers, and three Death Knights. Take some time to research "Death and Decay." It's awesome against men and materiel alike. Don't waste time upgrading the Ogres to Mages.

Build a Great Hall and Barracks near the ex-Dalaranian mine and refit your forces. The next phase is a tough one. The forces of Azeroth are numerous and firm believers in Cannon Towers. Again, you must use Catapults and Death Knights to soften up the defenses before the Ogres wade in for the final assault. Concentrate first on knocking out Churches, Town Halls, and Barracks; this cripples the Humans' ability to regenerate.

> ## TIP
> Because the scenario's objective is to destroy the wretched Humans completely, you could spend a lot of time mopping up. Construct a couple of Cannon Towers in the middle of the remnants of a Human village and open up on everything in sight, effectively leveling the city.

Once you've crushed the final Stronghold of Azeroth, there's nothing left but to find and slay the few remaining Humans. Ensure that the hunting parties have sufficient force to handle whatever they find. A mix of five or six units usually does the trick.

MISSION FIVE: DRAGONS OF BLACK ROCK SPIRE

When the Horde was driven back into the Black Morass, it was able to take only a small portion of its forces through the Dark Portal before the Portal was destroyed. Because the Alliance had rescued the Dragon Queen Alexstrasza and captured the Dragonmaw clan, you were no longer able to command these great winged beasts.

As you secure the rift and begin constructing a new Portal, a haggard Grunt approaches your encampment. His uniform marks him as a warrior of the Bleeding Hollow clan. He tells how those of his clan who failed to return through the Portal eluded capture and imprisonment by the Alliance armies. You also learn that many once-enslaved Dragons continue to feed upon the Humans and now roost at Black Rock Spire. If you can break through the Human defenses and gain the trust of these creatures, perhaps you can bring Ner'zhul powerful allies.

Marching Orders

- **Objectives:** Capture as many Dragons as possible. Capture the Dragon Roost high in the mountains.
- **Starting Location:** Southwest corner of the map.
- **Enemy Location:** Mid-southwest, northwest, and middle-ish. Roost is at northeastern corner.
- **Resources:** Six gold mines—southwest (two), northwest, north-center, mideast, southeast.

Beans and Battleaxes

You gotta eat, and you gotta pay the troops. These facts are the keys to this scenario. Although the Orc starts off with a powerful Horde, he doesn't own the Farms to feed them. Consequently, any further training must be put on hold until you build Farms sufficient to feed the greenskins. The Humans, on the other hand, need the gold mine just north of your location to finance a strong army.

First, build Farms. Detail a Peon to start right away while the other two mine. Raise the

Taking the Human's gold—the orcs raid the mine just above their base camp.

138

initial Farm at the southeastern edge of the village (below the woods) to block potential invaders.

After beating back the Human probe on the town's east side, take two Ogres, seven Grunts, and three Axethrowers through the same passage. Turn north at the first opportunity and continue until you reach the southeast corner of the Human settlement just north of your camp. Capture the mine located there; however, don't move west of the mine—it would draw a strong Human response.

This attack is crucial to ultimate victory. Possessing the mine doubles your gold flow and reduces the Humans' income. Plus, your losses bring your forces' nutritional needs more in line with their farming capacity.

The freed Dragons turn on the Elves at the scenario's end.

You may expand the work force (at the original camp) to ten Peons, set up a Lumber Mill and build four Towers, upgrade them to Guard status (so the Gryphon Riders will think twice about getting too close).

As soon as resources permit, raise a Great Hall near the northern mine. This should shore up Orc finances. As the money pours in, build a Blacksmith, two Barracks, an Ogre Mound, a Temple of the Damned, and upgrade the southern Great Hall twice (to Fortress). Research Death and Decay and train a strike force of three Catapults, six Ogres, three Axethrowers, and three Death Knights.

March north, sweeping all before you. Obviously, this group will need constant reinforcement. However, using the general tips given earlier in the book, this Horde should smash the Humans' two western settlements—destroying the pesky Gryphon Aviaries as it goes.

After leveling the northernmost settlement, proceed east to the mine located in the northern middle of the map. If necessary, you may stop here to regroup, build a Great Hall, Barracks, and, if needed, a Temple of the Damned. Slaughter the remaining Human enclave east of the mine, head to the Dragon Roost (northeastern map edge), and carry the day.

NOTE

A word on this northern excursion: It's not absolutely necessary to crush the northernmost Human settlement to save the Dragons. However, if you go for the (somewhat) middle-of-the-map gold mine first, you'll constantly be forced to fend off attacks on your rear. It's best to get the Humans out of the way first, then attend to business.

MISSION SIX: NEW STORMWIND

Finding the survivors of the Bleeding Hollow clan and gaining the Dragon Deathwing as an ally has strengthened your position in Azeroth. Your success has not gone unnoticed by Ner'zhul. He rewards your victories by assigning you a dangerous mission.

Gorefiend has sensed a focus of arcane energies within a Castle that has been raised upon the foundations of Stormwind Keep. Ner'zhul believes that this energy can only be the fabled Book of Medivh. Only a fool would leave such power unguarded, so your assault upon the new Stormwind Castle will be a bloody one.

Marching Orders

- **Objectives:** Destroy everything. Teron must survive.
- **Starting Location:** Southeast corner of the map.
- **Enemy Location:** Villages are in the southwest and northwest corners. Outposts are located in various other locations.
- **Resources:** Four gold mines–southeast, southwest, northwest, and mideast (east of pond).

Love Them Lizards

The keys to winning this mission are Dragons, gold, and Guard Towers. This encounter is primarily an air war. There may be other ways to win it, but using Dragons is the easiest. As with any scenario, especially those with high-cost units, keeping the gold river running is critical. Without a lot of capital, it's almost impossible to build and maintain a credible air force. Finally, until those Dragons are airborne, the primary defense against the Gryphon Riders is Guard Towers.

Axethrowers employed as a mobile anti-Gryphon battery.

Keeping this in the forefront of our green skulls, let's get down to killing some Human scum. Click first on the Great Hall; upgrade it. Remember, you want Dragons, and lots of them. The sooner you can build Dragon Roosts the better. Upgrade your Town Halls to Strongholds, then to Fortresses, then to Dragon Roosts.

> **NOTE**
>
> While we're on the subject of clicking, try poking Teron about 10 times in a row. It's good for a chuckle.

Next, send the three Peons to mine southwest of the Great Hall. Group nine Axethrowers and send them to the pass northwest of the Great Hall. Place the remaining Grunts and Ogres in front of them. Issue the "Stand Ground" order to them all. Pair Teron with an Axethrower and place them slightly behind the other troopers.

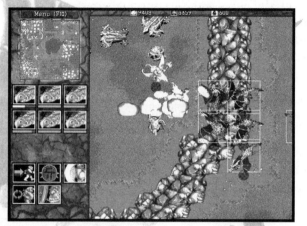

Dragons soften up the southwestern stronghold.

> **NOTE**
>
> Use Teron's Death Coil to terminate Gryphon Riders previously weakened by the Axethrowers. This buffs up the Death Knight's health.

Use the Axethrowers as a mobile anti-Gryphon battery. You need the Grunts and Ogres to block an assault through the northwest corridor, and Teron is the reserve.

Build and train four Guard Towers and seven (for a total of ten) Peons during the game's initial phase. Use three of the emerald-colored laborers to chop wood; the rest can mine. The Guard Towers should keep the Gryphons at bay. Because axes are such key weapons early on, upgrade them as soon as possible.

Village defenses are stable, and cash flow is steady. Now gather a strike force to capture the northeastern mine—five Axethrowers, an Ogre, Teron, and a Grunt or two should do the job. Trail them with two Peons and march north. As soon as you secure the mine, build a Great Hall and Barracks.

Now comes the midgame—perhaps the most crucial period of the scenario. In the northern camp, build four Guard Towers (again, for Gryphon shooting) and a second Great Hall, train Peons, and make money—*lots* of money. In the southern camp, make an Ogre Mound and, again, lots of money. Once you establish a solid line of capital, it's time to upgrade the southern Stronghold to Fortress, erect an Alchemist building, and start building Dragon Roosts in the north.

These Roosts are *the key* to the scenario. From this point on, devote 90 percent of your effort to pumping out Dragons. Start with three Roosts in the north. As your income permits, build more. By the scenario's end you should have seven or eight (and the income to keep them spewing winged lizards). As you train Dragons, send them down to the southern camp. Don't use them to fight off the incessant Gryphon attacks; that's what Axethrowers and Guard Towers are for. You must build up a squadron of Dragons in the lower camp. While the flapping fire-breathers accumulate, train three Goblin Sappers, a couple of Ogres, Axethrowers, and Grunts.

Fly your squadron of Dragons west to the Human Stronghold. Use them to level the defenses. Follow with Sappers, Ogres, and so on, trailed by two Peons. Have the Sappers blow through the rock surrounding the village, and use the other infantry to mop up any resistance. Bring in the Peons, construct a Great Hall, and commence accumulating gold.

The rest is relatively easy. By now you should have seven or eight Roosts and the capital (three mines) to keep them employed. Do nothing but make Dragons. Fly to the northeast corner and smash the men of Azeroth residing there. Then send your winged minions to fry any stragglers.

MISSION SEVEN: THE SEAS OF AZEROTH

After taking the Castle of New Stormwind, you search in vain for the Book of Medivh. As you sift through the rubble of the fallen city, you find the corpse of a Footman with a Human dagger in his side.

The spies of the Bleeding Hollow clan confirm that this blade was crafted by the weapon smiths of Alterac. These Humans are the same that were willing to betray their own brothers, and it may be that they have stolen the Book of Medivh for their own purposes. They will regret their decision.

To journey to Alterac, you must first establish naval superiority over the warships of the Alliance. The base at Kul Tiras has always been the Human's key to the might of their armada. You must establish a strong presence in the Great Sea in order to destroy Kul Tiras and prepare your way into Alterac.

Marching Orders

- **Objectives:** Build five Shipyards. Destroy all enemy ships.
- **Starting Location:** Mideastern near edge.
- **Enemy Location:** Nation of Azeroth, southeast; nation of Kul Tiras, center island—both northeastern islands.
- **Resources:** Four gold mines—northeastern island, center island, eastern and southern mainland. Five oil splotches—north-center, center (two), southwest-center, southwest.

Death from Above

Who says you need a powerful navy to control the ocean? This scenario is winnable with no more than a five- or six-ship navy (and, of course, Dragons).

Once again, your first priorities are Lumber Mills and Guard and Cannon Towers. The pathetic Humans have a couple of Aviaries on the northwestern island and will constantly pound your defenses with Gryphon Riders—at least until you get enough spear-throwing anti-Gryphon systems online.

Part of the L-shaped line of death.

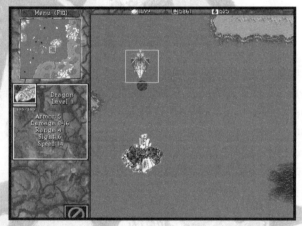

Searching for those pesky Submarines.

Send a squad of Grunts north to eliminate the warriors there. Then construct an L-shaped string of alternating Cannon and Guard Towers starting at the northern inlet and hooking under your village. This stabilizes the situation and gives you some much-needed time to concentrate on the economic betterment of your forces.

Focus your energies on two items—cash and Dragons. Dragons are beautiful reptiles, but they take a ton of cash to enslave. Sink your dough into about five Dragon Roosts. With a herd of Dragons on hand, establish local bestial flying superiority over your encampment and the surrounding waters.

Now erect two Shipyards, an Oil Refinery, and a Foundry. Drill for oil at the northern splotch. The one to the east is a lot closer, but the Humans on the center island will make you pay dearly for using it.

Make a small task force—a Juggernaught, two Destroyers, and matched Transports loaded with Ogres and Peons. Send these ships, escorted by six to nine Dragons, to the northwestern island. Use the Dragons, Juggernaughts, and Destroyers to level the defenses. Land the Ogres to mop up, the Peons to raise a Great Hall, and a couple of Cannon Towers to open up on surviving Human structures.

Spend any additional income on three Shipyards (remember, you need a total of five) and more Dragons. Group a bunch of air lizards (nine is ideal) and make a courtesy call on all the paleskins' flotillas, sending them to the bottom. That's it—well, almost. The Humans have a couple of Submarines sneaking about. Split the Dragon squadron and have them patrol the ocean in a crisscross pattern. As soon as they flush the Subs, the scenario ends.

MISSION EIGHT: ASSAULT ON KUL TIRAS

Now that you have cleared a path to the island of Kul Tiras, you must send your wave riders against the core of the Human fleet. With the naval forces of the Humans defeated, the Horde has free reign of the Great Sea. We have also learned that Admiral Proudmoore is no longer a member of the Alliance and does not have the support of its armies. Remove his armada and Kul Tiras will fall.

Marching Orders

- **Objectives:** Destroy the armada of Kul Tiras. Destroy Kul Tiras.
- **Starting Location:** Crammed together on the barren eastern isle.
- **Enemy Location:** Kul Tiras Village is north-center, naval base is center, and the accursed Aviaries are in the northwest corner.
- **Resources:** Six gold mines—southwestern island, mainland north-center (two), map center (three—one southwest of center, one north of center, and one center). Two oil splotches in ocean canal.

Invading the Mainland

The first thing you must do is get everyone off the eastern island. Load up the Transports and go west. Use a two-Destroyer, two-Juggernaught, single-Dragon screen, placed north of the eastern island, to keep the Humans away from your convoy.

When you arrive at your new home, build a Great Hall and five or six Farms. Keep the Axethrowers grouped together in their "mobile anti-Gryphon battery" formation. As soon as possible, build a few Guard Towers to keep the Gryphon Riders at bay.

The Orcish naval buildup.

With the home fires well tended, load the Transports with three Peons, half the remaining Trolls, and the Death Knight. Sail across the inlet, land these troops, and head for the south-center mine. Build a base here. Include an Ogre Mound (possible from an upgrade of the Great Hall at the original base), three Dragon Roosts, a couple of Barracks, and a Temple of the Damned. Use your wealth to upgrade all weapons and start a naval base at your southern paradise. An Oil Refinery, Foundry, and two Shipyards should do the trick. Build a medium task force—about two Juggernaughts with a six-Destroyer escort.

Do not go into nautical construction overdrive, because any ships left after you've thrashed the Kul Tiras navy will be wasted. Send this flotilla, along with a half-dozen Dragons, against the Kul Tiras naval base.

Regroup and refit. Concentrate on gathering a well-rounded force. Make sure, though, that you have plenty of Death Knights, Catapults, and Dragons.

Send the flying reptiles on a surgical strike to the Aviaries in the northwest corner, seriously flattening Kul Tiras air power for the foreseeable future.

NOTE

The adventurous may choose to go for the western Humans first. Use Goblin Sappers to blow a hole through the east-west woods and fall on the enemy's flank. This has the advantage of attacking the Kul Tirasians' soft underbelly, but it's harder to reinforce.

With the air power knocked back, begin a slow but steady encroachment on Human territory. Go for the two center mines next. Use your ranged weapons extensively.

The attack force mustered at the ex-Kul Tiras Naval Base.

TIP

Death Knights can be especially tough when working together. One casts Unholy Armor on his compatriot. While so protected, the second Death Knight moves within Death and Decay range of a significant structure and casts the spell—immune from return fire.

At first the going is exceedingly tough. Just keep refitting and moving forward. Each mine you capture lessens the Humans' ability to match your production.

TIP

Berserkers with regenerative ability do well in this type of battle. Once they take a few hits, roll them to the rear where they can recover their health.

Eventually you win the war of attrition, wiping out the Humans' center. Then it's merely a matter of turning west and taking out the remaining structures.

MISSION NINE: THE TOMB OF SARGERAS

Now that the Great Sea is once again under the dominion of our wave riders, Ner'zhul has a plan to increase the powers of the Dark Portal. While he was the tutor of Gul'dan, the shaman bound his soul so that Ner'zhul could keep watch over his disciple. Even though Gul'dan knew this link would serve to inform Ner'zhul of the Warlock's studies with the spirits that dwelt in the Twisting Nether, he was too arrogant to care.

Ner'zhul has ordered you to lead a small band to Sargeras's tomb in order to find the Jeweled Scepter of Sargeras. The remains of the Stormreaver and Twilight's Hammer encampment surround the entrance to the tomb, and the howling of their tortured souls fills the air. Although the inhabitants of this place died long ago, their bodies have been torn from earthen graves by the vile magicks of the Daemons and made to stalk this region for all eternity.

Marching Orders

- **Objective:** Slay the Daemon who guards the Jeweled Scepter of Sargeras.
- **Starting Location:** Southwest corner.
- **Enemy Location:** You name it, they're everywhere. However, the Daemon is at west-center of the map.
- **Resources:** Shipyard at the port; Temple of the Damned on Mage Isle; Lumber Mill on the eastern land mass; Blacksmith found along the trail.

The Slaying of a Daemon

These no-gold-mine scenarios are unique in the *Warcraft* world. Normally, everything you do is rushed–not so here. But you're still going to meet the same people and fight the same battles.

Before starting out, place the Grunts and Ogres in front, the Death Knight to the rear. Protect this messenger of darkness–the scenario depends on it.

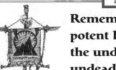

NOTE

Remember, the Death Knight's potent Death Coil has no effect on the undead, so his role in most undead battles is that of an interested observer. But don't worry, he makes up for it elsewhere.

Fight through the first undead ambush and regroup west of the village. Form a classic Grunts-in-front-Axethrowers-at-rear defense. Send the Knight to cast Death Coil on one of the Shipyard's defenders. It will probably kill the Human and cause the rest to charge. Run home with the Knight; when the guards hit your line they'll be decimated.

Head for the shipyard—don't sweat liberating the Farms. If you wander too far south, you trigger another undead ambush. Build a Transport, load everyone, and set sail for the island. Killing the Mage is job one.

You can handle the remaining undead in good time. Research Death and Decay and Raise Dead, load the Transport, and steam north.

Offload all but one on the extreme north edge of the mainland's eastern shore. Take the remaining passenger and land on the beach to the south. Move east of the woods and liberate the Trolls found there.

Once you get everyone back to the mainland, have the Death Knight cast Death and Decay on the Elven Archers.

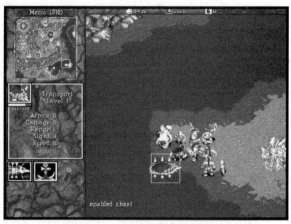

Assault on Mage Isle. Grunts hack away while the Undead stand around wondering what to do.

Then, to add insult to injury, raise them from the dead. Form the troops to slaughter the undead west of the Archers' former position. Follow up with Death and Decay on the Tower and its attendant Archers. Then use an Ogre to free the Orcs (he's fast enough to get out of town before what's left of the Tower gets him).

Get back on the boat. Ferry the troops south to the next coastline opening. Keep them close to the water until you're ready to fight some Humans with a very serious Paladin attack. Don't unload the Death Knight. The Paladin will eat him for lunch.

Laying it on the Elven Archers. The Death Knight casts Decay on the hapless longbowmen.

March forward and give battle. After slaying the Humans, bring the Knight ashore. Again, destroy the Tower with Death and Decay and move out. Capture the Blacksmith and Catapult. Upgrade everything except the Catapult.

Continue hiking toward the Daemon, baiting and ambushing the foot troops you encounter. Use the Death Knight against the Ballistae and Towers but keep a sharp eye out for Paladins. Set up shop a little south of the Daemon's place. Repeatedly send the dark one to hit him with Death Coil. When you've sufficiently weakened the holder of the Jeweled Scepter of Sargeras, draw him into your line and riddle his body with upgraded axes.

147

MISSION TEN: ALTERAC

Your capture of the Jeweled Scepter greatly pleases Ner'zhul. Word comes that you are to entrust it to the remaining warriors of the Bleeding Hollow clan; they are to return it to Draenor in all haste.

Deathwing and his Dragons deliver you to the Keep at Alterac. You could easily bring these curs to their knees, but they have hidden the tome you seek. They're also cunning enough to strike a bargain, knowing it's their only salvation. Should they tell you the location of the Book, however, they fear the retribution of the nations of Lordaeron and Stromgarde. They're willing to exchange the Book of Medivh for the destruction of these forces that sit along their borders.

You must eliminate the military outposts maintained by Lordaeron and Stromgarde. Then seal your pact by entering into Alterac, contacting the Human Mage who guards the Book, and escorting him to safety.

Marching Orders

- **Objectives:** Destroy the outposts belonging to Lordaeron and Stromgarde. Rescue the Mage from Alterac and return him to the Circle of Power.
- **Starting Location:** Northwest corner. (The Mage is in the southeast corner.)
- **Enemy Location:** Kul Tiras forces—between the rocks in a semicircle around the Orcs' starting position; nation of Stromgarde—northeast corner; Lordaeron's troops—southwest.
- **Resources:** Eight gold mines—three evenly spaced, running northeast to southwest, in the rocks fronting the Orc's position; three more south, between the river and western map edge; one northeast; one in map center. Two oil splotches—one at the river's bend; one at its southern end.

Running Metal Through Mortals

Despite the rescue-the-Mage wild card, this is a straightforward scenario. Your job is to kill Humans and flatten their dwellings. When the killing and flattening is done, bringing the Mage back to the Circle of Power is piece of cake.

Send everyone (except two Peons) to clear the three detachments of Kul Tirasian soldiers located in the semicircular ring that surrounds your forces. Attack each in turn. If you're careful, only the troops involved in the immediate skirmish will fight. Once you've slaughtered Humans, proceed to the mine located north of the map's center and set up shop. Send an Ogre, two Knights, and a Dragon back to guard the main base.

Speaking of home base, have the Peons you left behind build a Lumber Mill, a pair of Pig Farms, and the obligatory Guard Towers. As funds permit, erect a Barracks and Great

Hall. It'll be tight, but you need the ability to reinforce from within. Expect a charge from a herd of knights.

Meanwhile, back at the center-screen ranch, the cash should be piling up. As soon as possible, send a group of Peons to the mine you passed en route to your current location. Build a Great Hall and start mining. You need everything but the kitchen sink to win this one, so you might as well generate the cash flow to handle it. Construct four Dragon Roosts, two Temples of the Damned, an Altar of Storms, and two Barracks in the center city.

TIP

If the mines are unclaimed, construct a Guard Tower adjacent to them. Sometimes the computer attempts to mine gold without first securing the area. In this case, you can lay waste to a lot of enemy Peasants with a single Guard Tower. Now, if you feel really sneaky (not to mention wealthy), send a Death Knight to assist the Guard Tower. As the Tower kills Peasants, the Death Knight can use Raise Dead to recruit them.

It's time to take out the troops of Lordaeron. Use the standard tactics you've learned. First, secure the southern rock-belt mine. Then, slowly advance with Catapults and Death Knights in the lead. Have the Dragons supply air support.

TIP

Ogre Runes are particularly useful here. Cast them between the Catapults and an opposing formation. When the Catapults fire, the enemy charges, hoping to negate the threat to their front. Unfortunately for them, they walk into the Runes–killing most of the advancing Humans.

Guarding the home base gates.

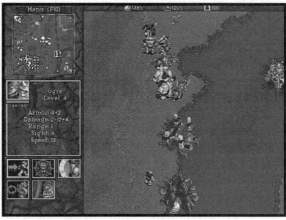

The raiding party.

149

Secure the Lordaeron village and, as always, construct Cannon Towers to mop up for you. Stroll down to the river, build a Transport, and send some Knights, Ogres, and a Death Knight across for the Mage.

By landing on the southern shore, you can avoid raising the ire of the Kul Tiras detachment at the northern end of the island. Escort the Mage to the Circle of Power with a couple of Grunts. By now the countryside should be safe for travel—at least for your side.

That's two objectives down, one to go. The nation of Stromgarde is a tough nut. They can't match your coin, however. Just take a little time to train a devastatingly powerful force, and then move in. Be methodical, conquer the city piece by piece, and don't forget to first soften the defenses with Catapults, Dragons, and Death Knights.

MISSION ELEVEN: THE EYE OF DALARAN

With the Book of Medivh in your control and the Jeweled Scepter delivered to Ner'zhul, only one artifact remains to be won. The Mages of Dalaran have created a device to focus their magicks in an effort to reconstruct the Violet Citadel. Ner'zhul desires this Eye of Dalaran to focus the dark powers of the underworld for the creation of his portals.

Teron Gorefiend has traveled to the Stronghold of the Human Mages at Cross Island, where they now rebuild their Towers amid heavy fortifications. You must break through their shoreline defenses, establish a base, and capture the Eye of Dalaran. No walls will protect them from the vengeance of the Horde.

Marching Orders

- **Objectives:** Destroy all Mage Towers. Destroy all of Dalaran.
- **Starting Location:** Western island.
- **Enemy Location:** Forces of Dalaran—northeast and southeast corner; nation of Lordaeron—coast and southwest.
- **Resources:** Four gold mines—north-center, south-center, southwest, mideast; two oil splotches—one north, one south of center in the moat-like sea.

From the Halls of Montezuma

This scenario gives you a chance to conduct a classic amphibious invasion and beachhead expansion. Our story opens with the Orcish navy embroiled in a bitter battle for the Straits of Lordaeron. You'll probably win no matter how you click; nevertheless, it's important to keep as many of your ships afloat as possible. Concentrate on massing fires against a single target. Send the Dragons—when they're not targeting Gryphons—to attack Battleships.

After defeating the Humans, load the Transports and form one large flotilla, keeping the troop ships to the west. Slowly slide down the Lordaeron coast, taking out Towers as you go.

When your task force approaches the southern edge of the first inland forest, land the troops.

Whisk by the woods, set up camp on the east side, and let the Sappers blow away the Aviary. Building a couple of Guard Towers is

The Orcish Hordes flow south toward Dalaran.

NOTE

As an alternative to the foregoing, land your troops just south of the second Lordaeron Tower (counting from the north) and build a Great Hall on the west side of the woods. Use Peons to cut a path through the woods to the gold mine. This strategy has the advantage of providing more room at the cost of a slower buildup.

Before heading north to take out the Mage Towers, conduct a seven- to nine-strong Dragon strike on the Lordaerons massing to the west. This keeps them off your back while you get down to the serious business of destroying the Dalaran Mages.

Once you've seriously crippled their defenses, use Death and Decay, Catapults, and Dragons to take out the island's Mage Towers.

Axethrowers guard the wooded path opened by the Peons.

important once you buy the Lumber Mill. Otherwise, those Gryphons will be all over you. Lay out the standard town stuff (make sure you have two Barracks early on) but watch the placement. Don't block the Peons' path to either the Great Hall or the Lumber Mill.

As income permits, creep south.

After you have Ogre, Death Knight, and Death and Decay capabilities, attack Dalaran's southern village. It's really not too tough if you get there in the middle to early part of the game. Consolidate forces, build Catapults, and train Death Knights and Dragons.

CAUTION

Watch out for the Paladins. They're absolute death for your Knights. Work them over with Catapults, Dragons, or Ogres, but never Death Knights.

151

MISSION TWELVE: THE DARK PORTAL

As the burning remains of your victims fill the air with acrid smoke, the sky fills with a figure as black as night. Deathwing descends, exhausted from his long journey from Grim Batol, bearing grave news from his brothers at Black Rock Spire.

The Alliance has sent a host of forces to the Black Morass and has engaged the forces of the Warsong and Shattered Hand clans at the Dark Portal. You must rally the forces of Shadowmoon to break through this siege and return the artifacts you have secured to Draenor. Only then can Ner'zhul's plan of opening portals to new worlds be realized.

Succeed and you will command vast armies as they ravage untold worlds. Fail and be slaughtered.

Marching Orders

- **Objectives:** Capture the Dark Portal. Destroy all Humans.
- **Starting Location:** Northeast corner.
- **Enemy Location:** Nation of Azeroth—west-center; nation of Kul Tiras—northeast corner; nation of Dalaran—northwest corner; nation of Lordaeron—southeast corner.
- **Resources:** Six gold mines—north-center, center, east-center, east edge, south-center, and west-center. Oil splotches—west, center, west-center.

The Grand Finale

Don't attack those Towers to the south. They'll wipe you out. Instead, send Deathwing over the forest on the east edge of the map. As he heads south you see two Towers. Use Deathwing, a Catapult, and some foot soldiers to destroy them both. March southeast along the edge of the eastern woods, where the forest meets the map edge. Blast a hole in the wall and continue south until you come to more foliage. Take care. If the traffic gets too congested, your units will try to go the long way around—and stroll through the heart of the Alliance. Follow the trees west until you come to a mine. Set up camp here.

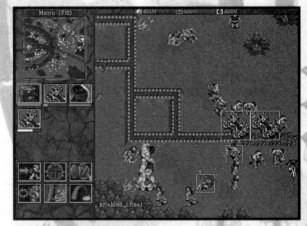

The Orcs stream through the hole in the wall.

Order the first military units on the scene to Stand across the forest gap west of the mine. Other Orcs should guard the breach in the wall and the gap between the wall and northern forest. As soon as possible, build Farms to plug these holes. Sprinkle some Guard Towers in front of your units covering the gap between the north and south forests.

Final defenses at the forest gap during a typical attack.

If you survive the initial Human attacks, start working on production. Buy the typical upgrades and buildings. Eventually your economic output is high and the attack frequency low. It's time to send an expedition to capture the mine at the center of the map.

Send Dragons to destroy the buildings leading to this mine. Don't mess with units on the other side of the southern gap. If you don't bother them, they won't bother you. When you come to the Guard Towers, pound on them from a safe range with the Catapults. Once you get to the mine, build a Town Hall, train some Peons, and start mining.

Once you have the second mine pumping gold, pour through the gaps in the rocky ridge and conquer the Humans residing there. Unfortunately, the village mines are empty, which raises the last significant obstacle to victory—gold depletion.

The mines you have are all you get, so take it easy on those pricey Dragons and Death Knights. I prefer Catapults, anyway, because of their faster rate of fire.

Learn the layout of the rest of the map using the Ogre-Mage spell, Eye of Kilrogg. The nation of Dalaran defends the three western islands. The Portal is on the center island. You see an oil splotch in the southwest corner of the map; this is a safe place to build ships. Don't forget to erect Guard Towers to discourage the Gryphons from hanging around the naval buildings.

Attack the north island from the west with your Dragon swarm. This island has no Destroyers, no Guard Towers, and only a few Archers. Once you kill off the opposition, land your Catapults and their guard (Ogres, Grunts, etc.) to mop up the buildings.

The south island is trickier. It comes equipped with Dragon-slaying Guard Towers, Destroyers, and a Gryphon Aviary. Bombard the Aviary from the waterside to prevent ground units from assaulting you. Keep a Juggernaught available to deal with Destroyers, and a Dragon or two to handle Battleships.

Having destroyed the Humans' ships and Aviary, level the Cannon Towers on the north side of the island. Land your troops, fend off any counterattacks, destroy buildings, and prepare for the final assault on the central island.

As before, use the Dragons to destroy the Cannon Tower. Lure the Gryphon out and over some of your Guard Towers. Then have fun as your Dragons enjoy a turkey shoot on the remaining units.

Chapter 10
Cheat Codes

To enable the *Warcraft II* cheat codes, press ⏎Enter while playing and type the appropriate message.

Cheat	Code
Cash	Glittering prizes
Enable Mission Jump	Tigerlily
Fast Build	Make it so
Finale	There can be only one
God	It is a good day to die
Jump to Mission	Orc14, Human14, etc.
Loss	You pitiful worm
Lumber	Hatchet
Magic	Every little thing she does
No Victory	Never a winner
Oil	Valdez
Show Map	On Screen
Special Sound Track	Disco
Upgrade	Deck me out
Victory	Unite the clans

Chapter 11
Battle.net Maps

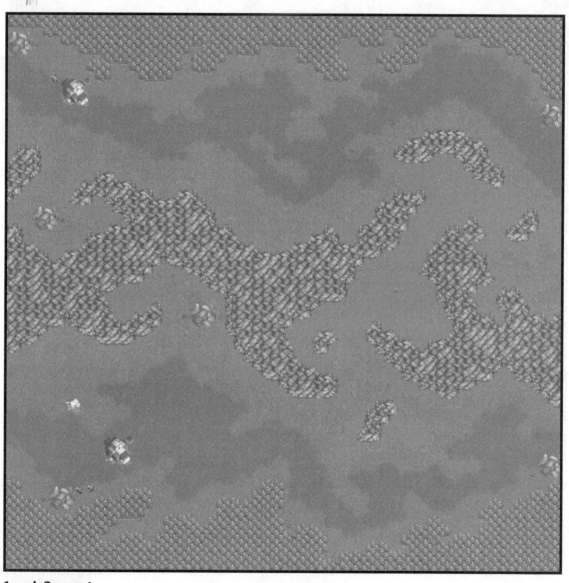

1wayin2wayout

3vs3

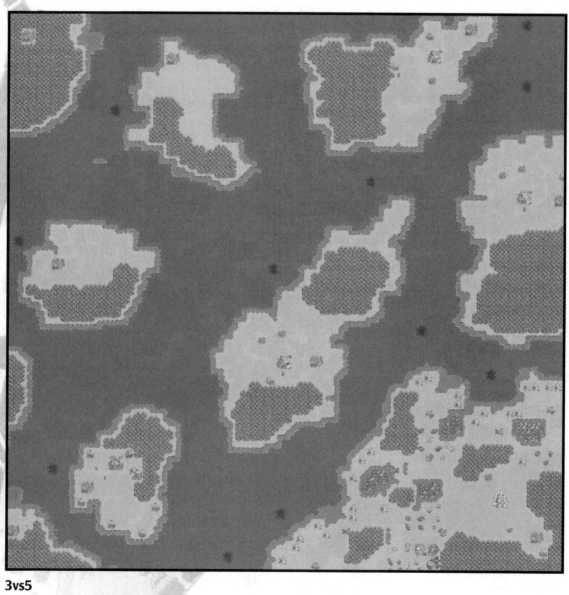

3vs5

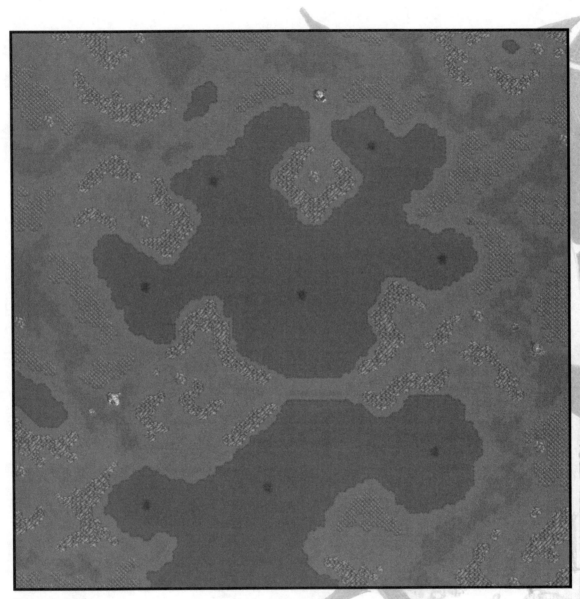

3ways2cross

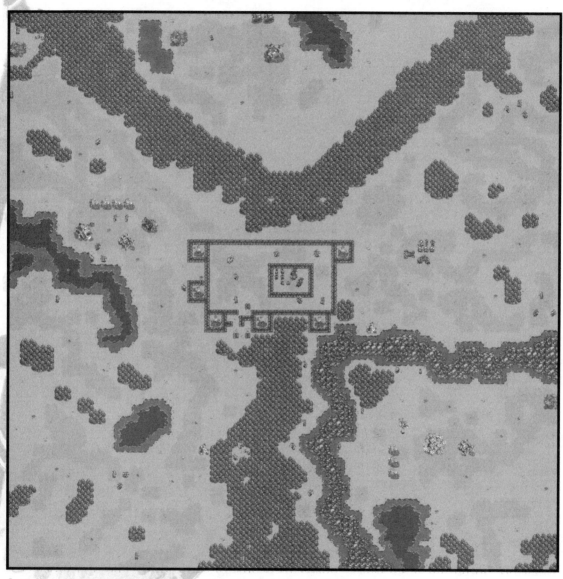

4_step

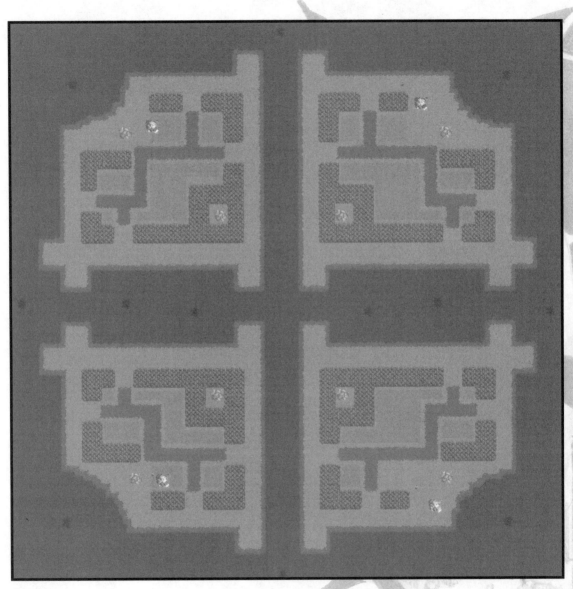

4corners

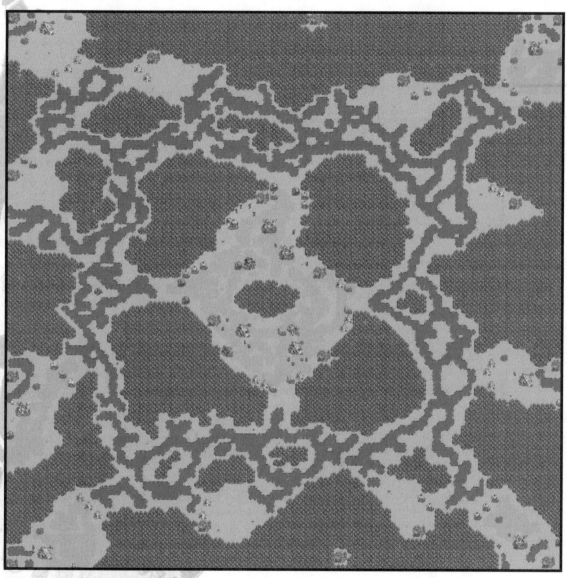

A Tight Spot BNE

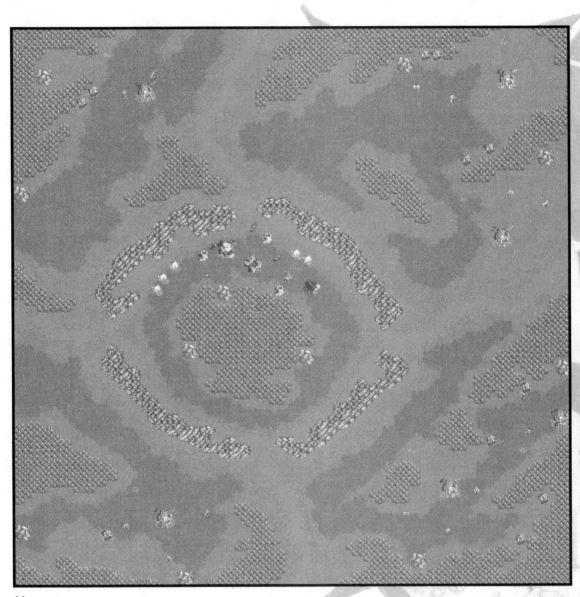

Alamo

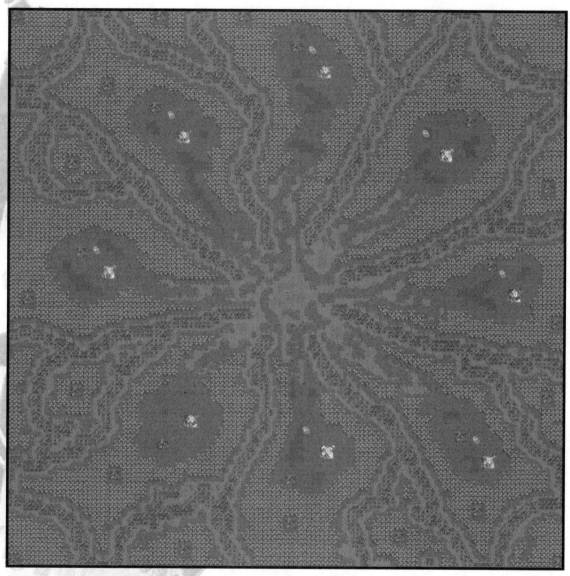

All You Need

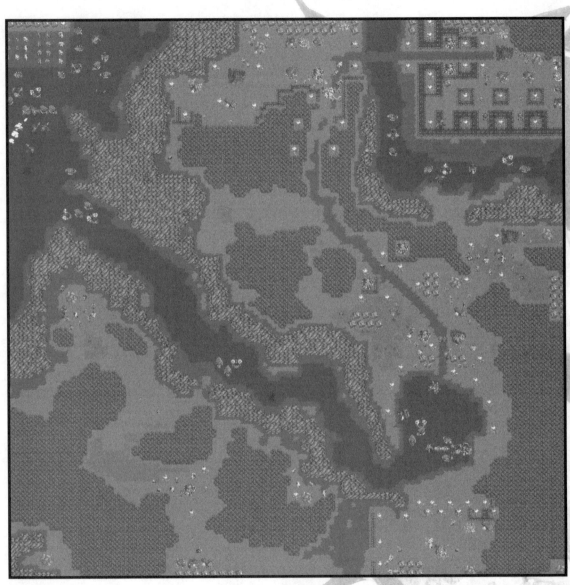

Anarchy

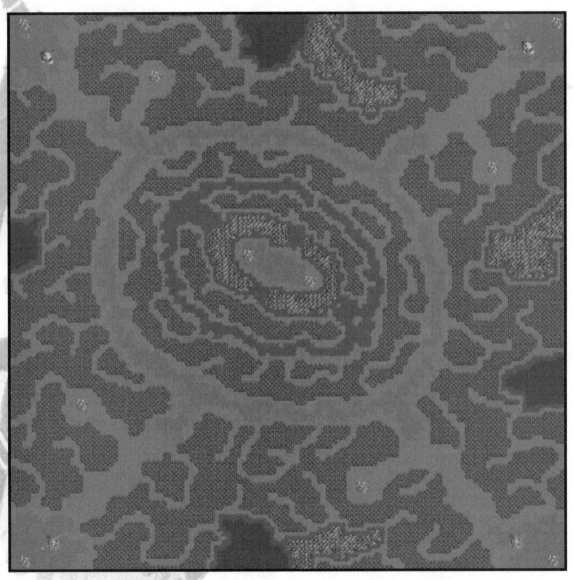

Ant Trails BNE

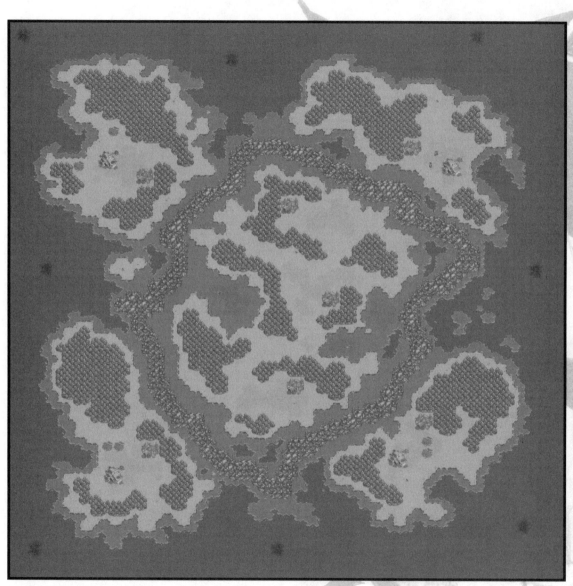

Arctic Circle BNE

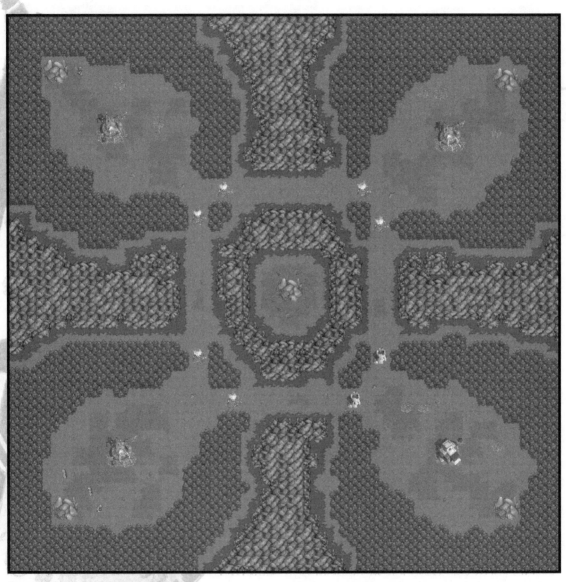

Arena

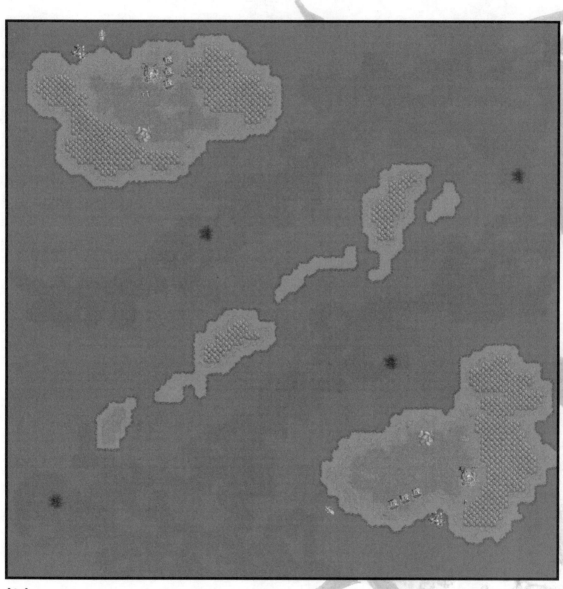

Atols

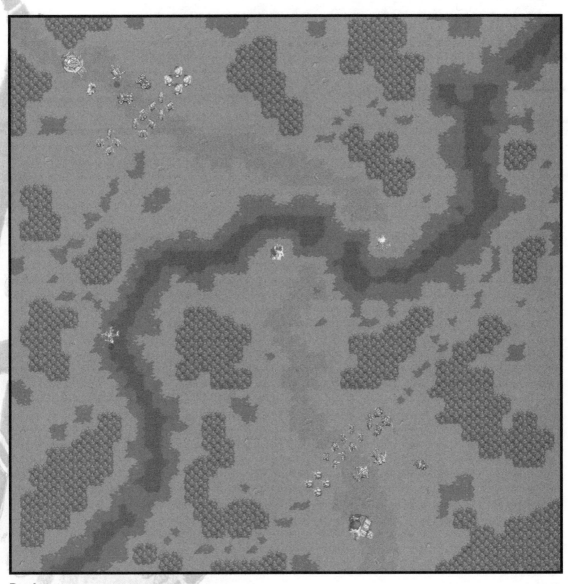

Battle1

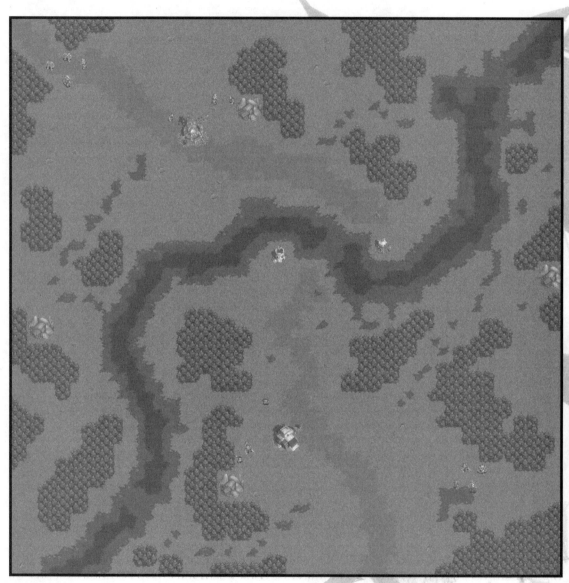

Battle2

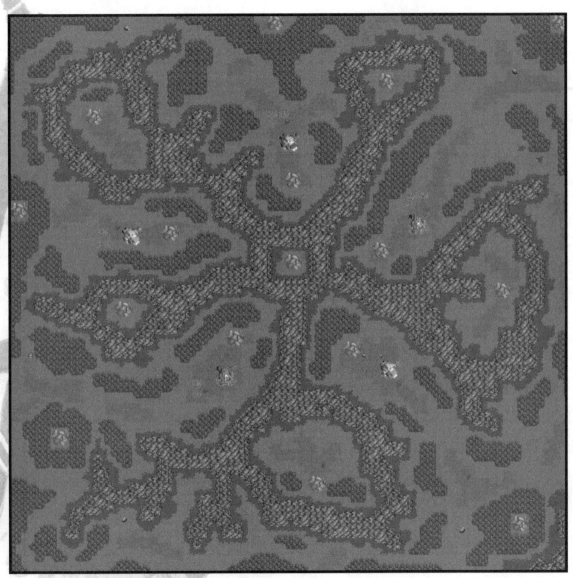

Big Rock Candy Mountain BNE

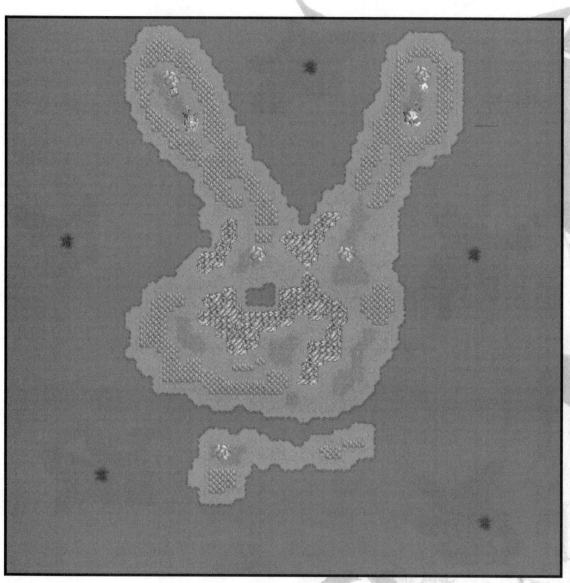

BigEars

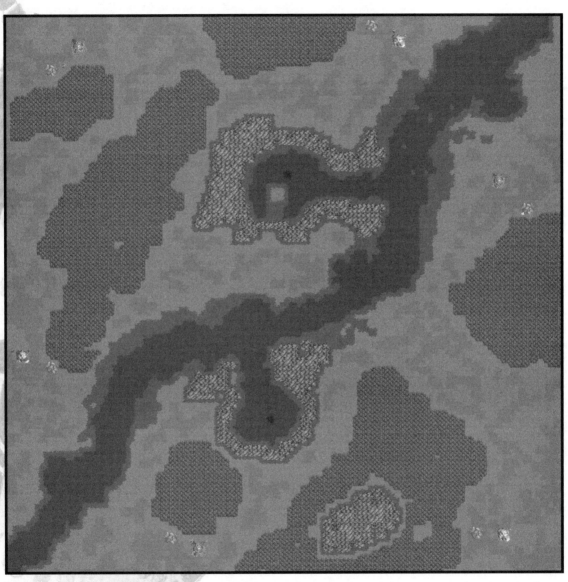

Blackgold

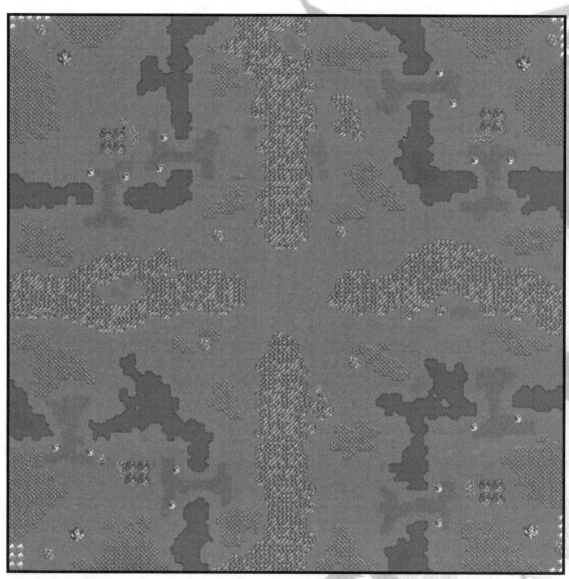

Bombs Away BNE

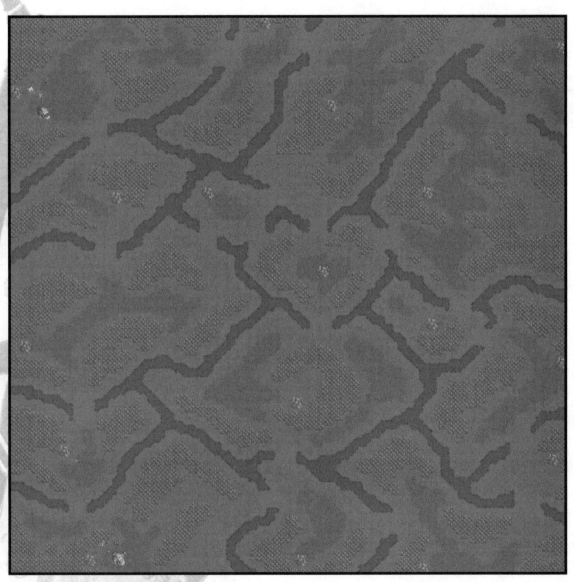

Bridge to Bridge Combat BNE

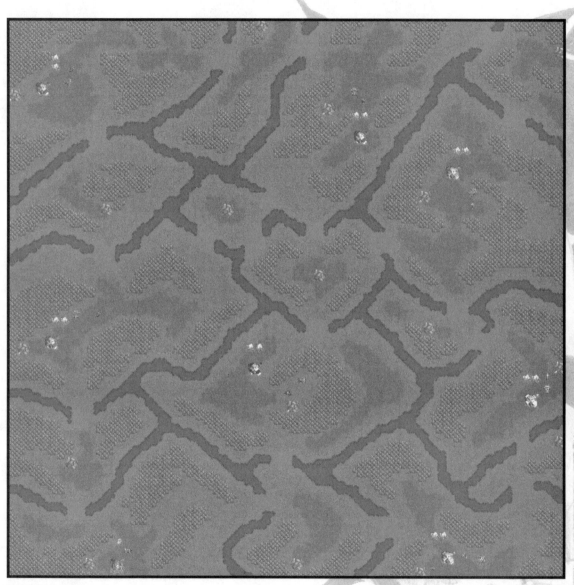

Bridge2bridge

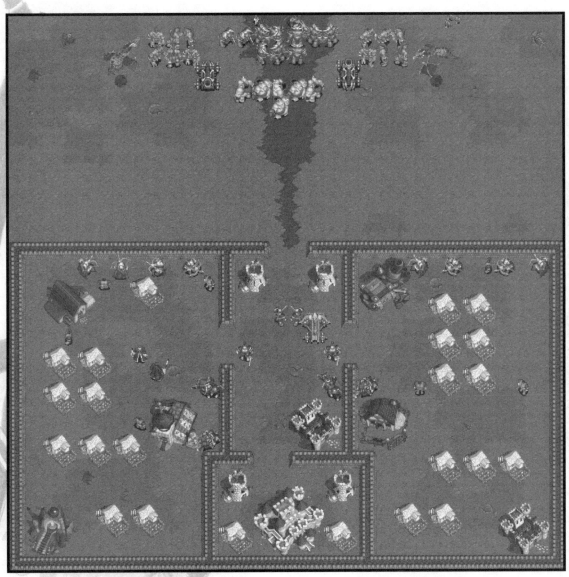

Burn_it

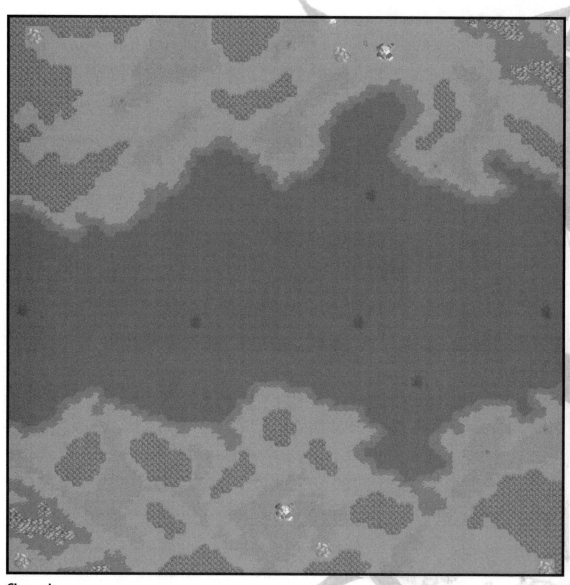

Channel

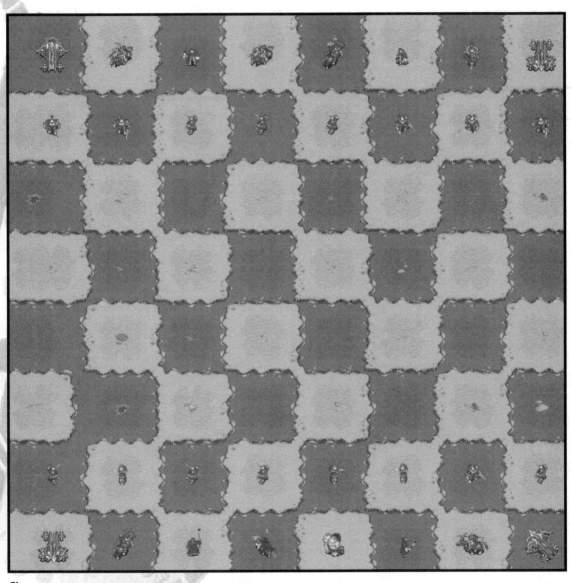

Chess

Collapse

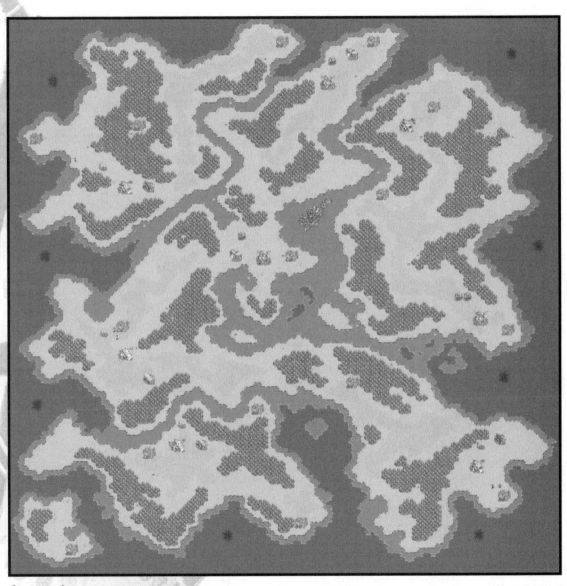

Cont2expl

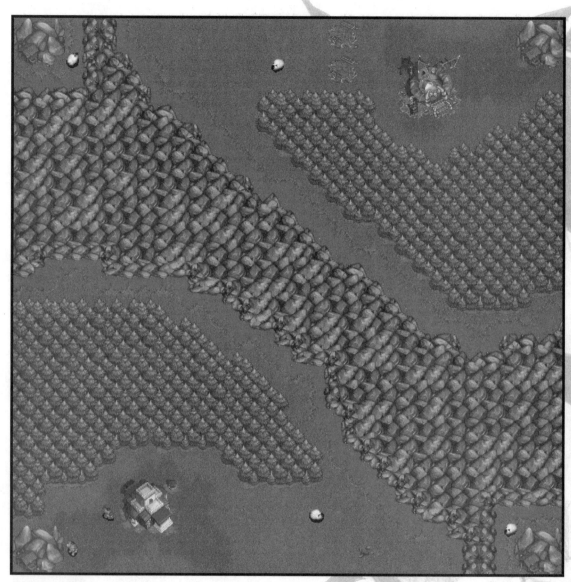

Cramped BNE

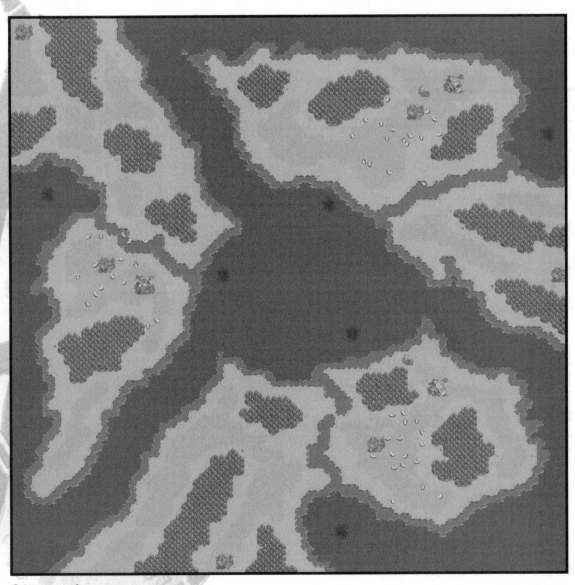

Critterattack

Crosshair BNE

Crossover

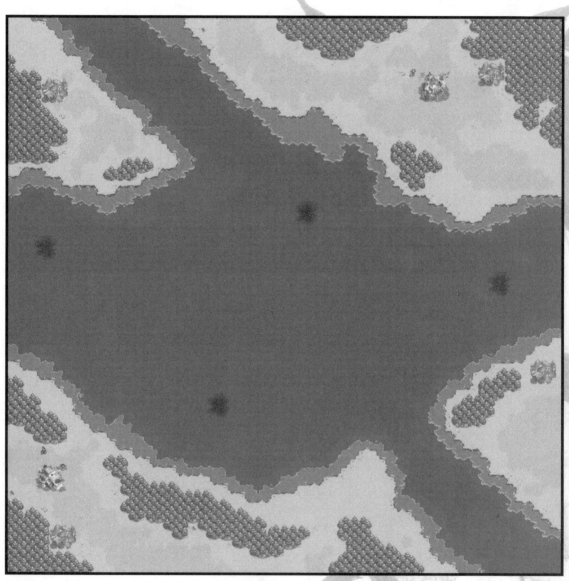

Crossthestreams

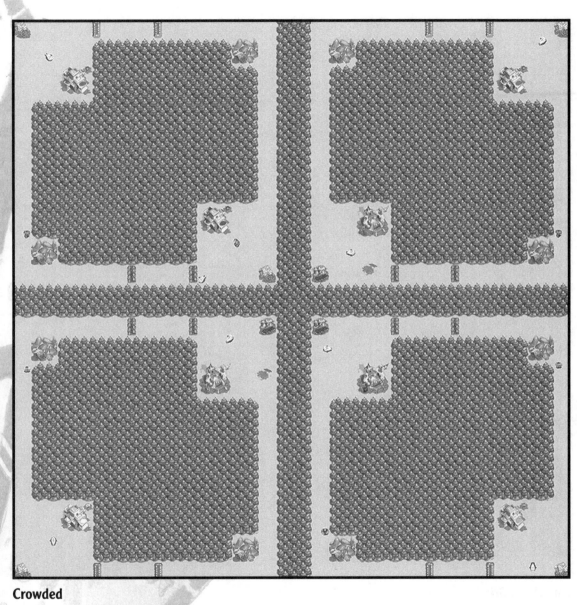

Crowded

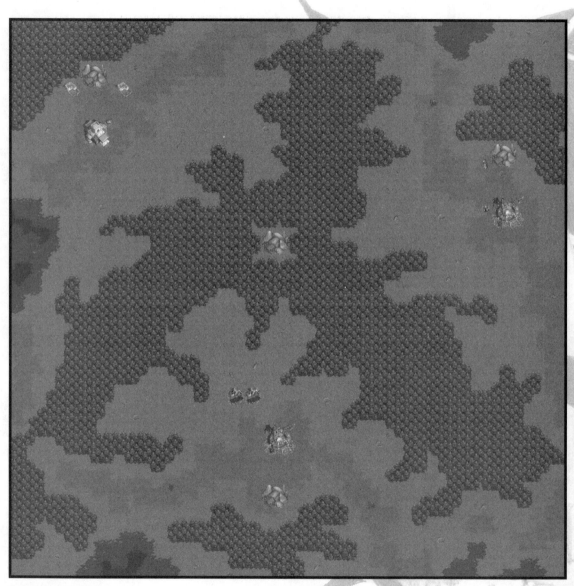

Dark Paths BNE

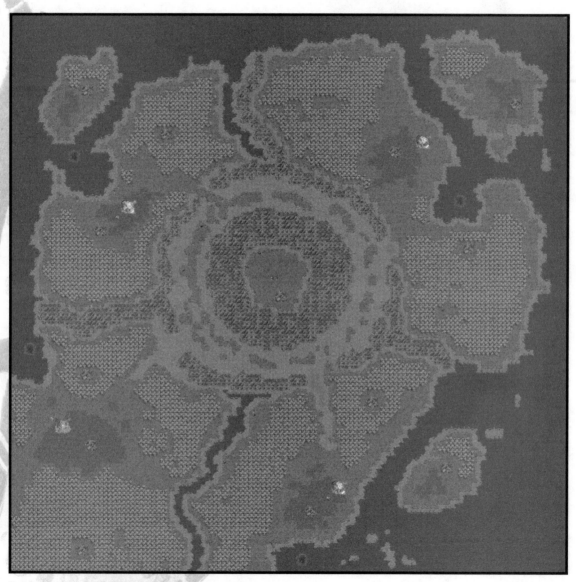

Dark Peninsula BNE

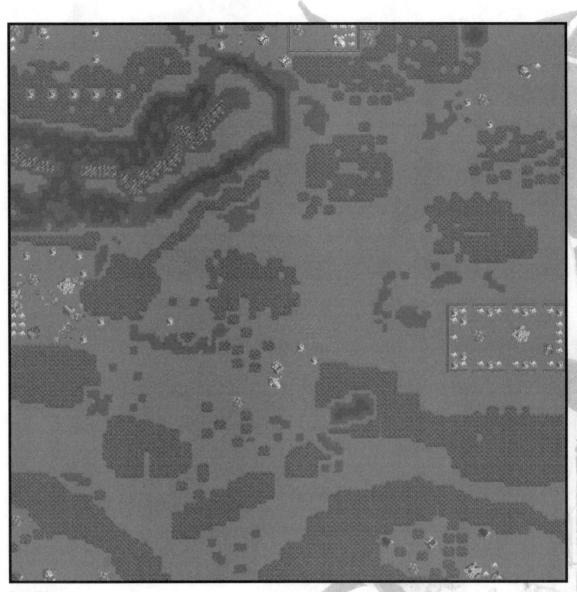

DeadMeet

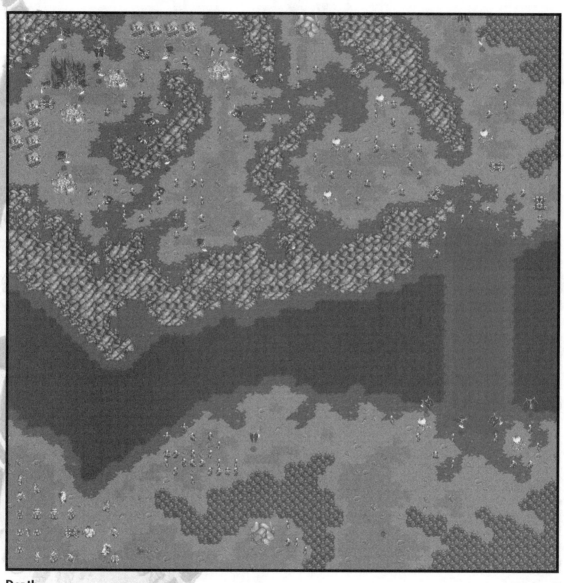

Death

Deathinthemiddle

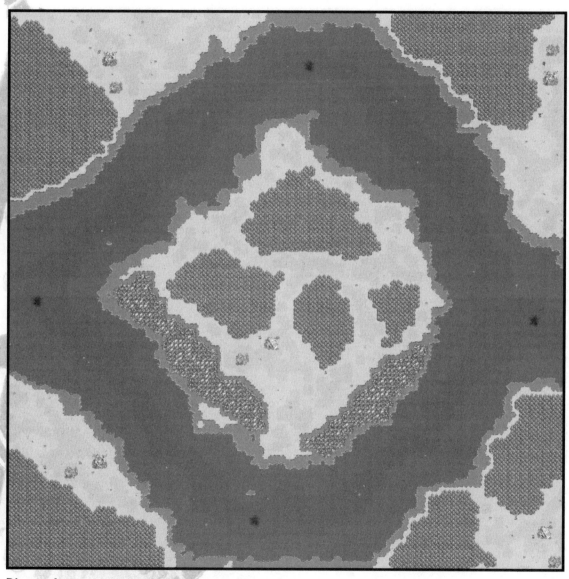

Diamond

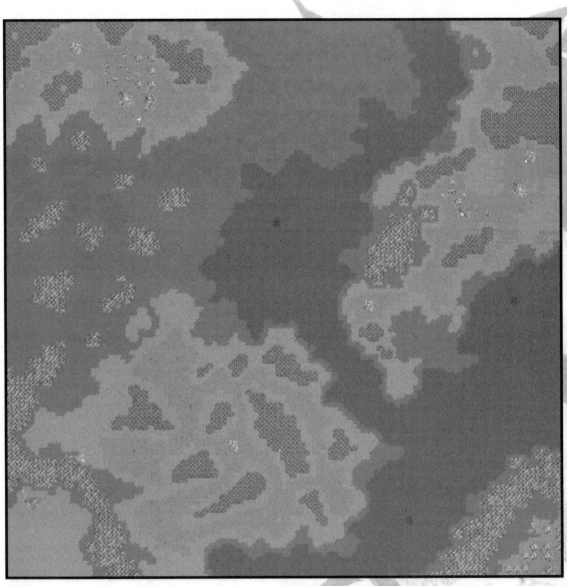

Dragon

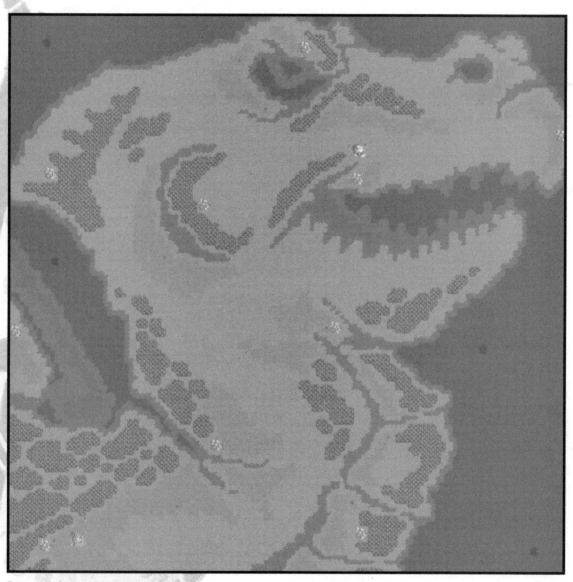

DragonIsle

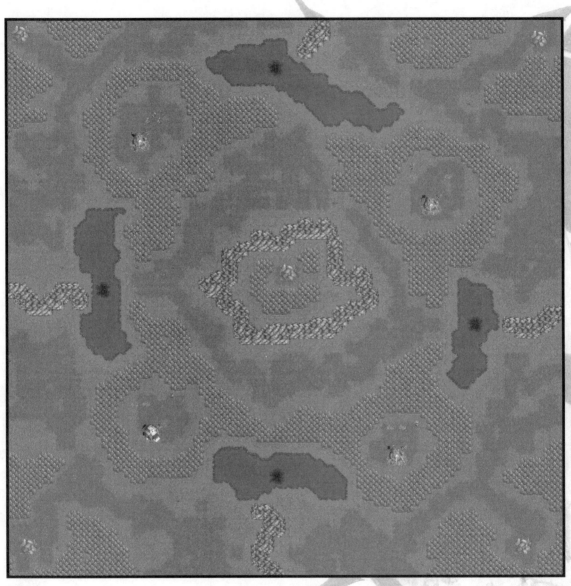

Dup

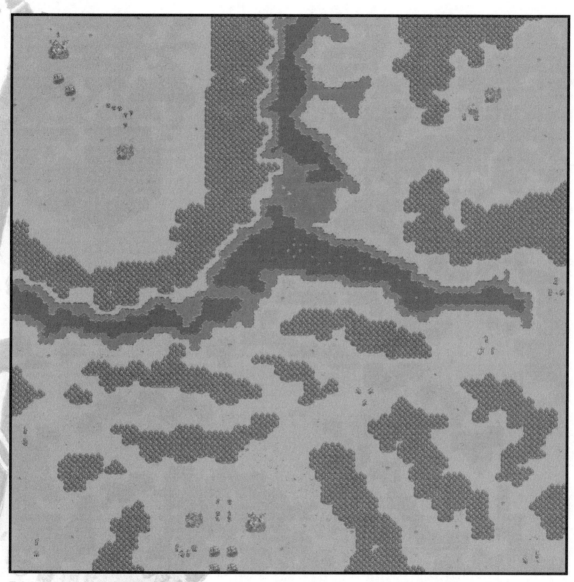

Falsie

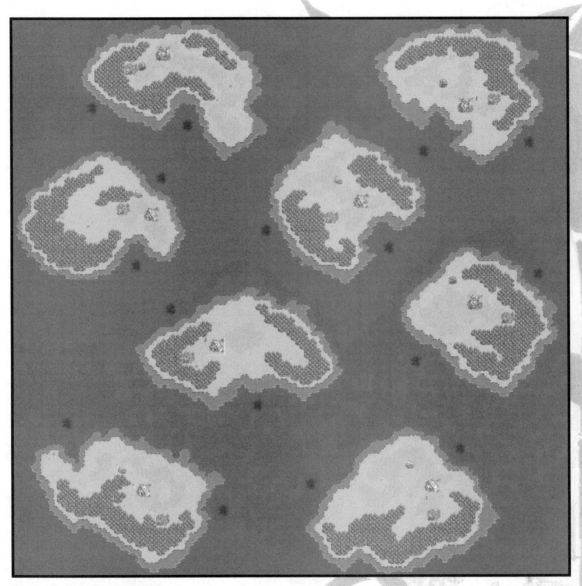

Fierce Ocean Combat BNE

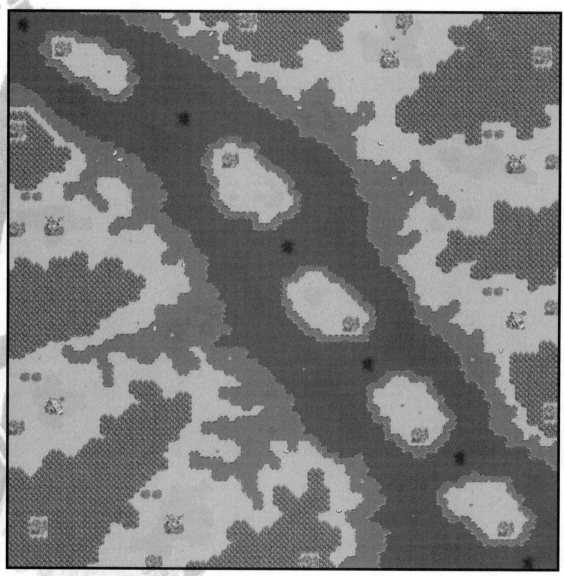

Fire in the Water BNE

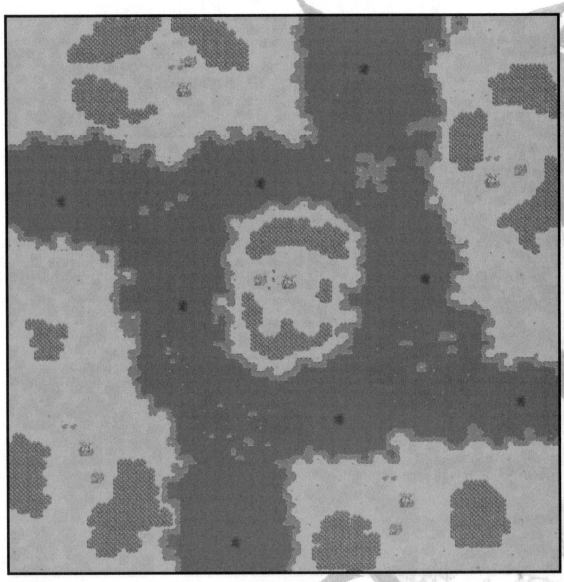

FireRing

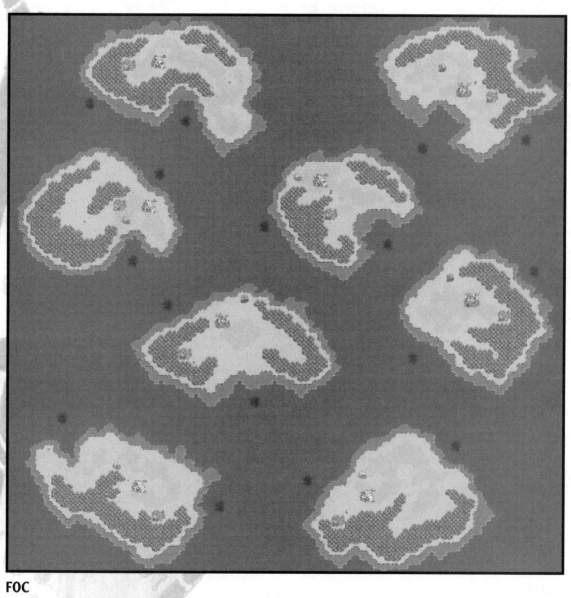

FOC

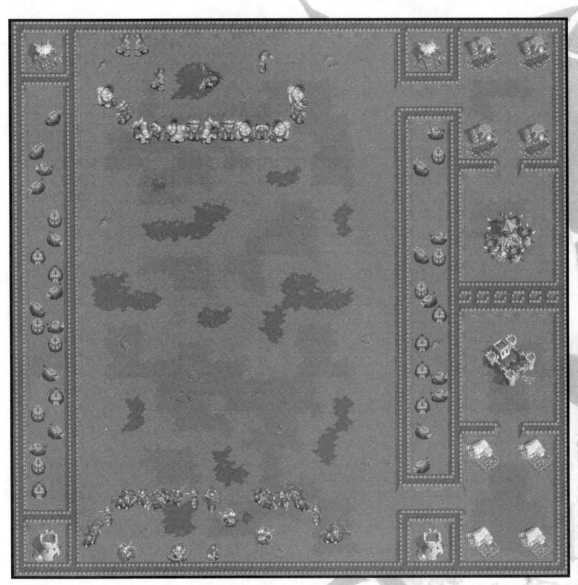

Football

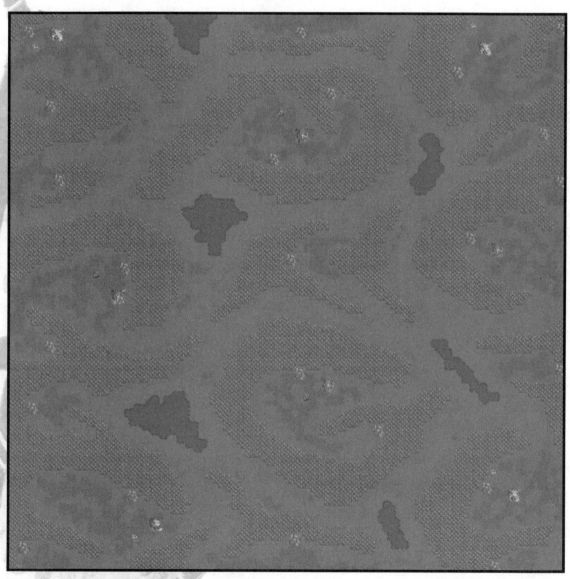

Forest Trail BNE

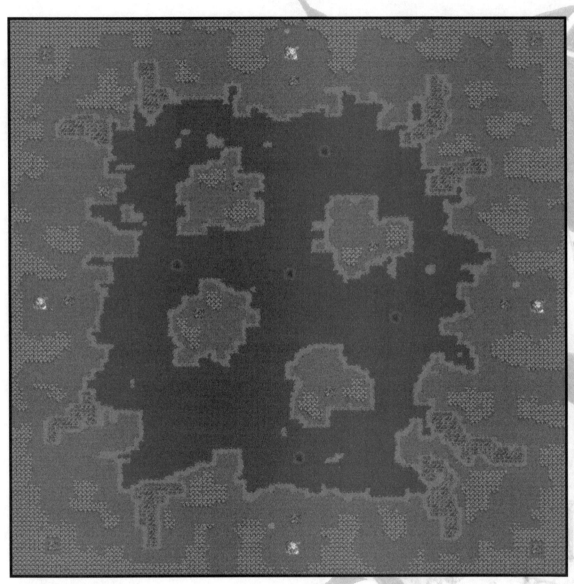

Forsaken Isles BNE

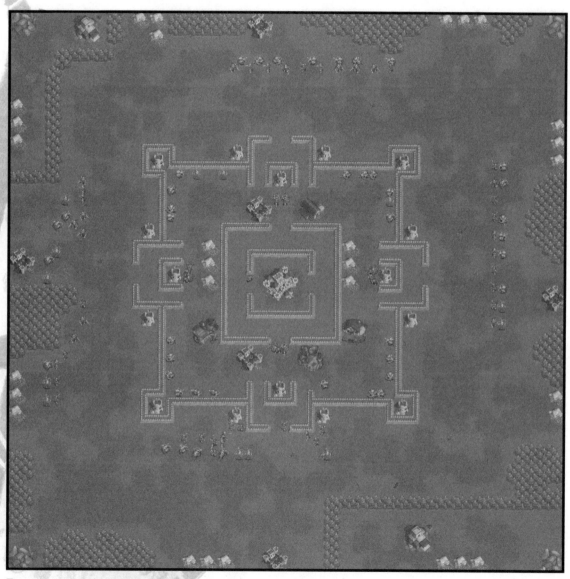

Fortress

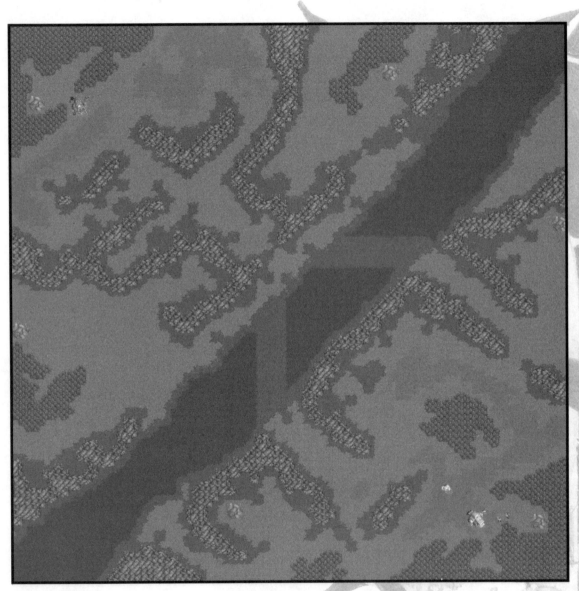

FortressofStone

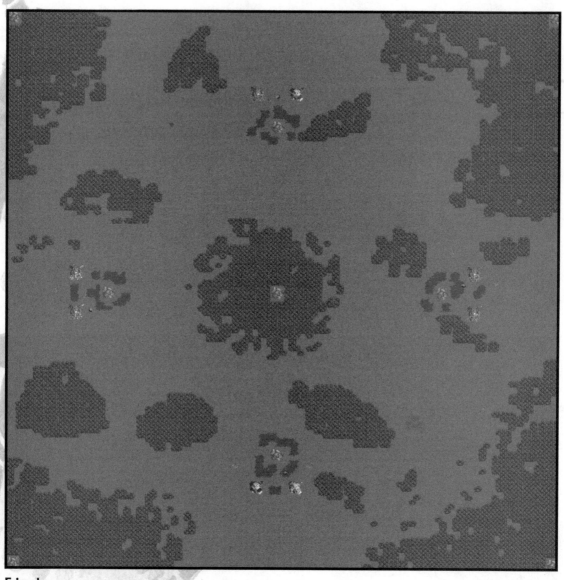

Friends

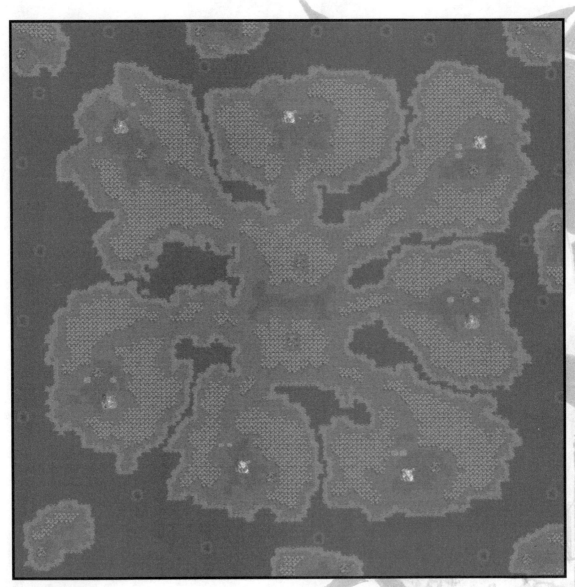

Frog Legs BNE

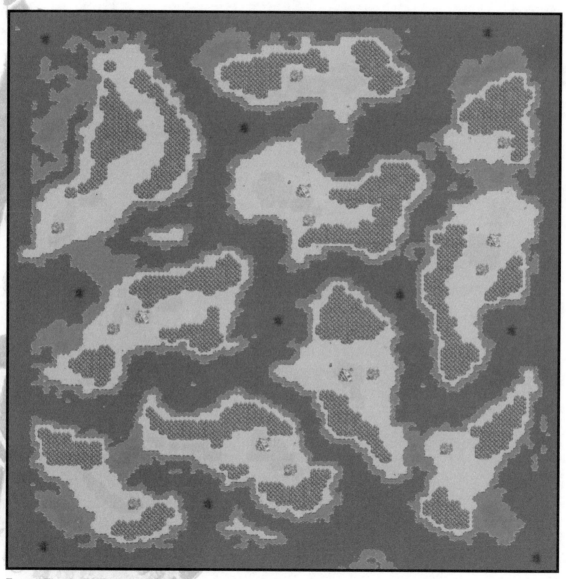

Frosty Fjords BNE

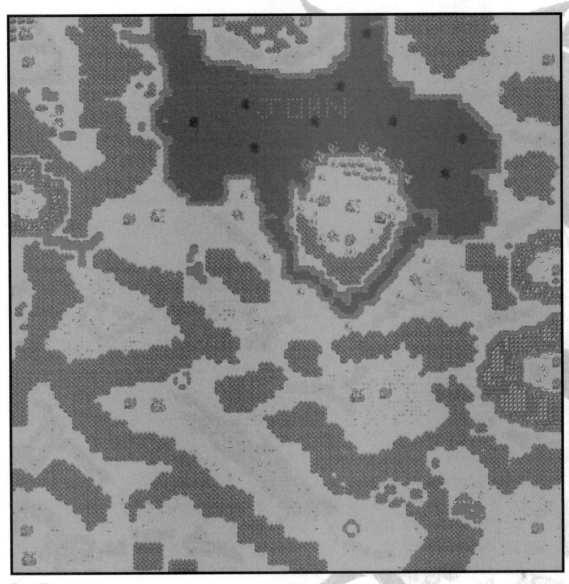

Fun4Three

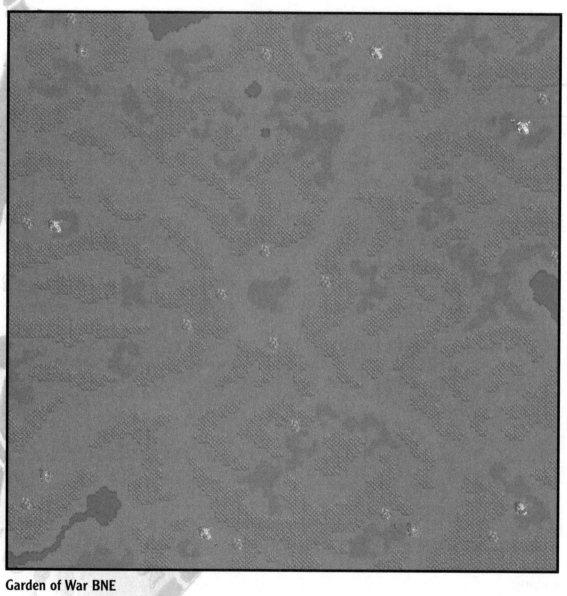

Garden of War BNE

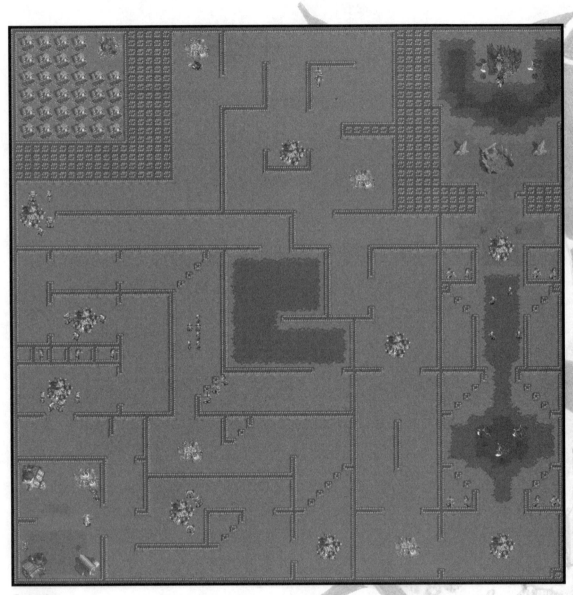

Gauntlet

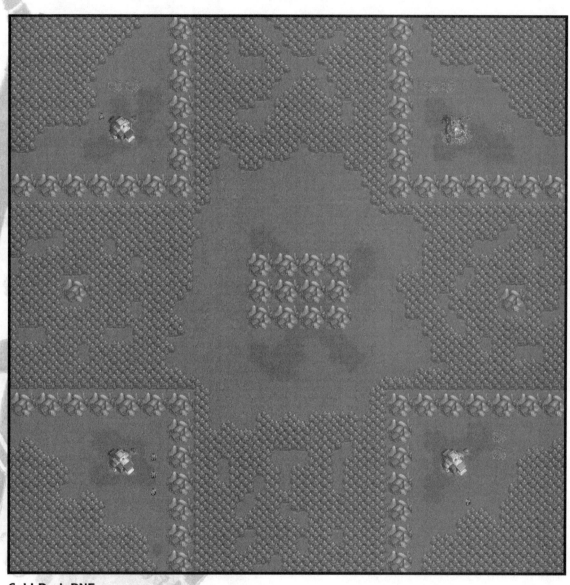

Gold Rush BNE

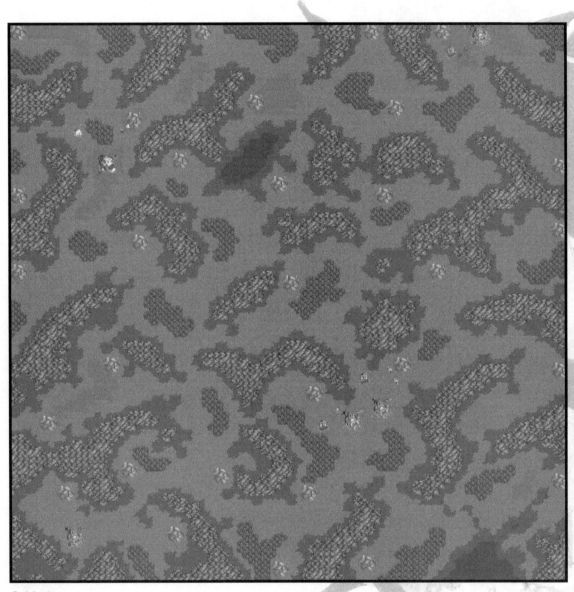

Goldmines

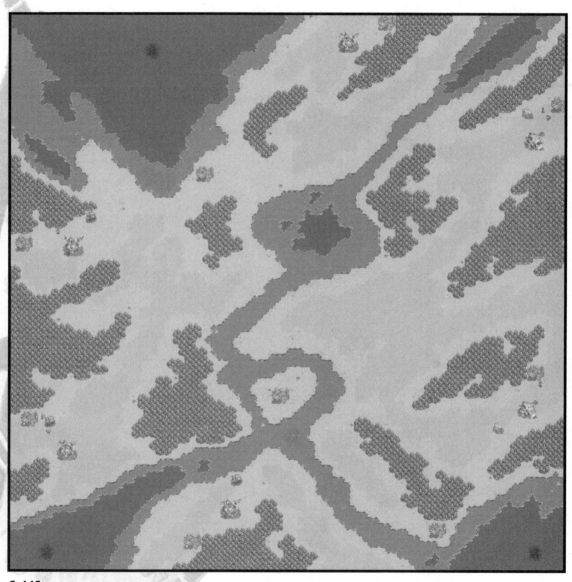

GoldSeps

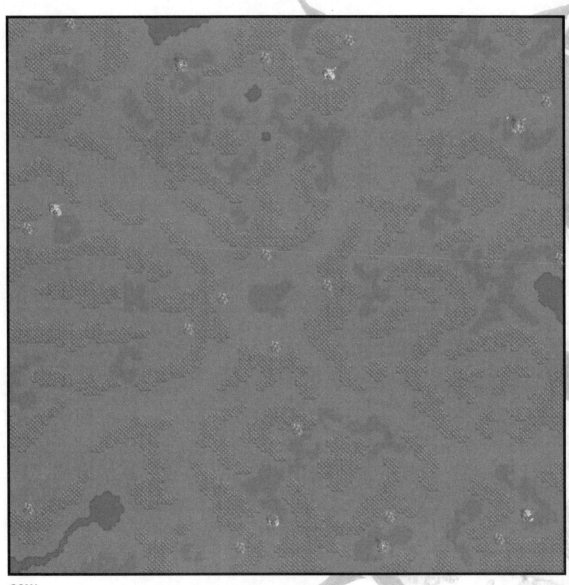

GOW

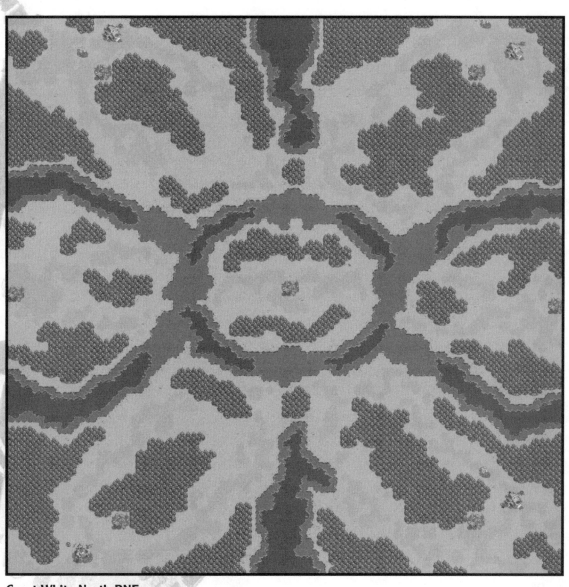

Great White North BNE

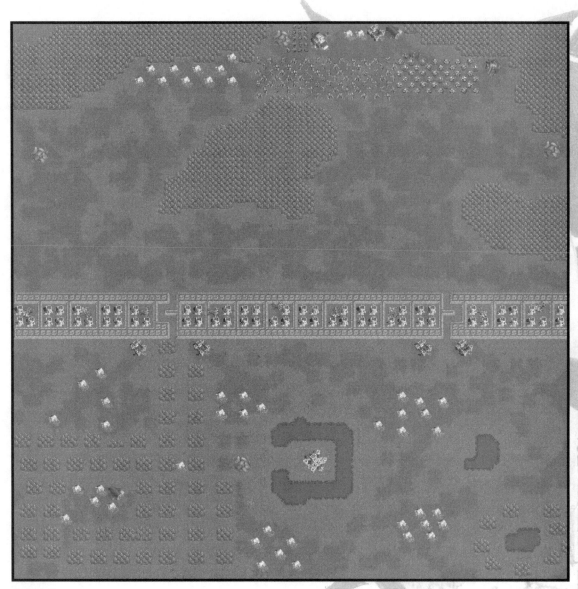

GrtWall

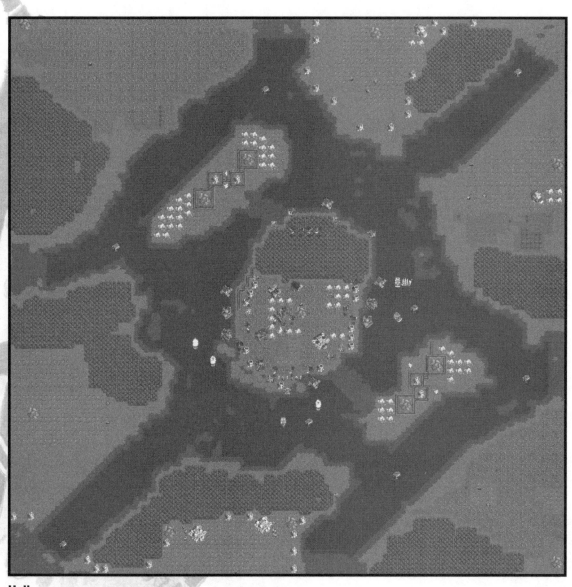

Hell

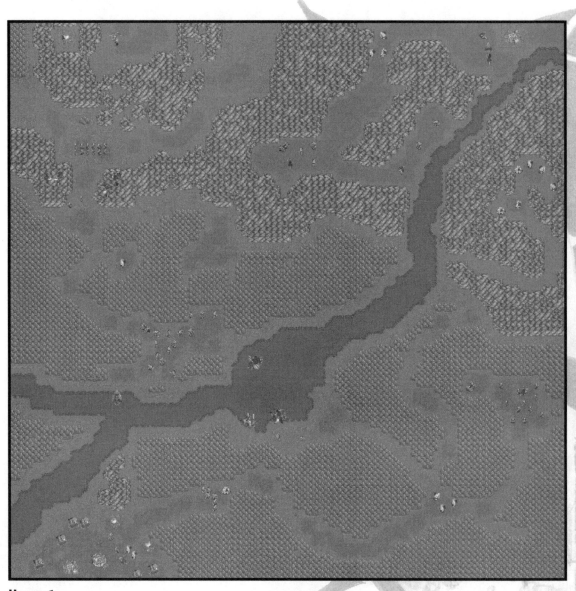

Heroes1

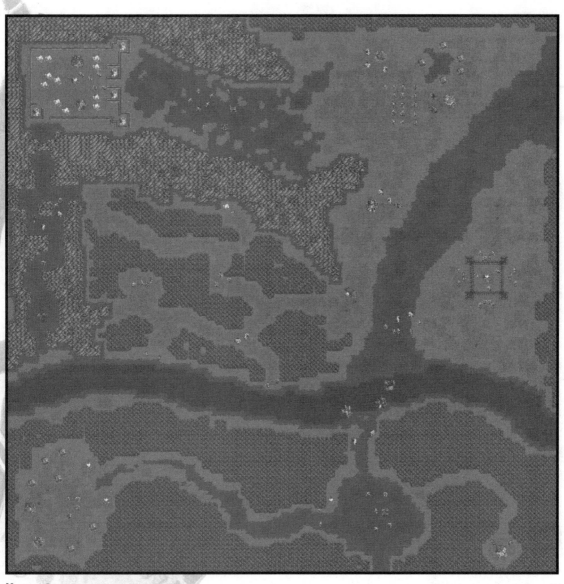

Heroes2

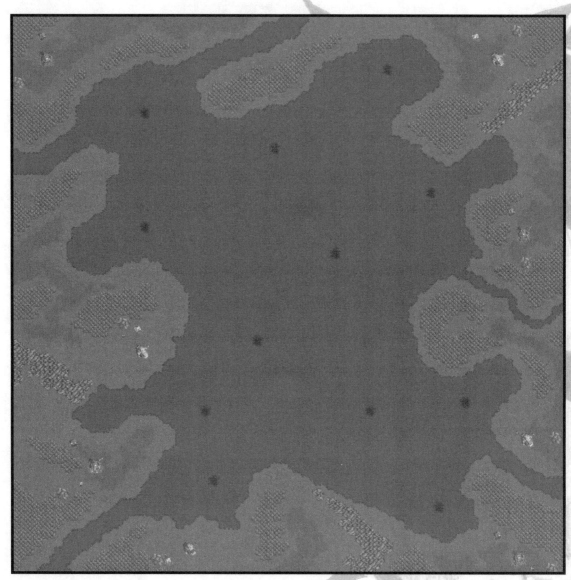

High Seas Combat BNE

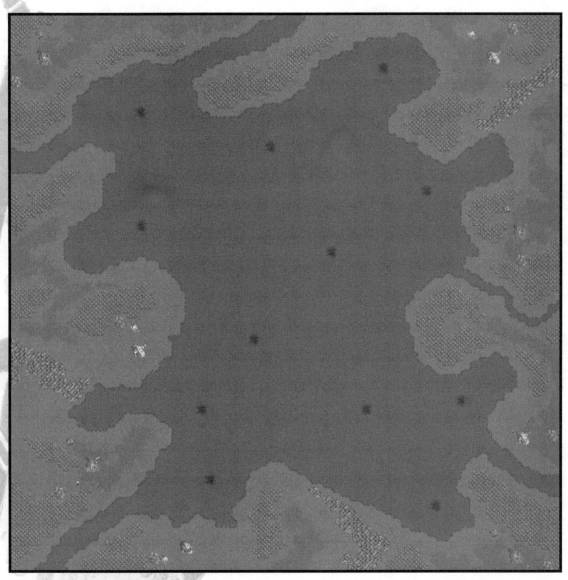

HighSeasCombat

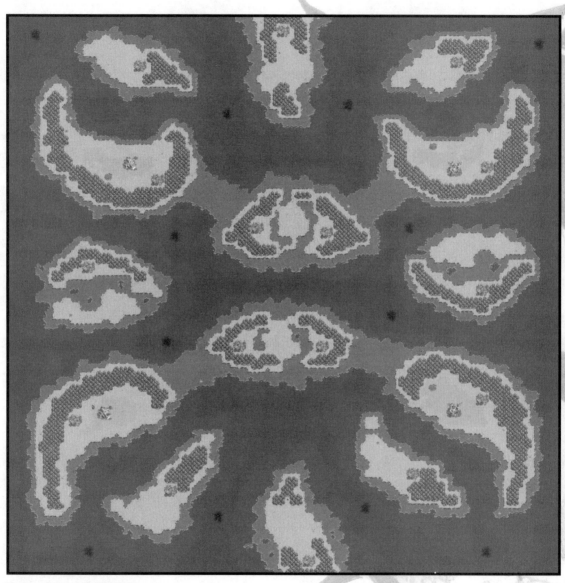

Horse Shoe Island BNE

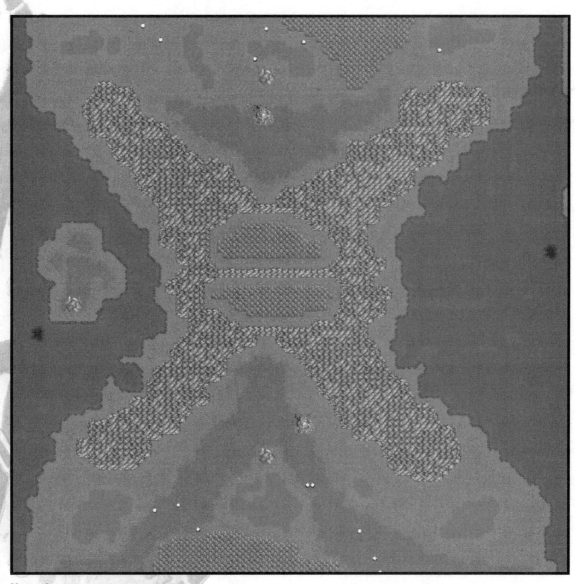

Hourglass

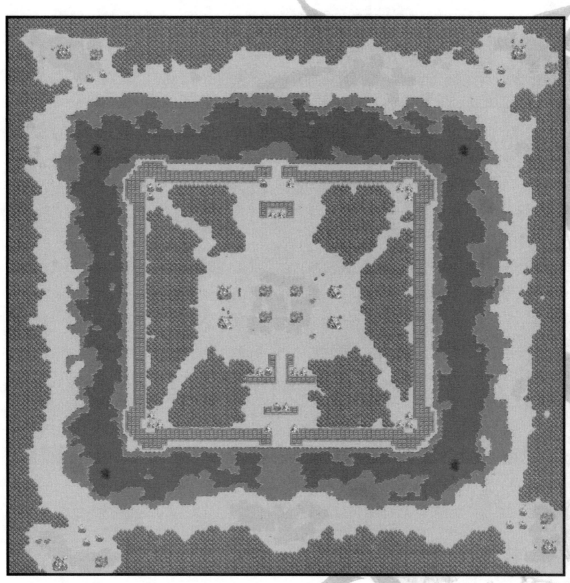

Ice Fortress BNE

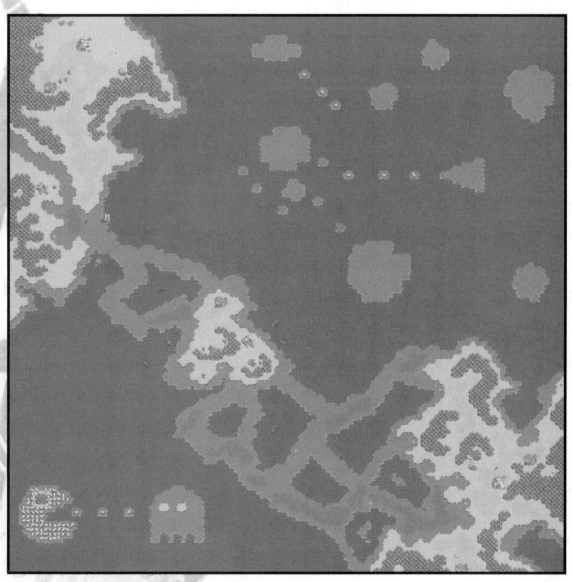

Icebrdge

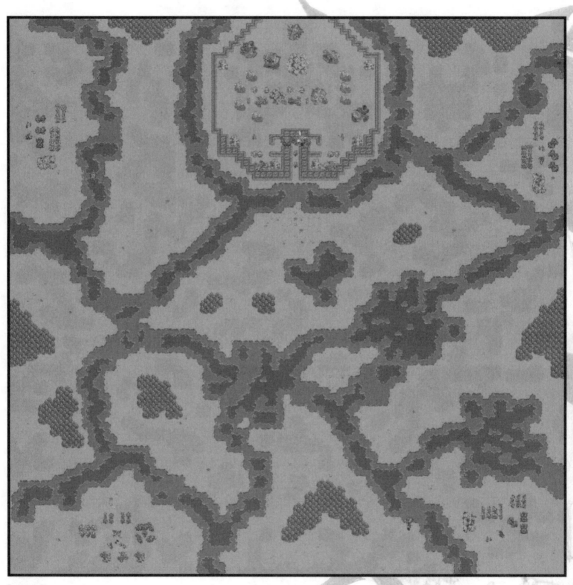

Icewall

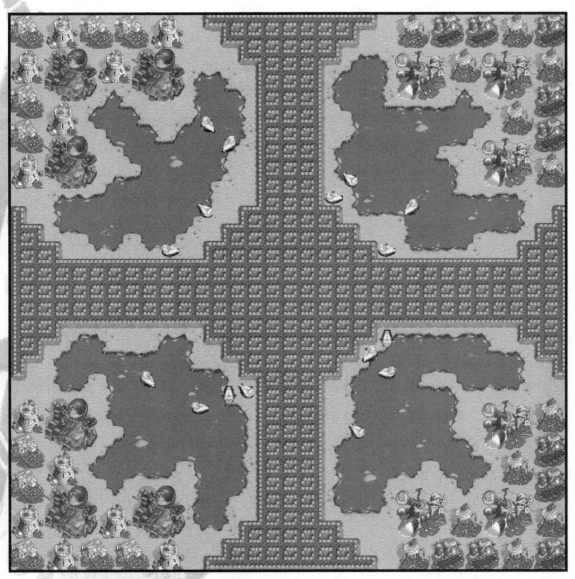

Instant Action BNE

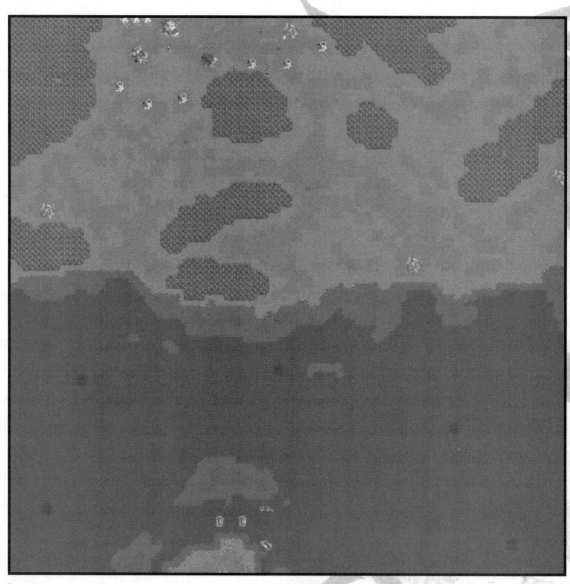

Invasion

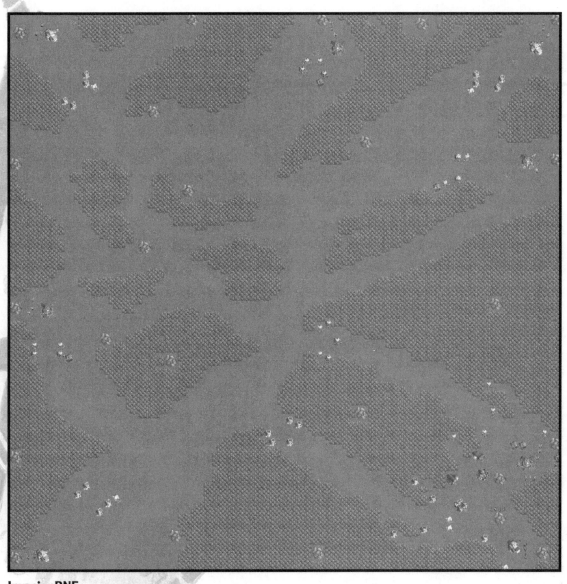

InvasionBNE

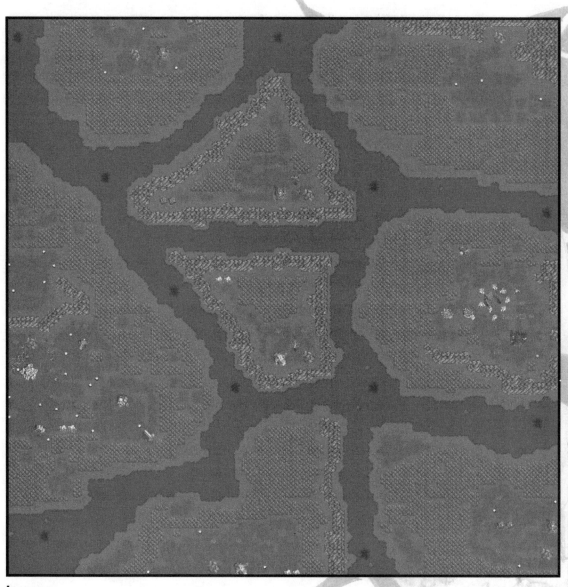

Ironcross

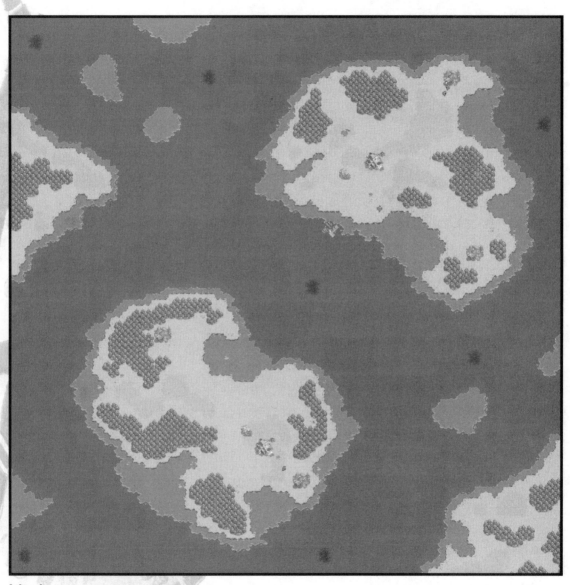

Islands

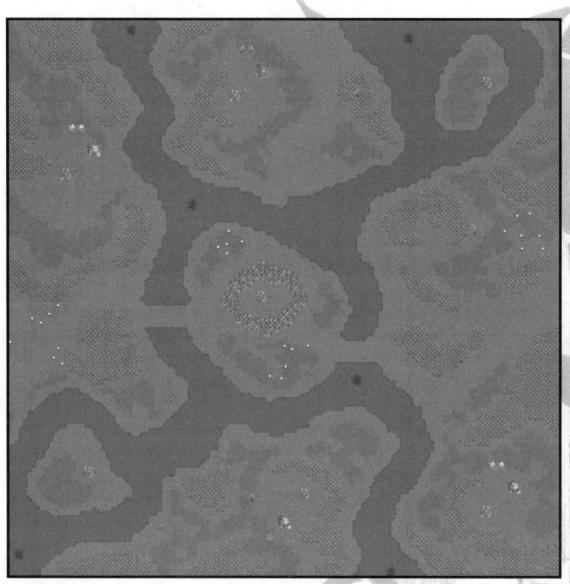

IslandsInStream

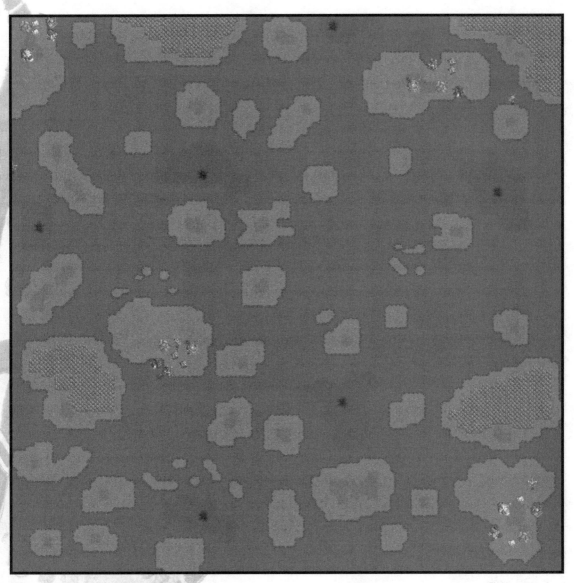

Isle

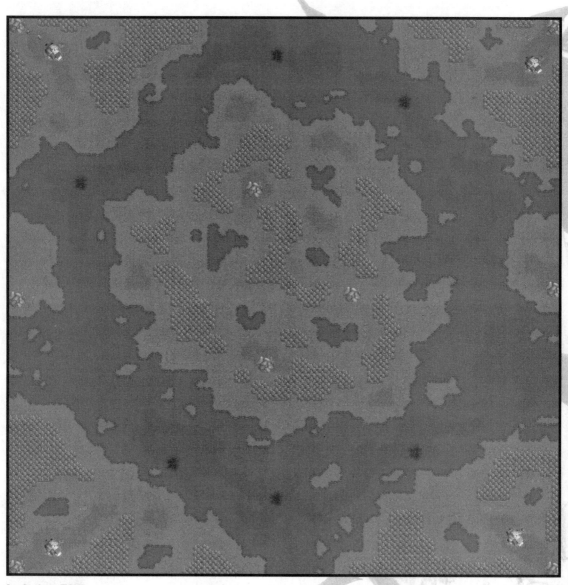

Isolation BNE

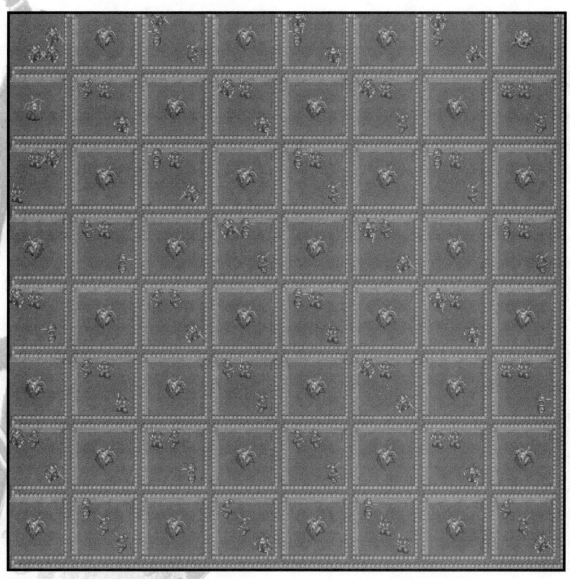

Jail

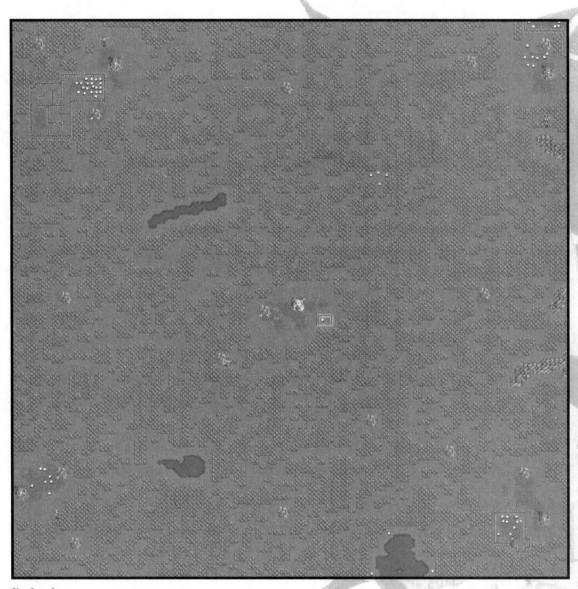

Jimland

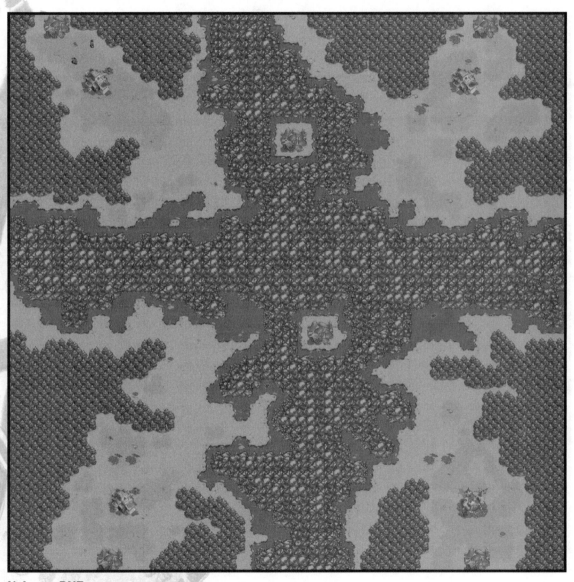

Kaboom BNE

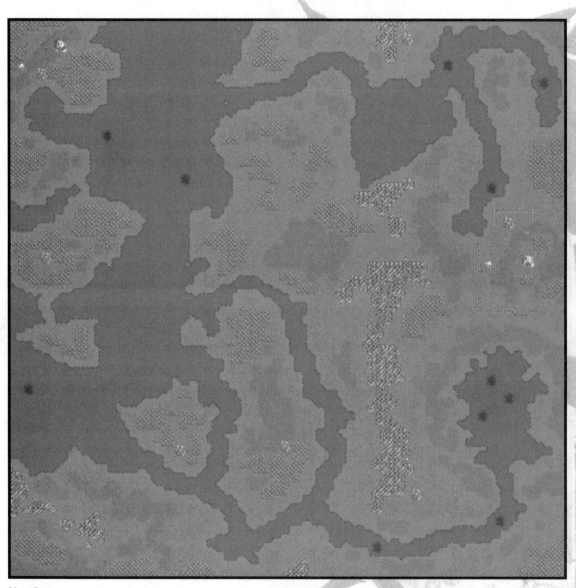

Kanthar

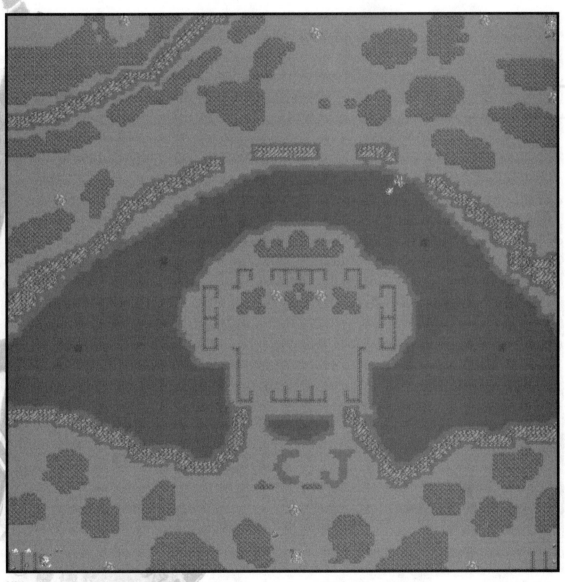

Khing

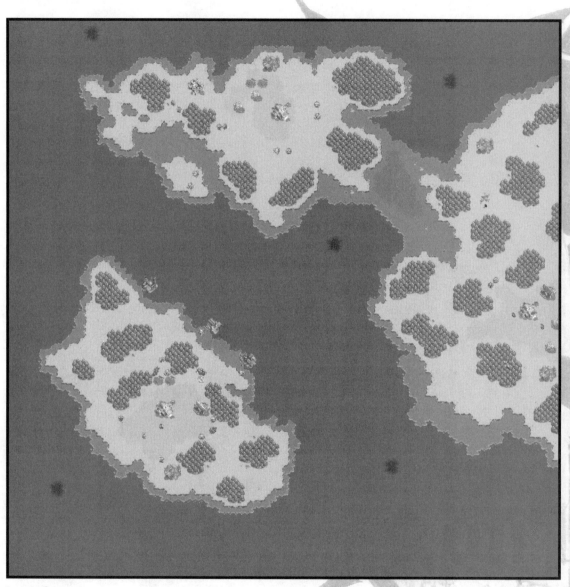

Land_Sea

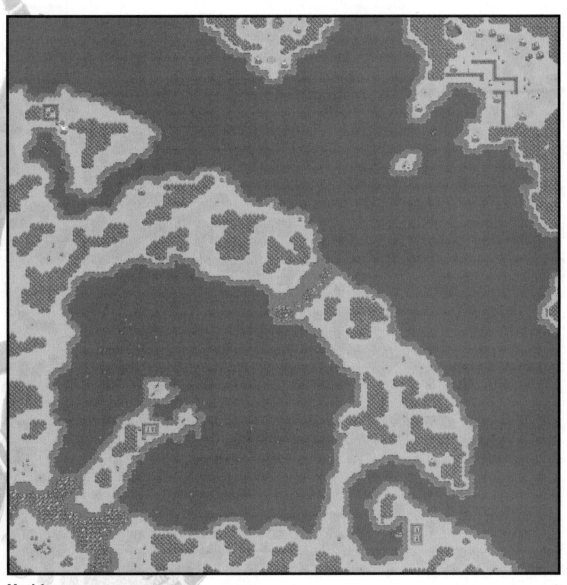

MagIsle

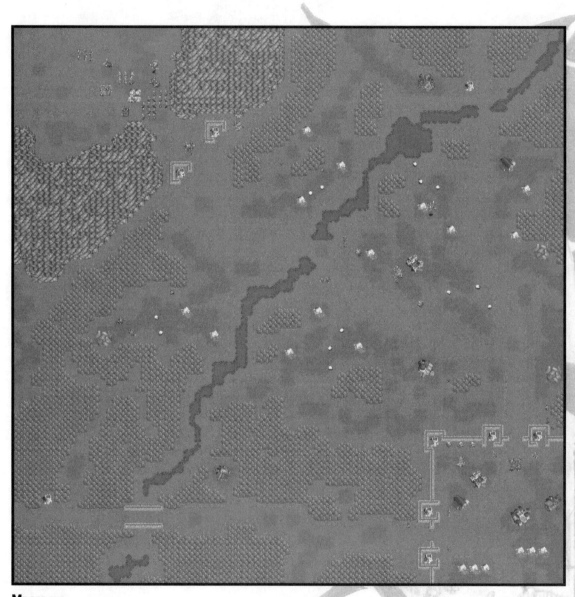

Massacre

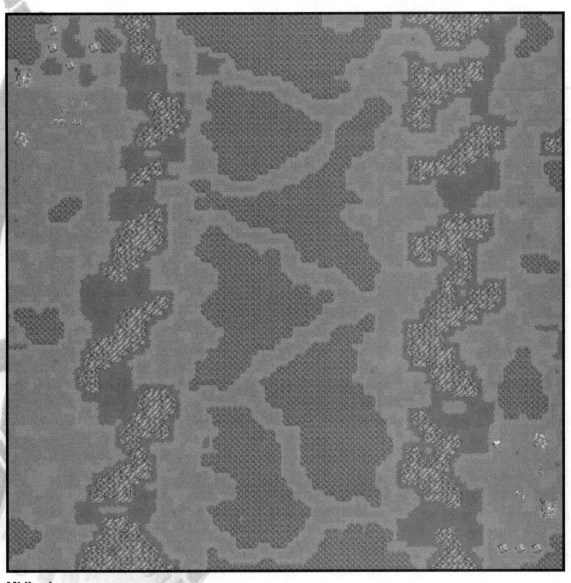

Midland

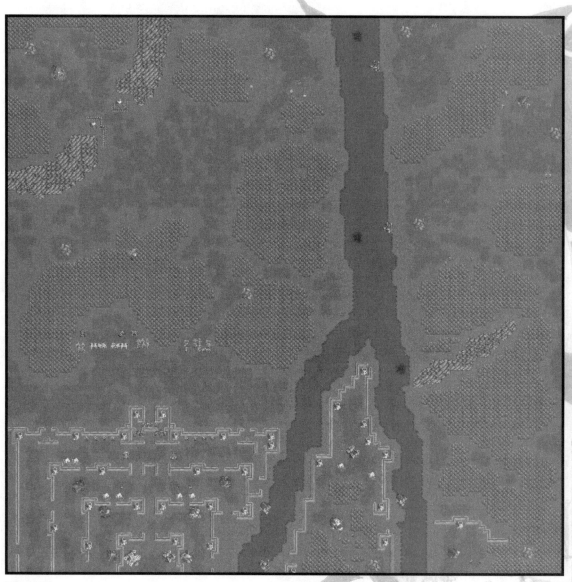

MinasTir

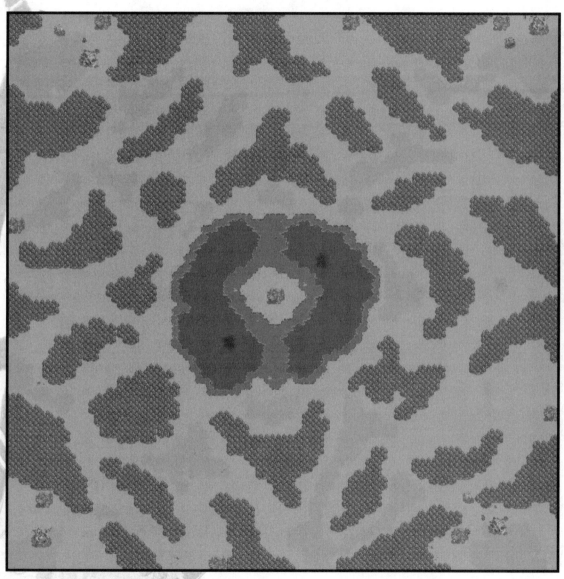

Mine in the Center

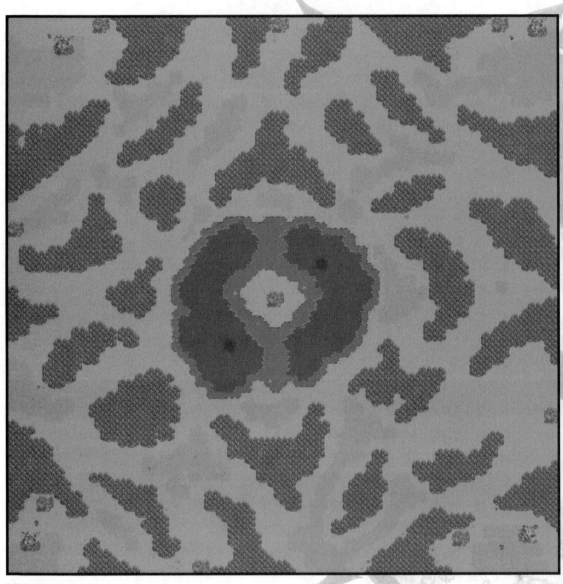

Minethecenter

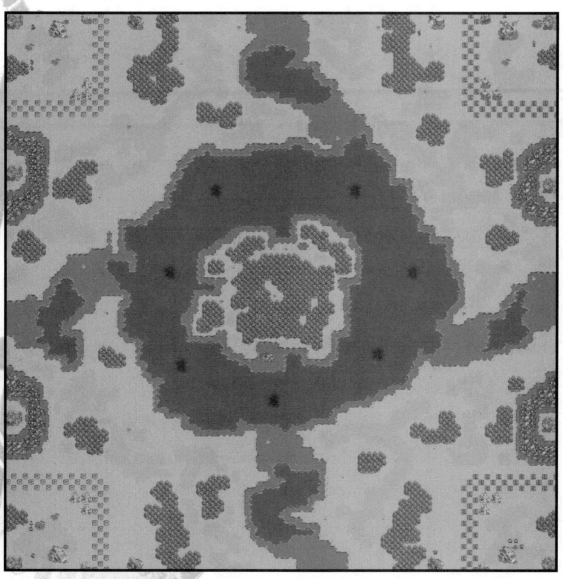

More Precious Than Gold BNE

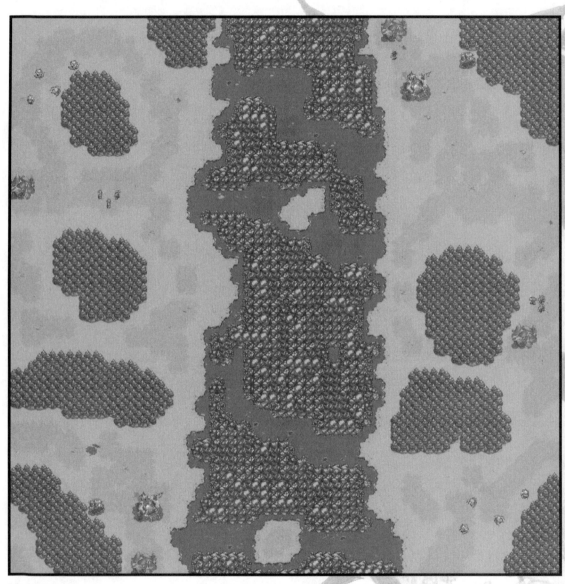

Mtnpass

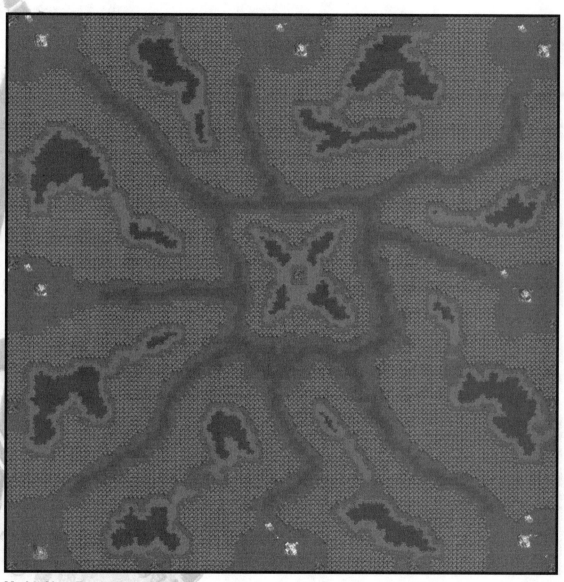

Mud in Your Eye

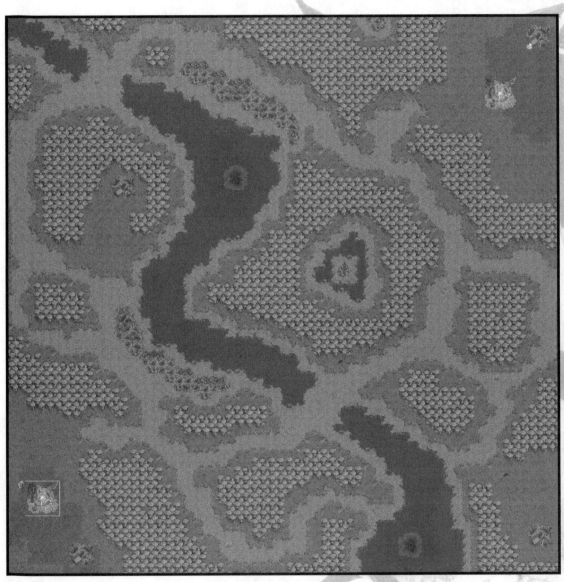

Murky River BNE

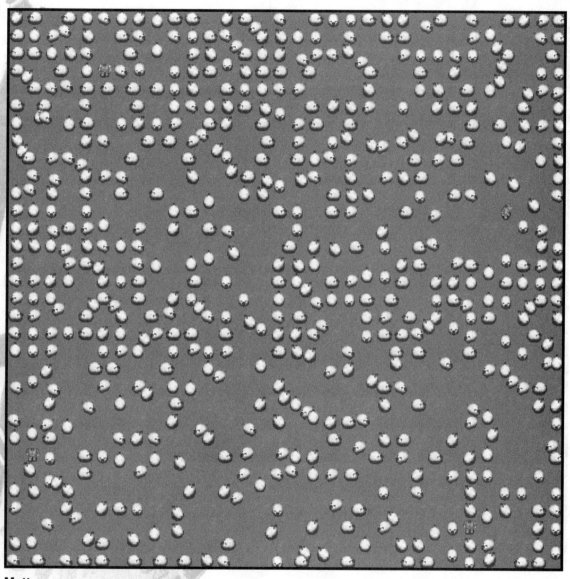

Mutton

No Way Out of This Maze BNE

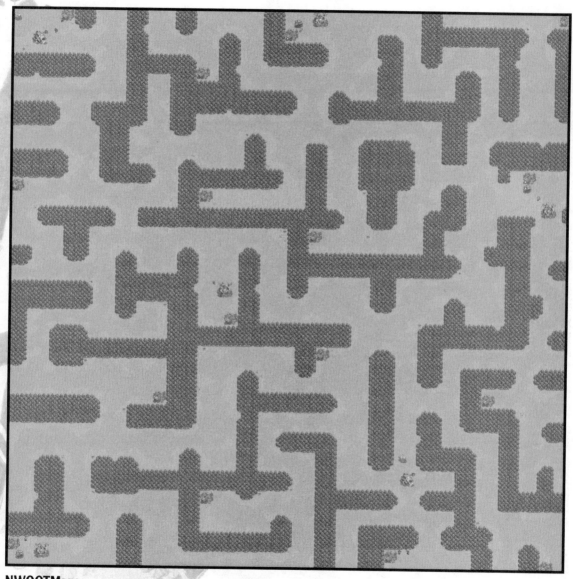

NWOOTMaze

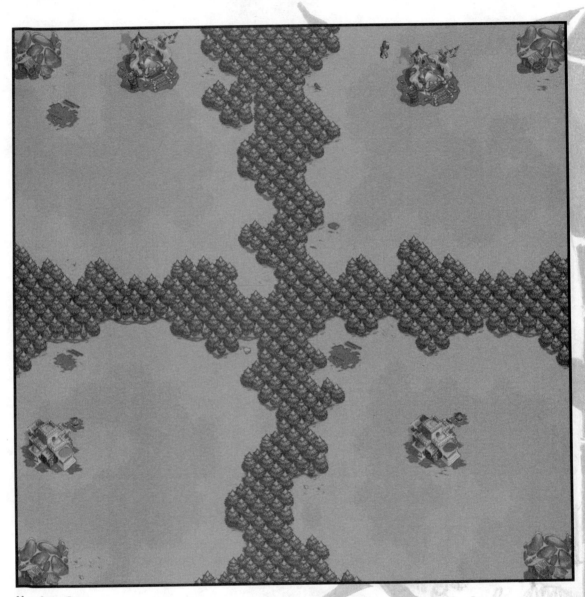

Nowhere2run

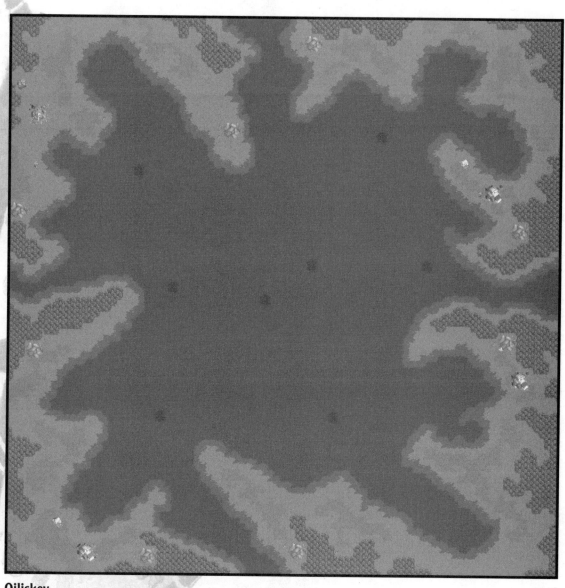

Oiliskey

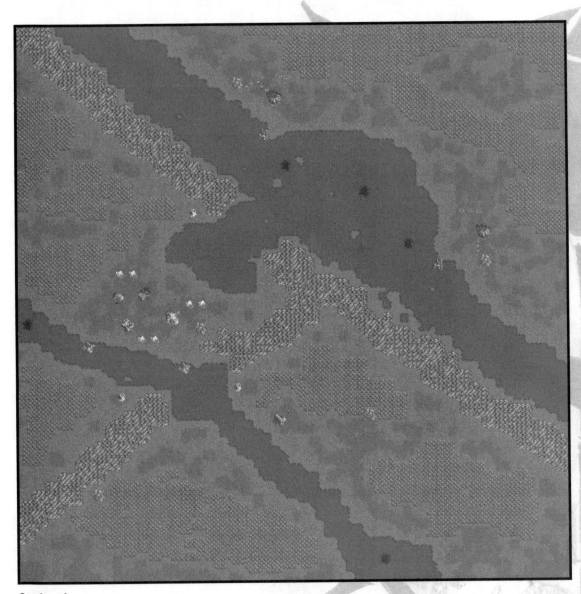

Onslaugh

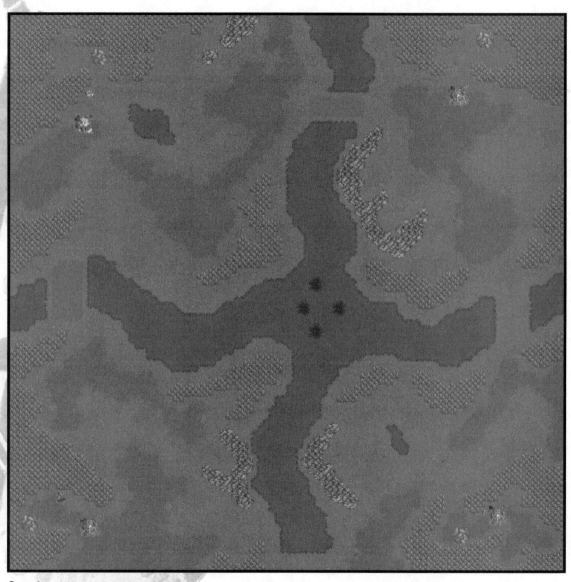

Oppcitystates

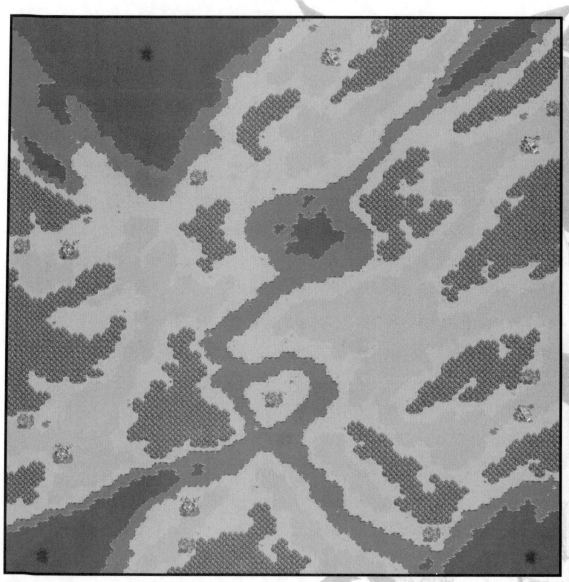

Opposites Attract BNE

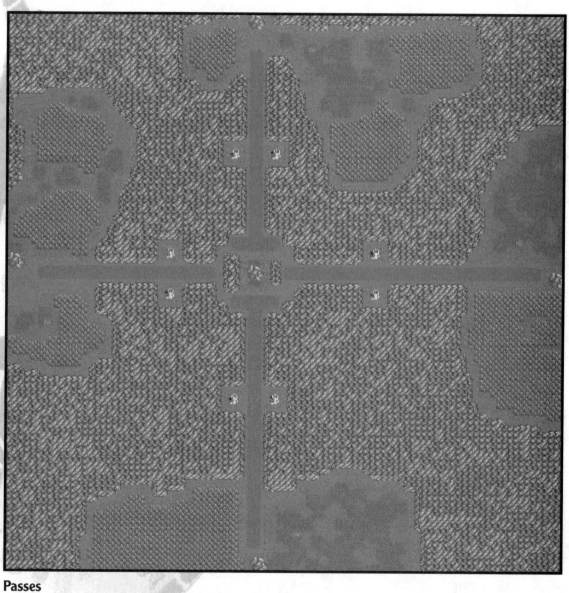

Passes

Plains of Snow BNE

Plainsofsnow

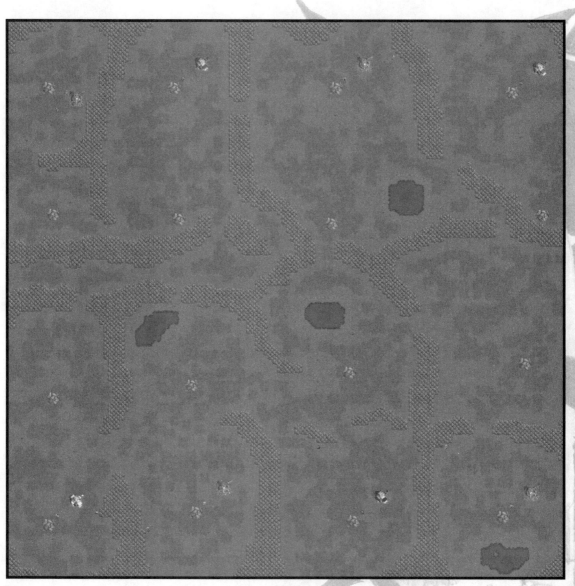

Plots

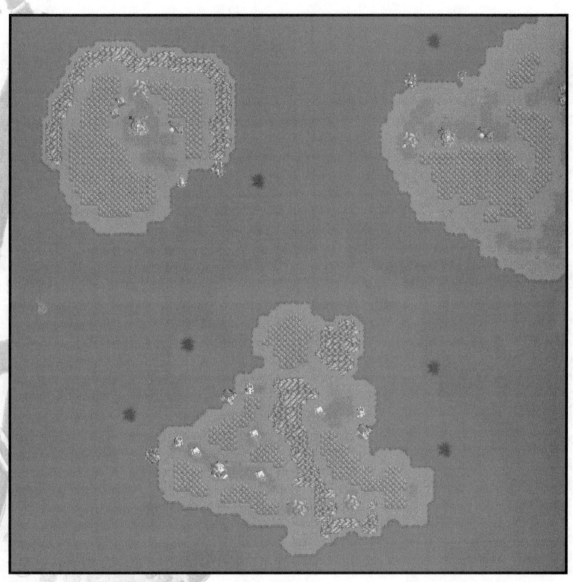

Raiders

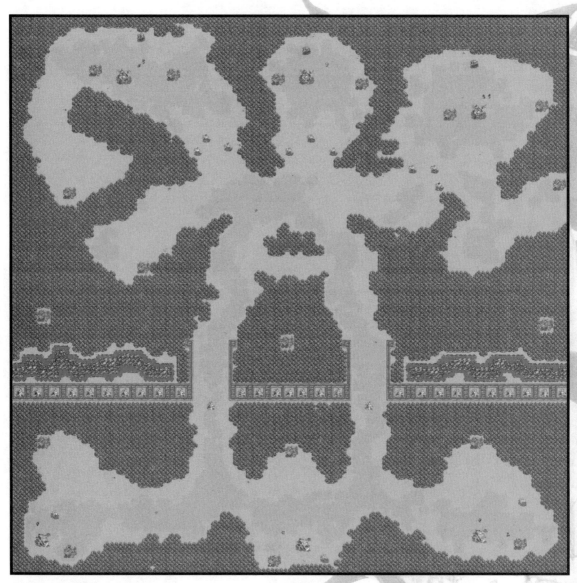

Ramparts BNE

Rescue

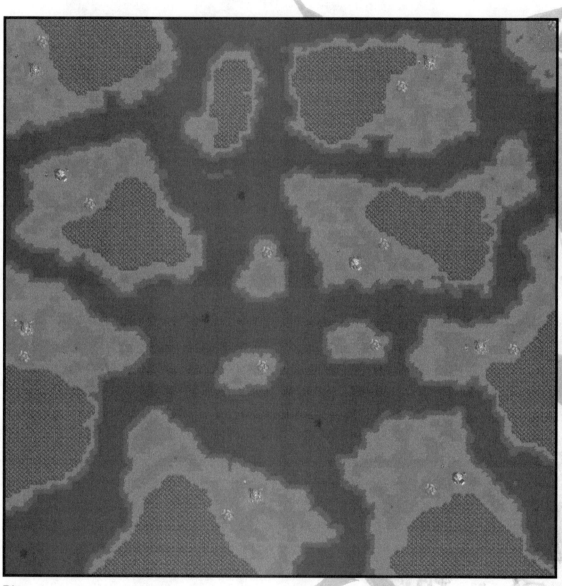

Ring

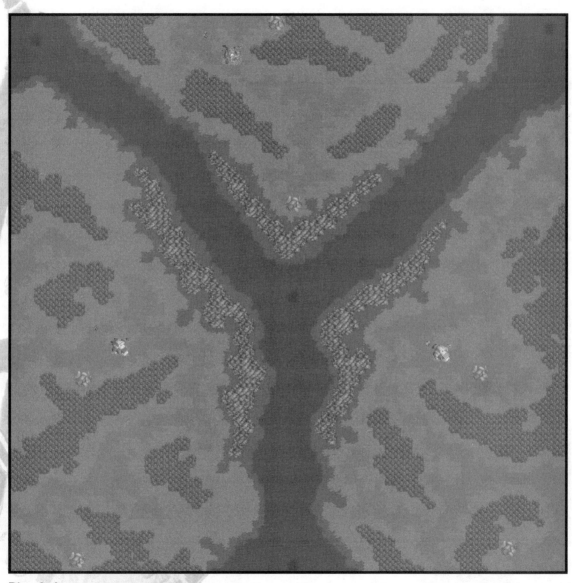

Riverfork

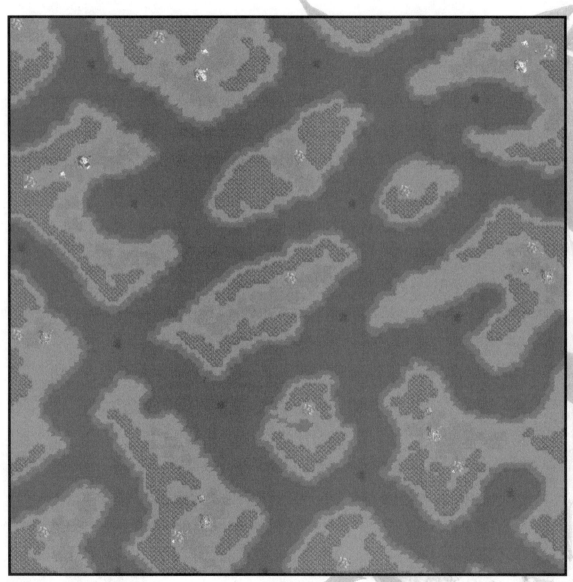

Rivers

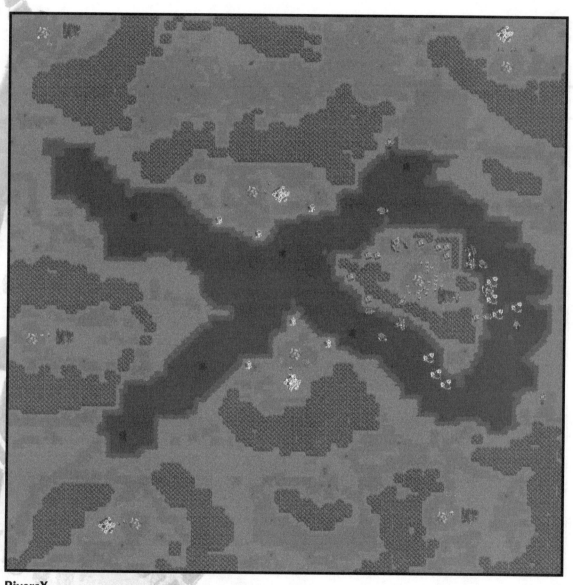

RiversX

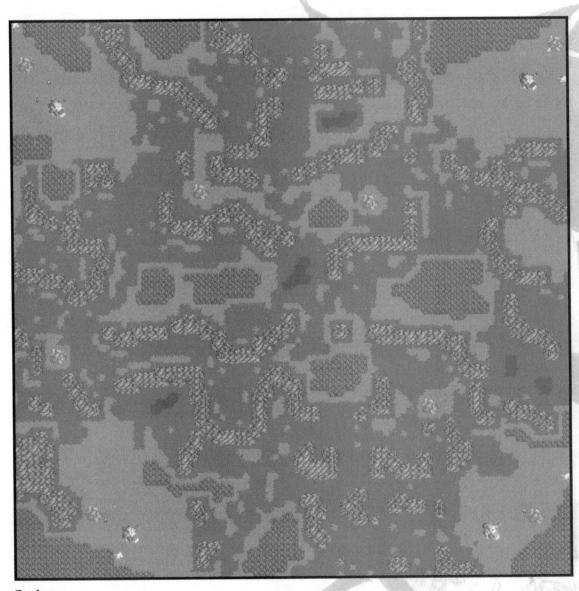

Rockmaze

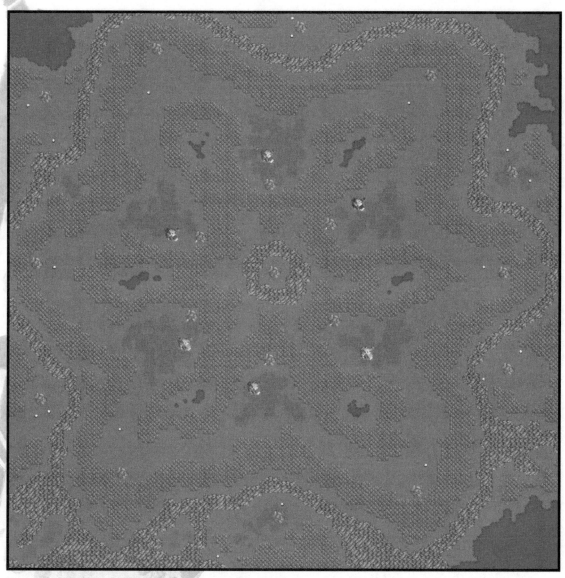

Rose Petal BNE

Sacrific

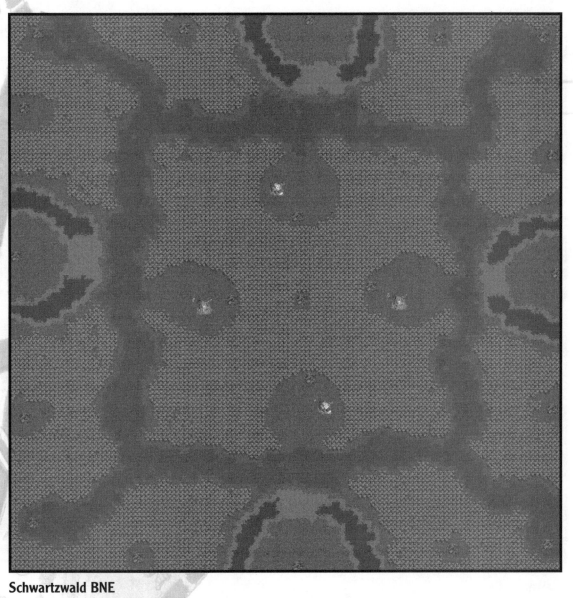

Schwartzwald BNE

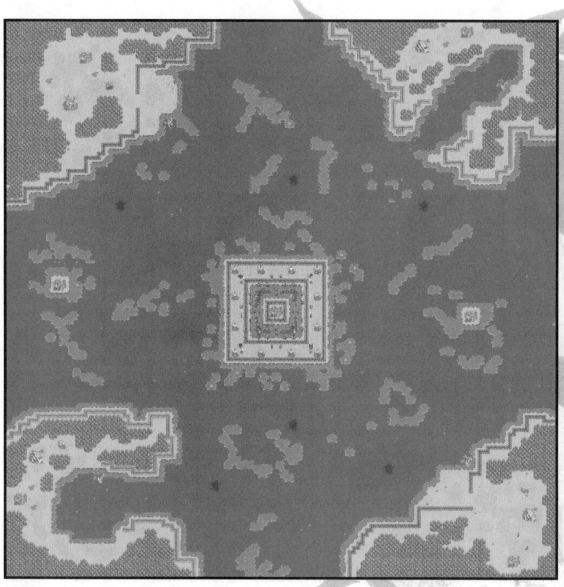

SeaWar

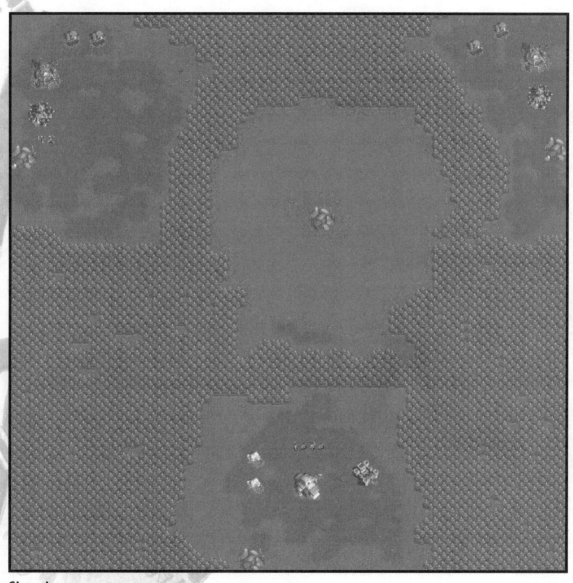

Shared

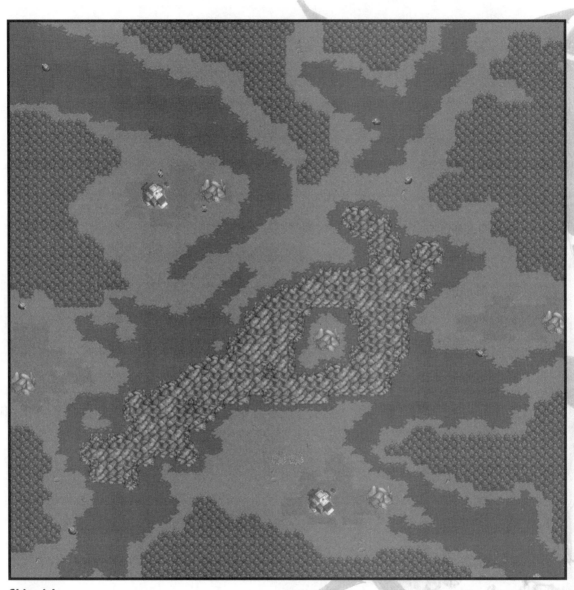

Skirmish

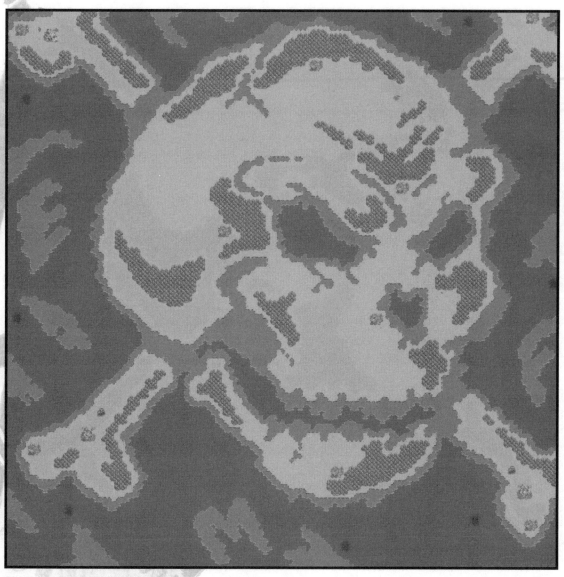

Skull Isle BNE

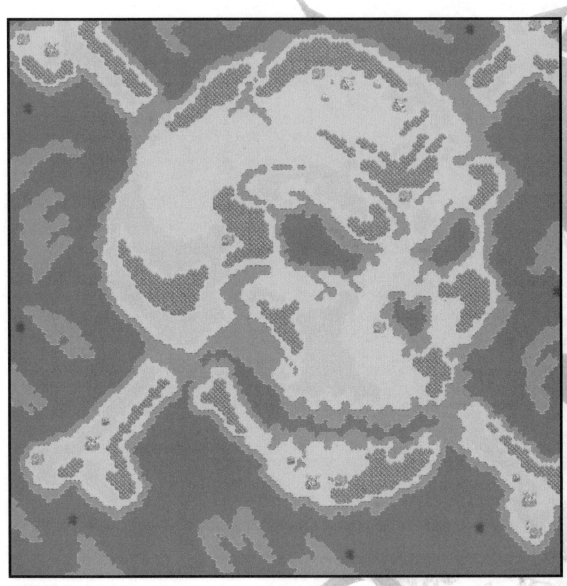

Skullisle

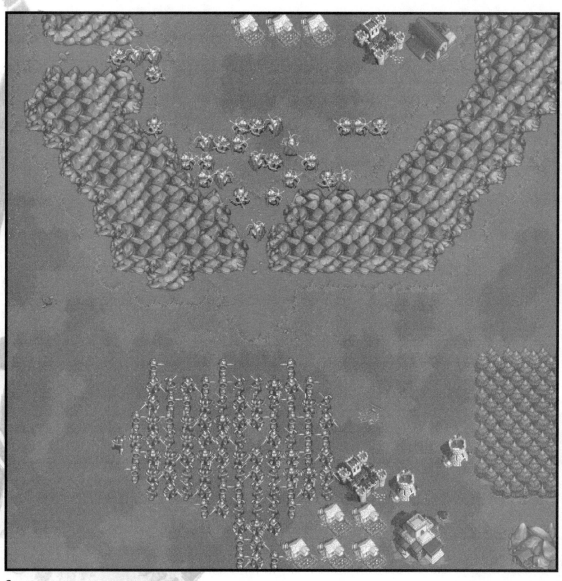

Sparta

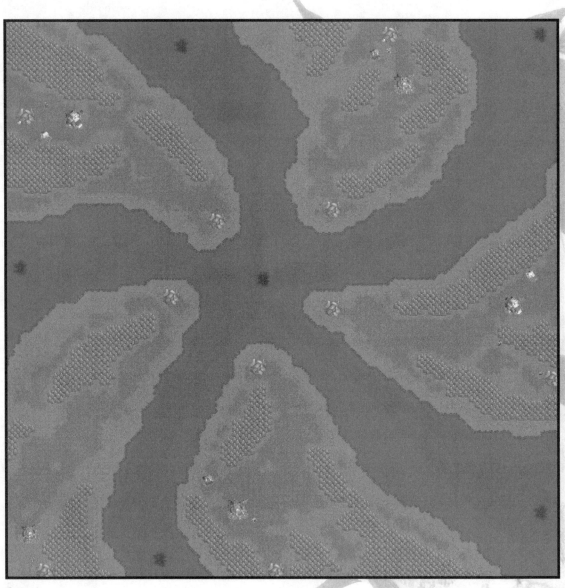

Spiral

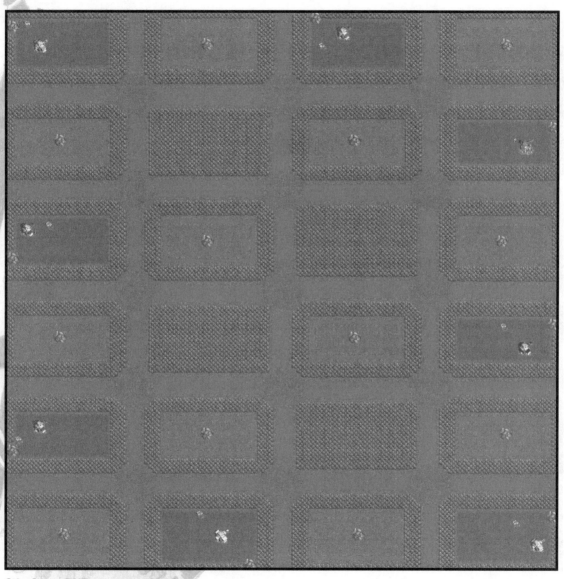

Stir Crazy BNE

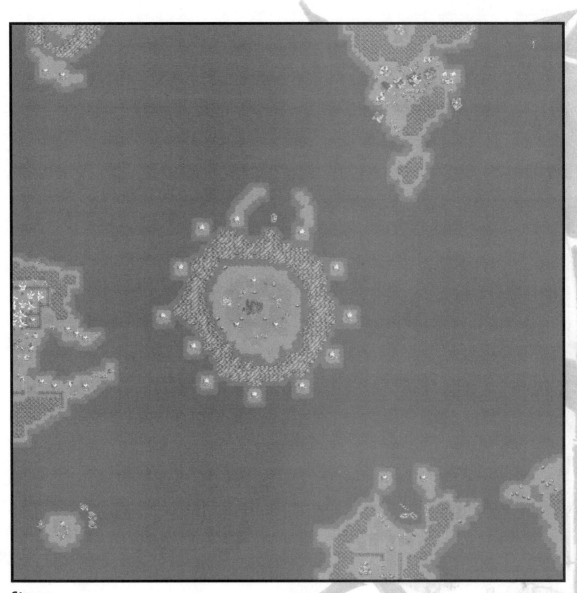

Stone

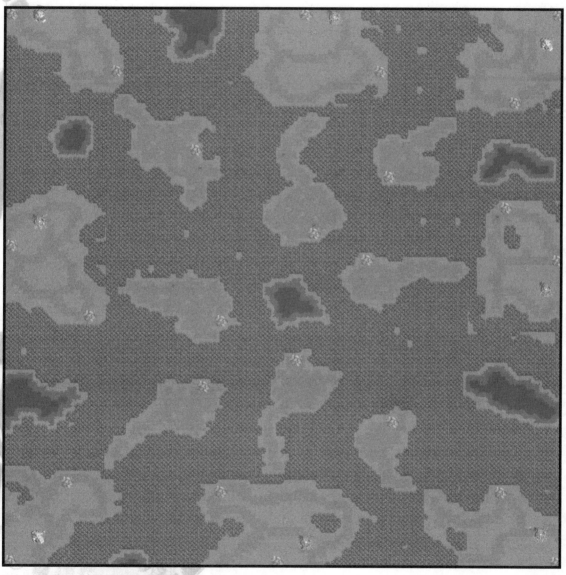

Taiga BNE

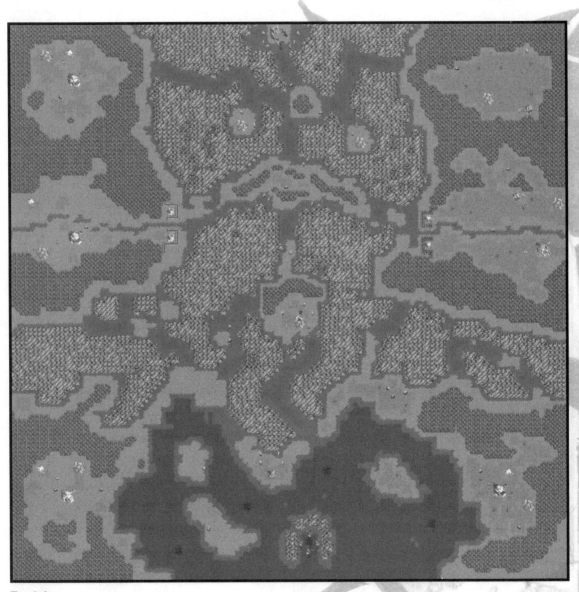

Tandalos

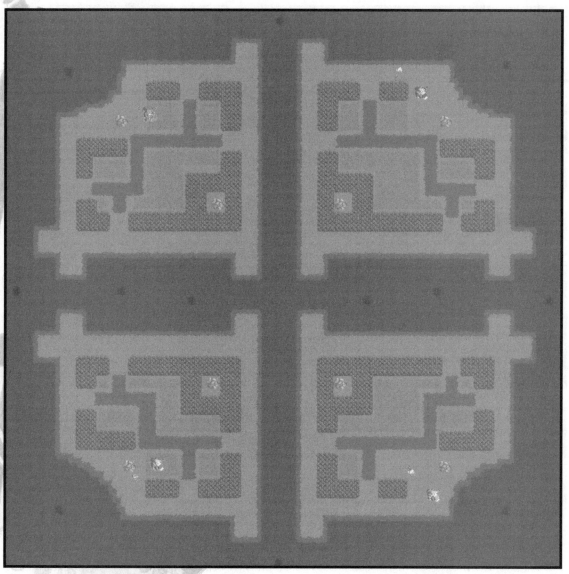

The Four Corners BNE

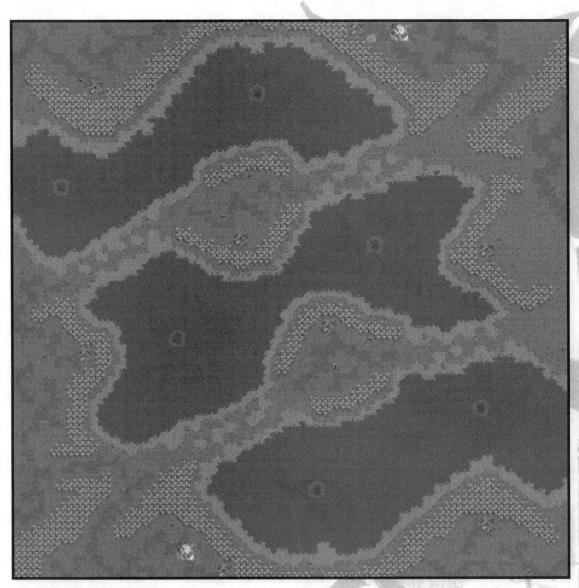

The River Kwai BNE

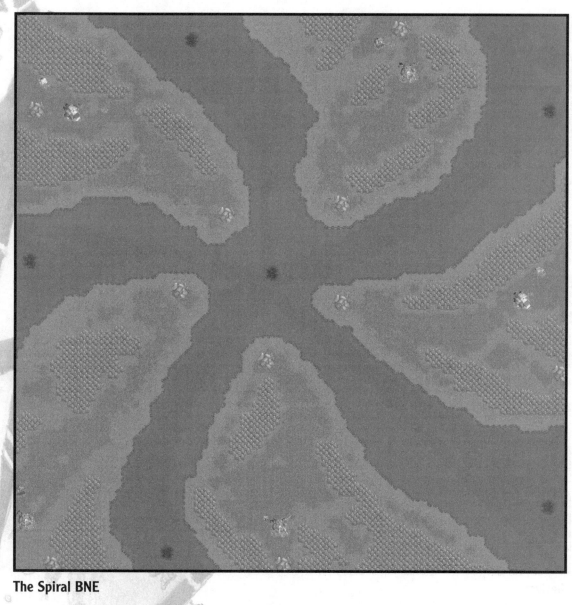

The Spiral BNE

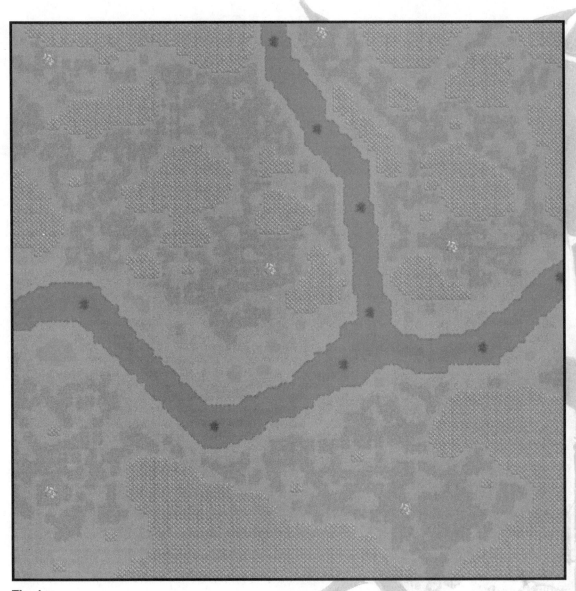

Theriver

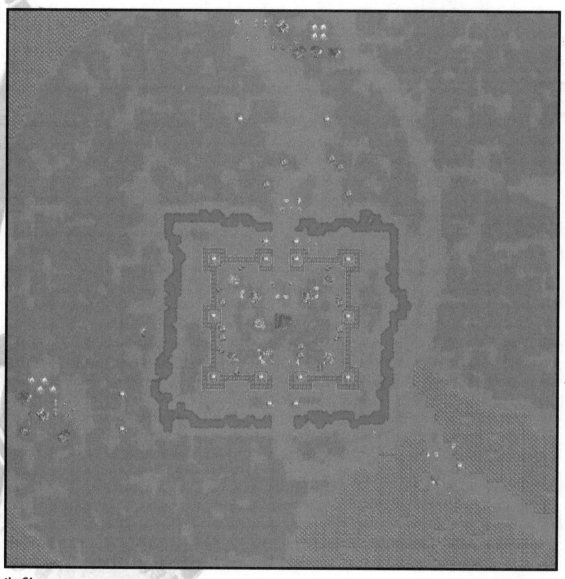

theSiege

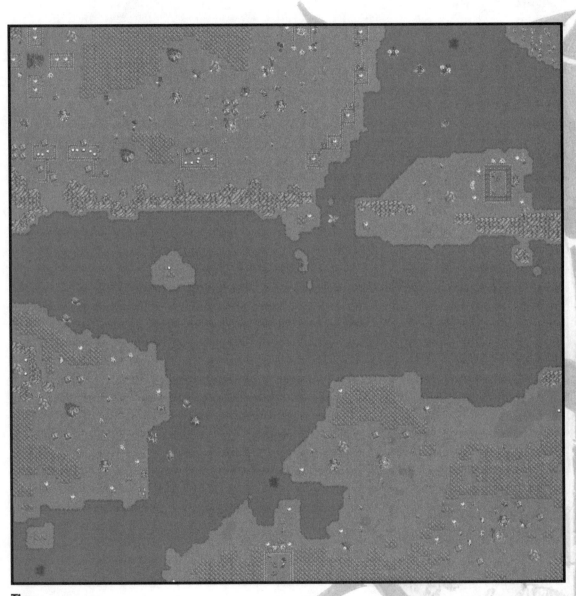

Time

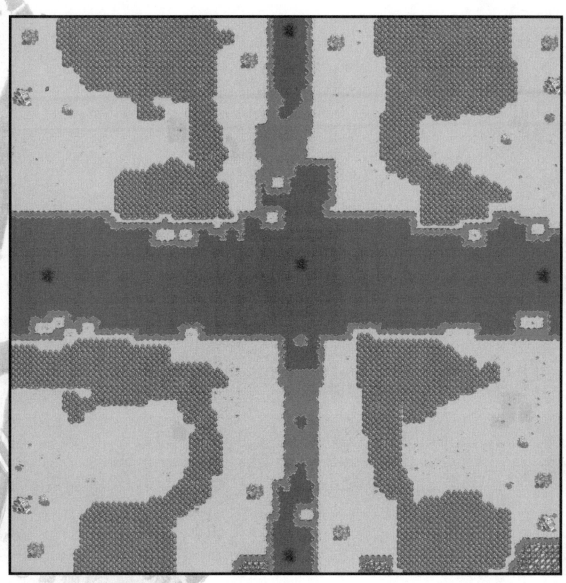

Tourney

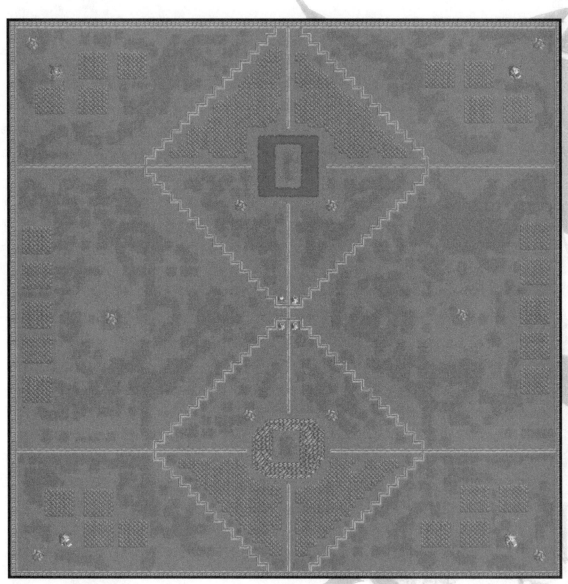

Training Ground BNE

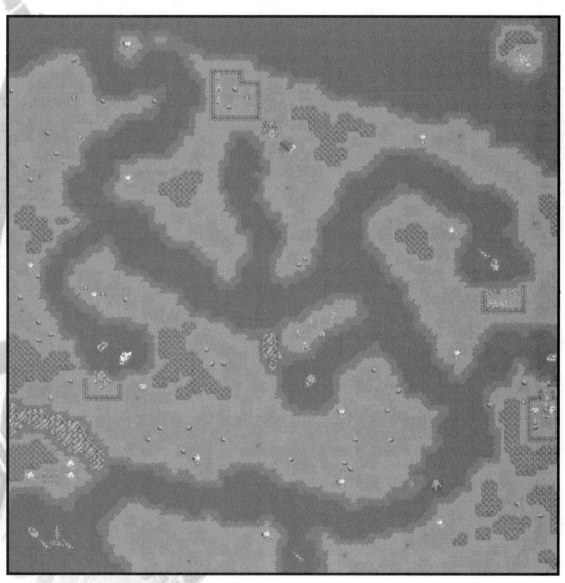

Trenchwar

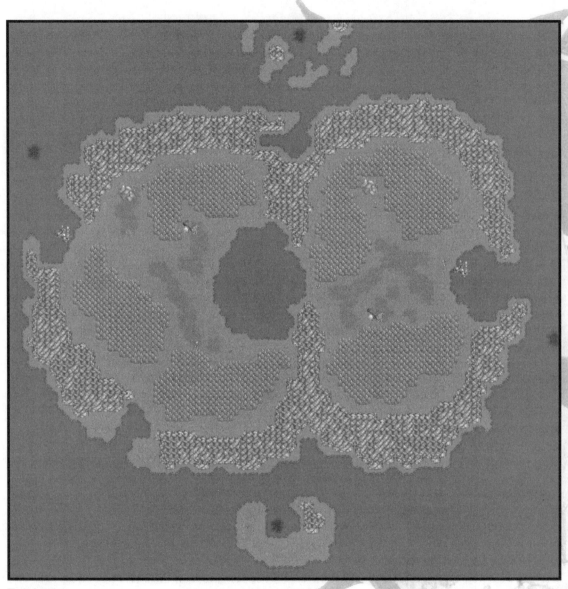

Twinharbor

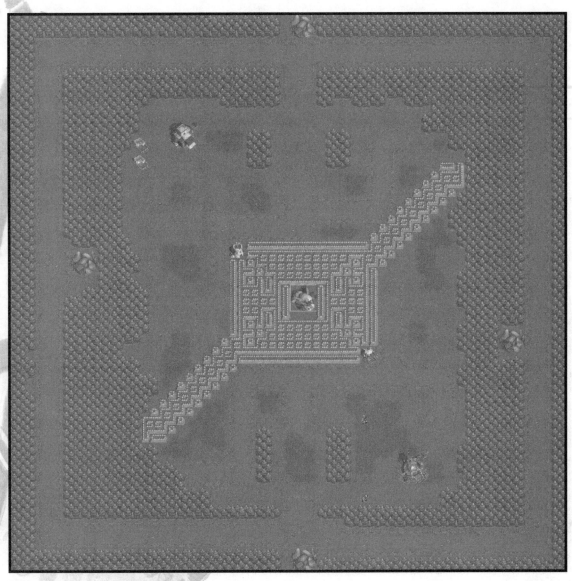

Upforgrabs

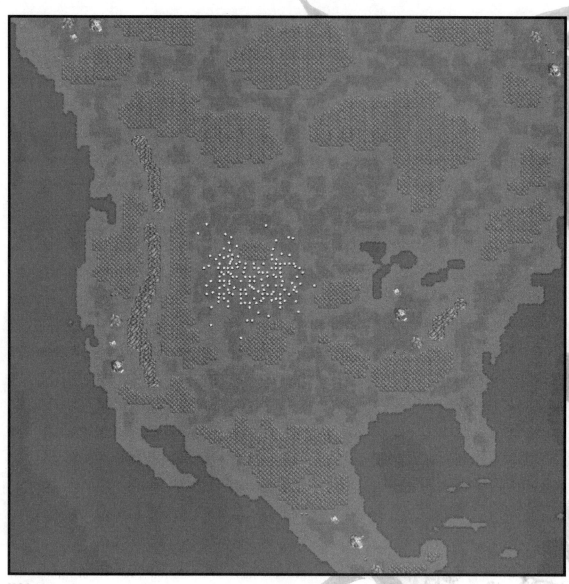

USA

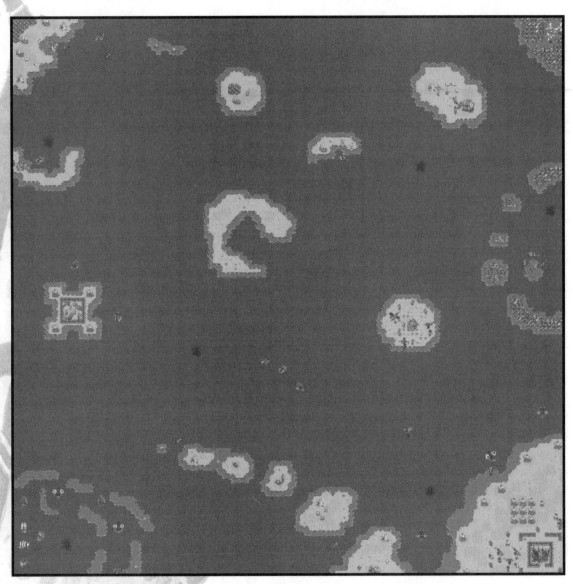

WaterRes

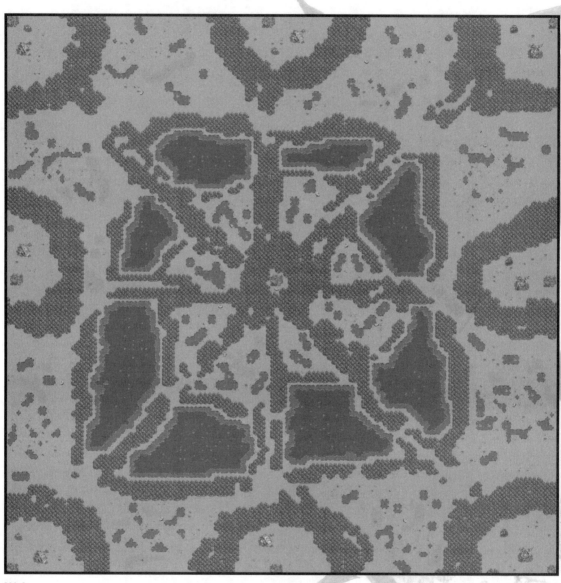

Web

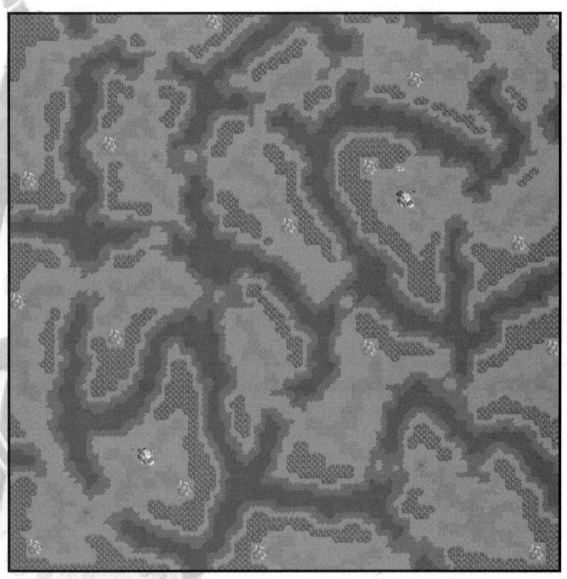

Widow's End BNE

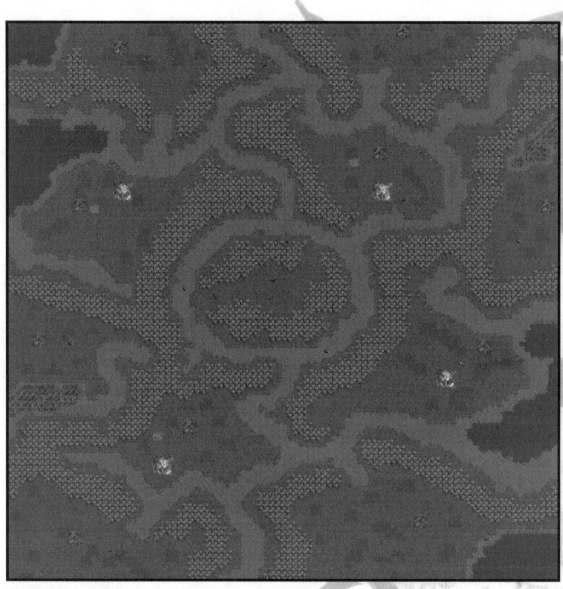

Winding Ways BNE

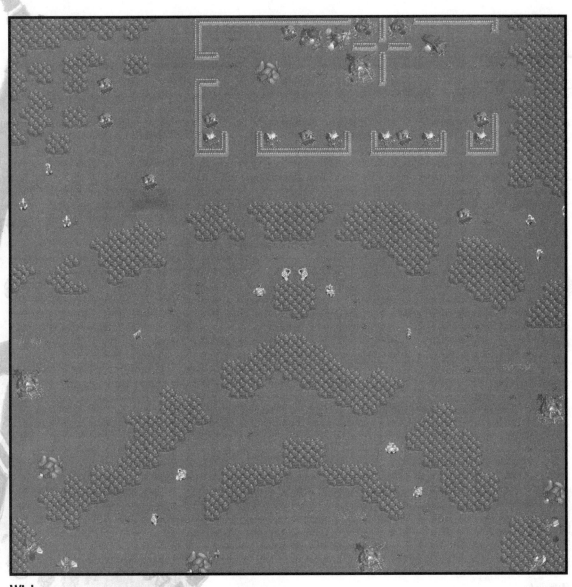

Wish

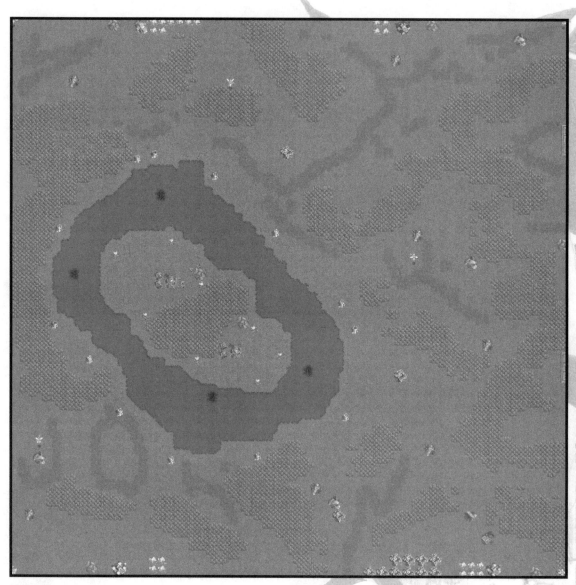

Wizard

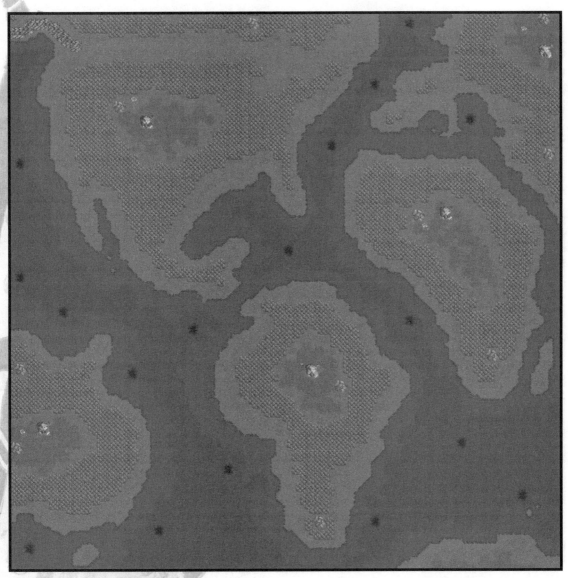

World Domination BNE

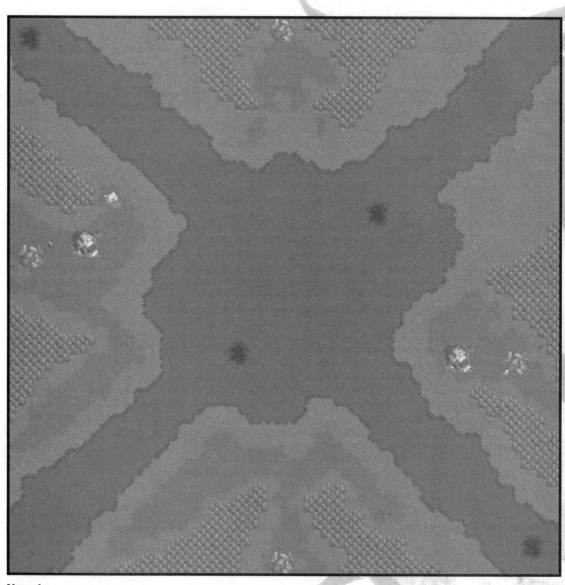

Xmarks